95p. D.G.H.

BRITAIN
in the 20th Century

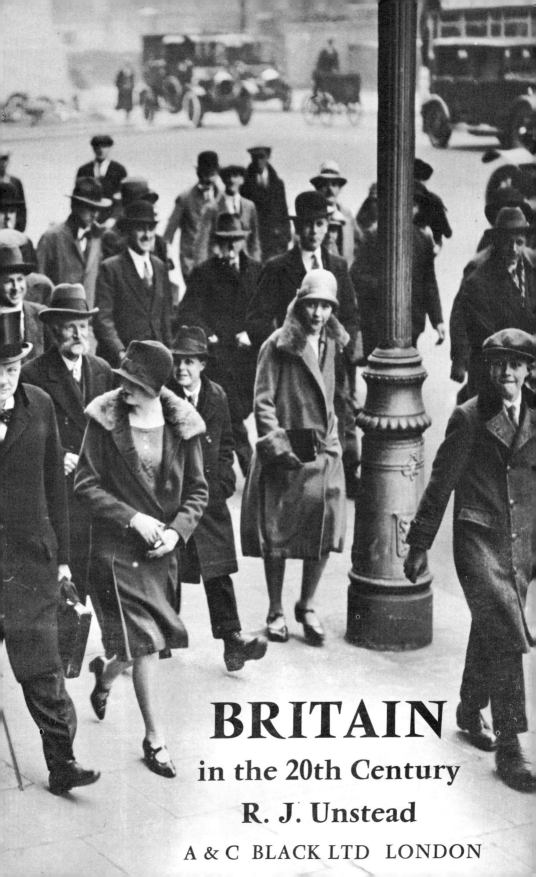

BRITAIN
in the 20th Century
R. J. Unstead
A & C BLACK LTD LONDON

A HISTORY OF BRITAIN

Also by R. J. Unstead

FOREWORD

THIS book describes British and world affairs in the first sixty years of the twentieth century.

To write about recent events is a risky, even a rash, undertaking. Happenings within my memory and the memories of older people are wrapped about with emotion and prejudice, and the truth is difficult to get at because many official papers have not been released.

However, at the risk of over-simplifying some issues and leaving out much that might have gone in, I have tried to describe in a continuous narrative the world affairs which have, since 1906, influenced and diminished Britain's position as a great power. My aim has been to tell what happened and why—leaving judgment to the reader.

R. J. UNSTEAD

FIRST PUBLISHED 1966
REPRINTED WITH CORRECTIONS 1970
SBN 7136 0768 8 (BOARDS)   7136 0769 6 (WITH JACKET)

© 1966 A. AND C. BLACK LTD
4, 5 AND 6 SOHO SQUARE LONDON WIV 6AD

MADE AND PRINTED IN GREAT BRITAIN BY MORRISON AND GIBB LTD., LONDON AND EDINBURGH

CONTENTS

Continued overleaf

CHEAPSIDE, LONDON, 1906

1 Edwardian Contrast

In history there are few abrupt beginnings or sudden endings. When the twentieth century began, the Victorian age had lasted so long that it seemed to be unchangeable. The old Queen was still on the throne and her portly, affable son was still awaiting the long-deferred call to take up his role as King and Emperor.

Our own age, the age of the twentieth century, began not so much on 1st January 1900 as in January 1906 when the Liberals won a General Election with a crushing majority.

The Liberal victory marked the beginning of a new age. In 1906 a government took office with fresh ideas about social reform; most of its members worked for a living and there were some who had been educated at elementary schools. For the first time, there was a sizeable group of Members of Parliament from working-class homes. The monarch no longer lived in seclusion at Windsor—for Edward VII was a popular figure, often to be seen enjoying himself, yet carrying out his duties with a new-found seriousness. There was less complacency about affairs outside the United Kingdom and the feeling was growing that Britain could no longer afford to ignore the existence of foreigners. Nervousness about German ambitions had already led to a friendlier understanding with France.

A young man named Morris had started making motor-cars at Oxford; there were experimental aeroplanes in France and America, and electric tramcars and underground trains in London. Maxim machine-guns, reduced in weight to less than 40 lb, were being adopted by Europe's armies; Marconi had sent wireless signals across the Atlantic; Thomson and Rutherford were working on atomic physics; medical science was being transformed through the use of X-rays, radium and new antiseptics. For the people's amusement, there were the first cinemas, the gramophone and the popular newspapers.

But if, in its concern with social reform, with science and with pleasure, 1906 resembled our own age, it was also a very different world from today.

7

Britain was rich and powerful. Her Empire covered a quarter of the globe's surface, the Royal Navy was more powerful than the combined strength of the next two most powerful nations, British merchant-ships carried half the world's goods and British money had built railways, mines and rubber plantations in distant places. To most people it seemed natural that this splendid state of affairs should continue indefinitely. True, there were occasional clouds on the horizon—the Boer War had been an irritating business and the German Kaiser seemed to go out of his way to be unpleasant—but with Free Trade and the British Navy, there seemed no reason why life should not go on getting better for everyone. As yet there was little realisation that America and Germany had already forged ahead in industrial production, that Britain was now in the afternoon of power.

It was a very good time for the rich. Income-tax was a shilling in the pound, servants were cheap (butlers at £1 a week, maids at 7s 6d) and there was plenty of money about. Unlike their fathers, the Edwardians made it fly. It was an age of extravagance when " Society "—the name given to the fashionable upper class—having broken away from the restrictions of Victorianism, displayed its wealth for all to see. It was a time of aristocratic house-parties, of great hostesses and famous beauties, when buxom tiny-waisted ladies, in satins, velvets and ostrich feathers, dressed more sumptuously than at any time since the eighteenth century.

At the summit of the fashionable world was King Edward with his circle of friends who included financiers, actresses and a successful grocer, for this was an aristocracy of wealth and charm, led by a king with vulgar tastes and an insatiable appetite for food, sport and the company of beautiful women. Shooting in Scotland, yachting at Cowes, racing at Ascot, dawdling in Paris and Biarritz, sipping the waters at foreign spas: all these helped the year along, and when the London " season " was over, there was the round of weekend parties at the great country houses. The style of these Edwardian weekends typified the opulence of that so-recently vanished age.

FASHION
1907

TEA ON THE
LAWN

As many as fifty guests would arrive on Friday afternoon. Motor-cars were still liable to break down, so most guests came by train and were met by a variety of carriages with wooden-seated waggons for the servants, since every man brought his valet and every lady at least one maid. On arrival at the big house, the guests were greeted by their hostess and escorted to their rooms. Meanwhile the resident servants, forty of them indoors and as many again in the gardens and stables, looked after the visiting servants according to the rank of their employers. After tea in the pink drawing-room, the guests prepared for dinner, for by now the servants had lit fires in every bedroom, turned on the bath taps and carried innumerable cans of hot water upstairs. The valets laid out their employers' evening suits and the ladies' maids laced up corsets and arranged hair into piles and curls. Dinner was served at eight-thirty. It consisted of seven or eight courses, liberally washed down with the appropriate wines; afterwards, there were cards, charades and dancing—the King particularly liked Scottish reels and, when he was feeling jocular, practical jokes of a singularly feeble kind such as pouring a glass of brandy over the head of an elderly equerry. At midnight, in case anyone felt hungry, a cold supper was served.

*Edwardian
house-party*

In the morning, tea and biscuits were brought to every room and the servants carried in the polished cans of hot shaving water, while downstairs another small army was dusting, polishing and blackleading the firegrates.

Breakfast was taken at half-past nine. The guests came down in ones and twos to help themselves from side-tables loaded with silver dishes containing porridge, kippers, bacon, eggs, kidneys and chops. There was also a cold table with ham, tongue, cold pheasant and grouse.

Saturday was devoted to sport. Parties went off to shoot or ride and after lunch there was croquet, archery or a run in a motor-car. For this adventurous sport, the ladies put on long sealskin coats, and thick veils as protection from the clouds of dust sucked up by the Dunlop tyres. So the weekend progressed. The guests changed their clothes endlessly, as one occupation gave way to the next. By evening, everyone was ready for another gigantic meal, for the dancing, the games, the love-making and the giggles at the latest story of the King's indiscretions. On Monday morning, the guests departed by train to prepare themselves for the following weekend.

HOUSEMAID AT
7s 6d A WEEK

*Middlesbrough
1906*

To a lesser extent, this style of life was copied by the prosperous middle class. The heavily-furnished homes of bankers and lawyers were staffed by a cook, butler and parlour-maid; charwomen did the rough cleaning and boys polished the knives and boots. Wives of shopkeepers and clerks employed a daily maid to answer the door and, out of all the women who worked, one in three was a domestic servant. In this Church-going world of governesses and nannies, of cosy drawing-rooms and seaside holidays, there was little knowledge of how the other half of Britain lived, of what life was like in an industrial town such as Middlesbrough.

In less than a century, Middlesbrough had grown from a hamlet with thirty-five inhabitants to a great iron town with a population of over 90,000. It possessed a town hall, a free library, some churches, schools and eight or nine hundred streets of mean little houses, each consisting of four or five rooms and a scullery. Nearly all the men worked at the iron foundries, where wages were fairly good—the best-paid men earned £2 to £3 a week, the lowest had 19s 6d and the majority from 25s to 38s a week, as much as clerks in Government offices, but their work was hard and unhealthy.

As always, the standard of life depended on the wife, whose

management made the difference between decency and squalor. Mrs A. with only one child, laid out her husband's wage of 19s 6d as follows—rent, 5s 6d; insurance, 7d; coal, 2s 5½d; household needs (soap, candles, matches), 1½d; clothing, 1s; husband's tobacco, 9d; debt, 1s 3d; and food, 7s 5d. Because she was frugal and self-denying, she managed far better than Mrs B. whose husband on £2 a week drank and gambled but, even so, 7s 5d a week gave her family only as much food as a better-off family would eat in two days.

These poorer working-class homes teetered always on the edge of disaster. Illness or the death of the wage-earner could mean loss of the home itself. The cost of a child's funeral or even of a pair of boots could lead to debt that had to be paid off by weekly instalments perhaps for years. Boots were a special problem for the men who had to have strong footwear for their work, so the children went barefoot and the women managed with second-hand pairs bought for a penny or two from the street barrows. " A working girl said . . . that she thought the mark of a ' real lady ' was that she wore . . . neat boots ".* Clothes were hardly ever new. They came mostly from second-hand shops and hawkers, and the workman went to work like a scarecrow " clad almost in rags, as, unwashed unshaven, his can of food swinging in his hand, he strides along in a greasy, torn old coat with holes in it, patched trousers . . . tied tightly below the knee ".*

But, except for the poorest, it was a life not without pleasure. In Middlesbrough there were the workmen's clubs and musical " socials ", two theatres and two music-halls (2d in the gallery) besides football matches and the perennial interest in horse-racing. There was a news-room at the free library, but it was estimated that out of a population of 90,000, 70,000 did not go to a church or chapel. With a six-day working week, Sunday was the only rest-day and since everywhere was closed except the pubs, it was customary for many workmen to spend most of the day in bed, reading the sensational newspapers. A good many who were unable to read were read to by their wives and children, but, at a time when working-class boys of ability had practically no chance of schooling beyond the age of twelve or thirteen, there were workmen who read history

* At the Works. A Study of a Manufacturing Town—Lady Bell (1907).

and economics and others who taught themselves French and German.

Drink was still a major evil. Time after time, households were ruined because the husband drank away half his wages and it was a common sight to see hopelessly drunk men and women reeling about the streets or fighting like animals. Scenes like this haunted the memory of many a child:

" I saw my brother look swiftly down the street at a second gang of urchins. It was following a navvy, a hatless figure with features flaming and eyes distorted with drink and fear. He was running and gasping as he ran . . .

" I heard the man whimpering for breath; and I smelled sweat and beer. I heard too the chorus of jeers and yells from the juvenile furies that followed. But between him and them was the real cause of his flight. It was a woman, ragged and shameful, her hair torn down, her blouse gaping and one eye laid open and bleeding on her cheek. She was mad with fury and screaming with pain, plunging wildly to right and left but striving by sheer power of rage to follow her man who had thus ill-treated her. The mob was at her skirts, urging her on . . ." *

Gambling was another cause of poverty but, apart from the death of the wage-earner, the worst threat to a family was illness. When he was off sick, a workman's wages stopped (unless he was a foreman) and his family was quickly plunged into want. To lessen this catastrophe, thrifty men paid 3d a week for the doctor and 4d or so into a sick club that provided a few shillings a week during illness. His union might also pay him 10s a week and, when all benefit ran out, his mates would pass round the hat at work. But even so, the debts incurred during illness or unemployment were a never-ending nightmare in the home.

Ahead of the workman there was no prospect of a serene retirement, but only poverty-stricken old age with the dreaded workhouse as the last humiliation. Sometimes, under a good employer, an old workman could be found a lighter job, and when he became too feeble to go on working, there was parish relief and the possibility of a home with a married son or daughter.

* *Over the Bridge*, Richard Church (1955).

EDWARDIAN POVERTY

Life in Middlesbrough in the early part of the century might have been hard and unlovely but at least there was work and a sense of community, even among the worst-paid labourers. Conditions were far worse in London's East-end and it was Charles Booth's survey,* published in 1903, that really shocked the Edwardians and, in particular, the Liberals. After eighteen years of picking his way in and out the foul courtyards of London's slums, where he found British citizens leading " the life of savages ", Booth calculated that almost one-third (30.7 per cent) of London's entire population were poor and that 8 to 9 per cent were " very poor " or nearly starving.

At York, Seerbohm Rowntree of the famous chocolate firm, carried out an even more searching investigation.† He worked out the income needed to keep people just well enough to do their work; he pared everything down to the barest essentials as though a housewife always bought the most nourishing food

* *Life and Labour of the People in London.*
† *Poverty. A Study of Town Life* (1901).

13

at cheapest prices, never cooked butcher's meat or wrote a letter or bought a penny gift; he assumed that her husband never smoked or tasted beer, that her children ate less than their parents, and did without toys. To live thus, without comfort and at a lower level than paupers in the workhouse, required an income of 21s 8d for a family of two adults and three children. Yet Rowntree found that one-tenth of the population of York were *below* this level of bare existence.*

"That in this land of abounding wealth probably more than a fourth of the population are living in poverty is a fact which may well cause great searching of heart," declared Rowntree and it was the knowledge of what he and Booth had uncovered that helped to bring the Liberals to power in 1906.

* Here is Rowntree's diet for children of 8–16 years. It was the most nourishing diet that could be devised for a cost of 2s 7d a week.

	BREAKFAST	DINNER	SUPPER
Sunday	Bread 6 oz Margarine ½ oz Tea ¾ pt	Boiled bacon 3 oz Bread 3 oz Potatoes 8 oz	Bread 6 oz Margarine ½ oz Cocoa ¾ pt
Monday	Bread 3 oz Milk ½ pt Porridge ¾ pt Sugar ½ oz	Potatoes 16 oz Bread 2 oz Cheese 1½ oz	Bread 6 oz Veg. Broth ¾ pt Cheese 1½ oz
Tuesday	,,	Veg. broth ½ pt Bread 3 oz Cheese 1½ oz Dumpling 6 oz	Plain cake 6 oz Milk ¾ pt
Wednesday	,,	Boiled bacon 3 oz Bread 3 oz Potatoes 3 oz	,,
Thursday	,,	Cocoa ¾ pt Bread 6 oz Cheese 2 oz	Bread 6 oz Broth ¾ pt Cheese 1½ oz
Friday	,,	Boiled bacon 3 oz Bread 3 oz Potatoes 8 oz	Plain cake 6 oz Cocoa ¾ pt
Saturday	,,	Suet Pudding 12 oz	Bread 6 oz Milk ¾ pt

In addition, lunch of bread 2 oz, cake 2 oz or biscuits 2 oz on weekdays only.

2 Liberals in Power

EDWARD VII
AND HIS NEPHEW
THE KAISER, 1906

In the House of Commons, there were two parties that mattered:
the Conservatives led by A. J. Balfour, the Marquess of Salisbury's nephew, and the Liberals led by Sir Henry Campbell-
Bannerman, an elderly Scottish millionaire with mutton-chop
whiskers and a hesitant manner that seemed to apologise for the
fact that he was the leader only by accident. For years the
Liberals had been weak and divided. The Boer War had split
them into three groups and their opponents believed that even
if they patched up their quarrels, they would provide so feeble
a government that, in Joe Chamberlain's words, they would be
speedily " hissed off the stage ".

However, the Conservatives also had their problems. They
had been in office for a long time, long enough to have upset a
great many people. Balfour's Education Act of 1902 * had
deeply offended the Nonconformists, and a Licensing Act which
aimed at reducing the number of public houses caused offence
because " the drink trade " thought it threatened their profits
and the temperance movement felt that it did too little to lessen
the evils of drink.

* The 1902 Education Act abolished School Boards and set up
local education committees with power to start secondary schools.
Great bitterness was caused by the assistance given to Church
schools out of the rates since, in many areas, the only school was a
Church of England school and Nonconformists objected to paying
rates for their own children to have religious teaching with which
they disagreed. Many refused to pay and some even went to prison.
Generally speaking, Nonconformists voted Liberal and Anglicans
voted Conservative.

15

Another cause of discontent was the famous Taff Vale case of 1901. A strike of railway workers in South Wales had been followed by a court action in which the employers successfully sued the trade union for damages, thus making it virtually impossible for any body of workmen to strike. A more extraordinary cause of alarm was the " Chinese Slavery " scare.

46,000 Chinese labourers had been imported into South Africa after the Boer War to restart the gold mines. They worked a sixty-hour week for 2s a day and were herded into squalid camps where their treatment was disgraceful. Yet it is difficult to explain why the British public was so roused. Their feeling was not so much pity as fear of cheap labour being introduced into Britain. Some Liberals, including Lloyd George, went so far as to hint that Chinese labour might take the jobs of British workmen; during the Election, gangs of unemployed men were hired to walk the streets in chains bearing placards with the words, " Chinese Slaves "!

Protection

But the real issue of the 1906 Election was Free Trade. A rare split divided the Conservative ranks when Joseph Chamberlain launched his campaign for " Protection ". He wanted to tax goods coming into the country in order to protect British employers and workmen from " unfair " competition—chiefly from Americans and Germans who, thanks to Free Trade, could sell cheap goods here while protecting their own markets by taxes known as tariffs. Chamberlain's real aim was to bind the Empire together by a special trading arrangement called Imperial Preference but, in attacking the sacred doctrine of Free Trade, he handed victory to the Liberals.

For sixty years Britain had prospered mightily and people believed in Free Trade as they believed in the Almighty. Yet here was Joe Chamberlain, the greatest figure in the Conservative Party, trying to put an end to it. The Liberals, Free-traders to a man, pointed out that Britain's chief import was food, and Asquith followed Chamberlain round the country denouncing his intention of taxing the poor man's daily bread. A famous poster depicted the " little loaf " of Protection beside the " big loaf " of Free Trade, and in the Election of 1906 the " big loaf " won a tremendous victory.

When the results came in—and in those days elections were spread over three or four weeks—the Liberals had won 401 seats against their opponents' 157, and there were in addition

83 Irish Nationalists and 29 Labour M.P.'s who were certain to support the Liberals on most matters.

" Unless I am greatly mistaken, the election of 1906 inaugurates a new era ", observed Balfour, who had himself been defeated at Manchester.

*   *   *   *   *

For the first time in history, Britain was to be governed, not by the aristocracy, but by a party drawn chiefly from the middle class. Perhaps the most significant feature of the new Parliament was the presence of twenty-nine Labour M.P.'s. They had been sent there by the Labour Representation Committee, for the Labour Party, as such, was not formed until later in the year. Their leaders, Ramsay MacDonald, a handsome, golden-tongued Scot, and Philip Snowden, an embittered cripple, were men of ability, but not even the most ardent trade unionist foresaw the day when they and their successors would form a Labour Government. For the moment, the Liberals, secure in their vast majority, smiled benevolently at the worthy fellows from the coal-mines and docks. *The Liberal triumph*

Between 1906 and 1914 the Liberals founded the Welfare State. They did not invent social reform, for the Conservatives had introduced many reforming measures, including Joe Chamberlain's Workmen's Compensation Act and Balfour's Education Act, but the Liberals tackled poverty and misfortune in a new spirit. Besides taking social reform into wider fields by giving assistance to adult male workers, they came to accept the principle that the State should take responsibility for *preventing* people from becoming destitute.

The new Prime Minister was Campbell-Bannerman, of whom *The Times* said " he really leads nobody, never has led anybody and is never likely to lead anybody ". But, in office, Campbell-Bannerman was a new man. Gone was his old dithering uncertainty and, although he still peered at his notes held two inches from his short-sighted eyes, he side-stepped those who would have replaced him by a younger man and, with an air of decision and authority, he picked his Cabinet from the ranks of eager politicians who now filled the House. He gave the Exchequer to Asquith, the Foreign Office to Edward Grey, the War Office to R. B. Haldane and the Board of Trade to David Lloyd George. These four were his leading ministers but there was a great deal of talent among the more junior M.P.'s,

CAMPBELL-
BANNERMAN

including Winston Churchill * who had left the Conservative Party over the Free Trade issue. At thirty-one, Churchill became Under-Secretary for the Colonies and quickly made his presence felt by deluging his colleagues with his views on each and every matter of government or policy. The Liberals regarded the explosive energy of the " little square-headed fellow " with a mixture of irritation and awe but the Conservatives looked on him as a base traitor to his Party and his class.

As a gesture of friendship to the Labour Members, Campbell-Bannerman made John Burns † President of the Local Government Board, so that the bearded docker who called the Prime Minister, " Sir 'Enery ", became the first ex-manual worker to enter the Cabinet.

Despite their huge majority, the Liberals were unable to start an immediate flood of social reform. Campbell-Bannerman had no clear programme, only a vague feeling that " progress " was a good thing; but, more important, the House of Lords, overwhelmingly Conservative, was able to block any measure by simply rejecting a Bill that had been passed by the Commons.

Curiously enough, the Upper House did not reject the Trade Disputes Act of 1906 which reversed the Taff Vale decision. The Bill was hotly attacked but it was passed, possibly because the Lords did not fully understand it or because the Conservatives hoped to win working-class votes. However, an Education Bill that attempted to solve the difficulty of religious

* 1874–1965. b. Blenheim Palace, eldest son of Lord Randolph Churchill. Educated Harrow and Sandhurst. Entered Army 1895, served in India and at Omdurman, 1898. Left Army for journalism, captured by Boers in South Africa, escaped and entered Parliament 1900 as Conservative M.P. Joined Liberals; 1906 Colonial Under-secretary; 1908–10 President of Board of Trade; 1910 Home Secretary; 1911 First Lord of Admiralty; 1915, after Gallipoli, joined Army in France; 1917 Minister of Munitions; 1919–21 Secretary of State for War and Air. Rejoined Conservatives; 1924–29 Chancellor of Exchequer; 1939 First Lord again; 1940–45 Prime Minister; 1951–55 Prime Minister.

† Burns was in fact a Liberal, as were many other trade unionists. In 1906 the Labour Movement was far from united. Apart from the Independent Labour Party (I.L.P.), whose leader Keir Hardy was now joined in the Commons by MacDonald, Snowden, Clynes and others, there was a Marxist organisation called the Social Democratic Federation (led by Will Thorne and Ben Tillett) and the Fabian Society whose leaders included the Webbs, G. B. Shaw and H. G. Wells. Labour members affiliated to the Liberal Party were called " Lib-Labs ".

instruction in schools was so drastically handled by the Lords that it had to be withdrawn. When the same fate befell the Plural Voting Bill,* it was clear that the Liberals could only put through laws that the Lords accepted and Lloyd George, in particular, took note of the fact.

Some minor reforms were passed. Local authorities were given power to provide school meals for needy children, an Act of 1907 arranged for medical inspection at schools, grants to secondary schools were increased and a few more State Scholarships to universities were provided.

Meanwhile, Haldane reformed the British Army and created the Territorial and Reserve Forces. At the Board of Trade, *First reforms* Lloyd George was feverishly busy. This Welshman, brought up by his uncle, a village shoemaker, had qualified as a solicitor in 1890 and had entered Parliament, where for fifteen years his eloquence and knowledge of Welsh affairs had made him the most prominent of all the back-benchers. Now that he was in office, Lloyd George seized the chance to prove his capacity. His Merchant Shipping Act of 1906 improved the conditions of seamen at sea and in the ports; he took the first Census of Production in Britain, settled a major railway dispute and a shipyard strike and set up the Port of London Authority to plan the development of England's greatest port.

* At this time an elector could vote in any constituency where he owned property. Even if his property was scattered, the practice of holding a General Election over several weeks meant that he could still vote several times. In 1918 Plural Voting was restricted to the right to vote in two places only: it was finally abolished in 1948.

While Campbell-Bannerman encouraged his restless sub-ordinates and gave them their head, his own greatest achieve-ment was a settlement in South Africa where full self-government was given first to Transvaal and in 1907 to the Orange Free State. Balfour described this as a " reckless experiment " but it led to the formation of the Union of South Africa which became a Dominion of the British Empire.

Asquith Prime Minister

By the end of 1907 Campbell-Bannerman was seriously ill and, although he remained full of plans and hopes for the future, he was forced to resign in April 1908 and in the same month he died. Edward VII, who had already informed Asquith * that he was to be the next Prime Minister, was staying at Biarritz but, not wishing to interrupt his holiday, he summoned Asquith to France where the royal hand was kissed in a foreign hotel.

To his own place as Chancellor of the Exchequer, Asquith appointed Lloyd George and he brought Churchill into the Cabinet as President of the Board of Trade. With these two human dynamos under a Prime Minister so tough and remorse-less in debate that Campbell-Bannerman used to call him " The Sledgehammer ", sparks were certain to fly in Parliament and in the country at large.

Old Age Pensions

For his 1907 Budget, Asquith had set aside £2 million towards a future introduction of Old Age Pensions and now, in 1908, although Prime Minister, he insisted on presenting the Budget he had already prepared. At the age of seventy, a single person was to receive 5s a week and married couples 7s 6d if the income was less than £26 a year for a single person and £39 for a couple. A strange exception was that the pension was not to be given to anyone who in the previous five years had been convicted of a serious crime. Even for 1908 the pension was small but it benefited five million persons whose gratitude at being saved from the workhouse was often pathetic in the extreme. The cost of the scheme was to be met from general taxation since, as yet, there was no insurance plan.

Naturally, there was opposition, the fiercest coming, strangely enough, from a small group of die-hard Liberals. Lord Rose-bery, a former Liberal Prime Minister, denounced the pensions

* Herbert Henry Asquith (1858–1928), b. Morley, Yorks, educated Oxford University, a brilliant scholar and lawyer, M.P. 1886. Home Secretary 1892–95, Chancellor of Exchequer 1905–08, Prime Minister 1908–16, i.e. for eight and a half years until " ousted " by Lloyd George. Became Earl of Oxford and Asquith 1925.

A TAILOR'S 'SWEAT SHOP' IN EDWARD VII'S REIGN

as " a scheme so prodigal of expenditure that it might be dealing a blow at the Empire which might be almost mortal ", but Asquith had his way and Britain moved on to the road that led to the Welfare State.

1908 saw a series of furious battles over a Licensing Bill and two more Education Bills. All three were defeated, partly by the Lords but also by the passionate emotions that were aroused on the subjects of drink and religion. The Home Office brought in a Childrens Act that set up juvenile courts and remand homes, and Churchill at the Board of Trade proved as vigorous as his predecessor in pushing through the Act that created the Port of London Authority, and in pressing for an eight-hour day in the coal-mines. In the following year, 1909, he introduced the Trades Board Act to regulate wages and conditions of work in tailoring, paperbox-making, lace- and chain-making, four trades notorious for using " sweated labour "—i.e. persons, many of them women, children and aliens, who were forced to accept low wages and to work at home or in foul workshops. The first Labour Exchange was opened in 1910 to help the unemployed to find work, and for the task of organising similar exchanges all over the country Churchill chose W. S. (afterwards Sir William) Beveridge.

Yet, while these reforms were in hand, the Liberals steadily lost support. Their only popular achievement was the Old Age Pension scheme, and the Conservatives were cock-a-hoop when the traitor Churchill was defeated in a by-election * at Manchester, though he soon succeeded at Dundee.

By-elections were much livelier affairs than nowadays:

By-elections

" The law on election expenses was so weak that any outside organisation could join in. In every constituency where there was a contest the Imperial Tariff Committee rented shop windows to show ' dumped foreign goods '. The Free Trade Union retaliated by renting windows to show specimens of horse flesh and black bread on which the protected workers of Germany were supposed to live. The coal-owners financed a Coal Consumers League which made a speciality of torchlight processions in protest against the Eight Hour Bill in the mines. The publicans organised against the Licensing Bill, every bar becoming a Conservative Committee-room. The United Kingdom Alliance paraded its banners in favour of the Licensing Bill, every chapel vestry becoming a Liberal Headquarters. Anglican and nonconformist clergy thundered against each other in their pulpits over church schools. There were election jingles for the children to sing and plenty of unemployed who, for a shilling a head, would demonstrate in favour of anyone. On the fringes demonstrated the Suffragettes, breaking up the meetings of both sides, but especially of the Liberals, by shrieking ' Votes for Women! ' " †

Into this excited atmosphere came the news of a crisis in the Balkans and the alarming discovery that the Royal Navy was seriously threatened by the growth of the German Navy. McKenna at the Admiralty asked for six dreadnoughts ‡ at once and eighteen in all and when the Government decided that four were enough with four more later, music-hall audiences chanted " We want Eight, and we won't wait ". As Chancellor of the Exchequer, Lloyd George would have to find an extra £15 million in taxes to pay for the ships, at a time when finance was stretched by the fact that the Old Age Pensions were proving to be far more costly than Asquith had calculated.

* At this time, an M.P. who was appointed to the Cabinet had to be re-elected.
† *The Liberals in Power*, Colin Cross (1963).
‡ See page 32.

The little Welshman was exhilarated by this challenge to his ingenuity. Difficulty could be turned into an opportunity to defeat the Lords, to bring in fresh social reform and to build the battleships that the Navy wanted.

The 1909 Budget was deliberately dramatic. Lloyd George called it a " War Budget for raising money to wage war against poverty and squalidness ", though by modern standards it was unbelievably mild. Its chief proposals were increased income-tax on large incomes, so that the rate rose from 1s to 1s 2d on incomes over £3000 with a supertax on those over £5000 a year, increased taxes on public houses, on tobacco and drink, taxes on motor-cars and petrol to pay for improvement of the roads, a tax on mining royalties to go into a Miners' Welfare Fund and some small taxes on land that roused particular fury.

The People's Budget

The howl of protest that greeted " the People's Budget " was absurd if anyone had stopped to contrast the country's needs with the small amounts of extra money that even the richest citizen had to find. But the Opposition rightly perceived that this was the thin end of the wedge and that the " robber gull's " Budget was only a start to the process of " soaking the rich ".

In attacking Lloyd George, the Conservatives took on a tartar. In speech after speech in different parts of the country, he poured contempt and ridicule upon their defence of mon-opoly and privilege until he goaded them into their greatest folly. The House of Lords rejected the Budget and Lloyd George cried exultantly, " We have got them at last! ".

For 250 years it had been accepted that whatever else the Lords might reject, they must not throw out a Money Bill. A General Election had to be held on this issue and although the Liberals came back with a much smaller majority, the Budget was passed and Asquith brought in his plan to curb the House of Lords. He prepared a Parliament Bill that would prevent the Lords from rejecting or amending money bills and from holding up other bills for more than two years. Naturally, the Lords put up a strenuous fight against a plan that would so seriously reduce their power.

The sudden death of Edward VII in May 1910 brought a truce to the struggle but after the accession of George V, the Lords persisted in their opposition until Asquith announced that a General Election would be held on the sole question of the Lords' power to prevent laws being passed.

GEORGE V,
1910

*Defeat of
the Lords*

In December 1910 the Liberals and Conservatives tied with 272 seats each but since there were 42 Labour M.P.'s and 84 Irish Nationalists, Asquith could be certain of victory. When the Lords understood that George V had agreed to create sufficient new Liberal peers to swamp the Conservatives' majority, they gave in and the Parliament Bill became law.*

If the Liberals now looked forward to entering calmer waters, their hopes were vain for they were on the threshold of an era of violence which eventually engulfed their Party, the nation and the whole of Europe.

The Taff Vale judgement had been reversed but in 1908 the trade union movement suffered a severe blow in the Osborne Judgement. The secretary of the Walthamstow branch of the Amalgamated Society of Railway Servants, W. V. Osborne, obtained a court ruling that it was illegal for a union to compulsorily levy money from its members for the support of the Labour Party.† The unions, already irritated by the slow progress of reform and by rising prices at a time when some employers were cutting wages, turned to violent methods of airing their grievances. The writings of Karl Marx and a movement known as Syndicalism ‡ influenced some of the leaders, notably Tom Mann who went to France to learn the new doctrine of revolutionary trade unionism.

In 1910 there were strikes by miners, boilermakers and railway workers in the Newcastle area, trouble in the Lancashire cotton industry and a ten-month strike by miners in South

* On this same day (10th August 1911) the Commons voted themselves salaries—£400 a year for an M.P.

† The political levy was restored in 1913.

‡ Syndicalism comes from the French word for trade unionism. Its aim was to influence Parliament by direct action—strikes, sympathetic stoppages and sabotage leading to a general strike of all workers.

BEN TILLETT ADDRESSING A CROWD IN HYDE PARK ON LABOUR DAY

Wales. Serious rioting took place at Tonypandy, a man was killed and the chief constable asked for troops to reinforce the local police. Two companies of infantry and some cavalry were sent from Salisbury Plain. Churchill, the Home Secretary, stopped them at Swindon in hope that the riots would subside. *Strikes* They did not do so immediately and the arrival of the soldiers and a body of Metropolitan police caused deep resentment. Thereafter, Churchill was regarded as the man who had used troops against the workers.

The following year, 1911, brought more strikes. Seamen at Southampton struck for a wage increase, and when they won it their success galvanised other workers into action so violent that it surprised even Tom Mann and his friend Ben Tillett, the dockers' leader. A strike in the London docks was followed by a more serious one in Liverpool where two men were killed in a bloody clash between troops and rioters. Railwaymen joined the strike which spread into the Midlands and South Wales, where, at Llanelly, looting took place and two men were killed when soldiers opened fire. Mann was sent to prison in 1912 for urging soldiers not to obey their officers on such occasions and in the bitter atmosphere of riots, bloodshed and talk of " murdered " workers, the newly-formed Labour newspaper, the *Daily Herald*, took as its slogan " Strike and Strike Hard! ".

Further unrest and increased bitterness between employers and workers led to the so-called " Triple Alliance " of the miners, railwaymen and dockers who, at the suggestion of Bob Smillie, the Scottish miners' leader, were to combine for a general strike that would paralyse the country. However, arrangements had not been completed when war broke out in 1914 and, after a moment's hesitation, during which Ramsay MacDonald resigned the Chairmanship of the Parliamentary Labour Party, the trade union movement dropped its strike plans and co-operated with the Government.

Suffragettes

Less serious than the strikes was the vexatious behaviour of the Suffragettes, led by Mrs Emmeline Pankhurst and a number of well-to-do women, who had expected that the Liberal Government would bow to their demand for votes for women. When Asquith advised delay, they resorted to unbelievable violence, breaking windows, chaining themselves to railings, setting fire to houses and railway stations and damaging valuable paintings and works of art. Imprisoning the culprits only increased the Government's embarrassment, for the women went on hunger strike and in some cases became so ill that they had to be released. By the " Cat and Mouse Act " * of 1913, they could be rearrested at any time and this served to quiet things down until, at the outbreak of war, Mrs Pankhurst called off the campaign. The war service of thousands of women did far more to convince men that women should have a vote than did their breaking of windows and digging up of golf courses.

During these stormy events, the Government brought in the Shops Act to give a weekly half-holiday to workers, but the great measure of 1911 was the National Insurance Act. This was the creation of Lloyd George who had examined a health insurance scheme already set up in Germany, and of Churchill whose part was to work out a plan of unemployment insurance through the new Labour Exchanges.

* The name arose from the gibe that the government was treating the imprisoned suffragettes in the way that a cat plays with a mouse —letting it go and catching it again.

" Four spectres haunt the poor; old age, accident, sickness and unemployment ", said Lloyd George. " We are going to drive hunger from the hearth. We mean to banish the workhouse from the horizon of every workman in the land."

The Act had two parts: Part I dealt with sickness and Part II with unemployment. With a few exceptions,* Part I covered all workers earning less than £160 a year. Each would pay 4d a week while his employer paid 3d and the State 2d, hence Lloyd George's famous cry that the worker was getting " 9d for 4d ". The benefits were free medical treatment and sickness pay of 10s a week for men and 7s 6d for women for six months. Some 14 million people came into the scheme despite the fierce opposition of Conservatives, doctors and private insurance companies. Churchill's unemployment insurance covered only about 2¼ million workers, mainly in the shipbuilding, engineering and building trades, and the rate of contribution was 2½d a week by workmen, employer and State to provide unemployment benefit of 7s a week for up to fifteen weeks.

The National Insurance Act, 1911

* * * * *

From the beginning of the century, Irish affairs had taken on a menacing air. The Irish people had endured centuries of misgovernment and, although the Act of Union 1800 had joined Ireland to the United Kingdom, its native inhabitants always felt that they were second-class citizens in their own country. Gladstone had realised that the Irish must be given Home Rule but he failed to convince his Party or the Commons.

Ireland

Gradually the Irish became aware of their own nationhood. Poets such as Yeats and Synge awakened their pride and there were widespread attempts to revive the ancient Irish language. Nothing that the English could do in the way of a benevolent land policy or a friendly administration could weaken the Irish determination to free themselves from the hated oppressor.

Asquith and the Liberals were " Home Rulers " but their huge majority made it easy for them to put Irish affairs on one side. However, in 1910, when they tied with the Conservatives, they needed the support of John Redmond's Irish Nationalists. Thus, with the Lords shorn of their power, Home Rule seemed just round the corner.

* Soldiers, sailors, teachers and state employees.

SIR EDWARD
CARSON

There was however the problem of Ulster, that part of the North where Protestants were in the majority. In 1910 a pugnacious lawyer named Edward Carson became chairman of the Ulster Unionist Council and pledged himself and nearly half a million Ulstermen to defeat the " conspiracy " to set up Home Rule. They feared that a Roman Catholic Parliament in Dublin would deal harshly with the Protestants in the North and, in 1912, when Asquith introduced the Home Rule Bill, the Ulstermen were ready to fight. By 1914 both they and the Nationalists in the remainder of Ireland were drilling with rifles. Ireland was on the brink of civil war. The British Army, which included many Irishmen in its ranks, was shaken and feelings between the Liberals and Conservatives were so hostile that it appeared not unlikely that democracy would collapse.

The Conservative leader, Bonar Law, declared: " There are things stronger than parliamentary majorities . . . I can imagine no length of resistance to which Ulster can go in which I should not be prepared to support them." F. E. Smith, afterwards Lord Birkenhead, openly said that if Home Rule was granted, the Conservatives would refuse to recognise the law.

In March 1914 occurred the so-called " Curragh Mutiny " * when a number of Army officers declared that they would prefer to be dismissed than to obey orders to fight in Ulster, and in July Carson declared that Ulster would rather be cut off from the rest of Ireland than accept government from Dublin. " Give us a clean cut or come and fight us! " he cried. It was only the outbreak of war in Europe that postponed civil war in Ireland.

* The Curragh camp was near Dublin. Fifty-seven officers of the Third Cavalry Brigade and Brigadier-General Gough informed their C.-in-C. (General Paget) that they would accept dismissal " if ordered north ". Called to Whitehall, Gough and his colonels insisted on a written assurance that they would not be ordered to enforce the Home Rule Bill on Ulster. J. E. Seely, the Secretary of State for War, weakly agreed and General Sir John French initialled the written statement. Gough returned to Dublin in triumph but Asquith and his Cabinet could not allow Army officers to dictate policy. Seely was forced to resign. No action was taken against the officers. Strictly speaking, there was no mutiny as they had not disobeyed any orders. Paget and Seely were really to blame for having earlier suggested that officers whose homes were in Ulster might " disappear ".

3 Causes of the Great War

THE Liberals who came to power in 1906 were a peace-loving set of men whose aims were to heal the wrongs of Ireland and to promote social reform. Even Winston Churchill was opposed to spending money on the Royal Navy, but in less than a decade the peaceable Liberals found themselves faced not only by riotous strikers, fanatical women and trigger-happy Irishmen, but by the greatest conflict that the world had ever known.

As always, the roots of war were deep and entangled. The Western nations, for all their wealth and progress, had not devised a way of solving their disputes without war. Nationalism, hurt pride, sensational Press-scares and even perhaps a deep longing for violence may have been more potent causes of war than the actual events that brought about the explosion. Had the nations been set on peace, the arrival of a gunboat in a distant harbour or even the murder of an Archduke would not have provoked a war.

Bismarck, " the Iron Chancellor " of Germany, had completed the unification of his country when he defeated France in 1870. Thereafter, he wanted peace but France would neither forget the loss of Alsace-Lorraine nor forgive her own humiliation. So Bismarck built the Triple Alliance with Austria and Italy and encouraged France to interest herself in North Africa. When the young Emperor, or Kaiser, William II dropped Bismarck and began to show a thirst for military glory, France and Russia made a treaty (1894) that seemed to balance the peace but, in fact, led to war.

Like Britain, France suffered from a series of violent strikes in the pre-war years and the country was divided by an attack on the Roman Catholic Church that led to confiscation of Church property in 1906. Clemenceau and Briand, two of France's best-known premiers, did not hesitate to use troops against Syndicalist strikers but, in general, governments were weak and constantly in and out of office so that Frenchmen came to despise politicians and to distrust their leaders.

These weaknesses at home did not prevent France from pursuing her ambitions in North Africa. Rivalry over Egypt led to anti-British feeling but, thanks partly to King Edward's cordial attitude, relations between the two countries became more friendly. Britain recognised France's claim to have a special interest in Algeria and Morocco but this new-found friendship was far from pleasing to Germany. In 1905 the Kaiser visited Tangier to announce his country's " great and growing interest in Morocco ", and his pugnacity appeared to pay dividends when the French meekly dismissed their Foreign Minister, Delcassé, and agreed to an international conference. However, the conference rebuffed Germany and the Kaiser had to retire empty-handed. The Sultan of Morocco was to allow France (and Spain) to " police " his territory but, more important, the crisis led to secret talks between British and French military staffs. No official decisions were taken and Grey did not tell the entire Cabinet about the talks, but they were a sensible precaution at a time when the German Chief of Staff in Berlin was openly speaking of the need for a " prompt war " against France.

Triple Entente

To counter the German tactics, Britain's next move was a friendly approach to Russia. In 1907 their long-standing differences over Persia * and Afghanistan were settled and this meant that Russia and France, already allies, were now joined by Britain in a Triple Entente that balanced the Triple Alliance of Germany, Austria and Italy. This apparently satisfactory arrangement was to prove disastrous for, with everyone scenting danger, any affront to one partner was bound to be taken up by the others. Britain tried to salve her conscience by avoiding actual alliances. In fact, she selfishly wanted the rewards of friendship without definite obligations.

By now, all leading countries except Britain had systems of compulsory military service and the German Army was by far the strongest in the world, especially as France had temporarily cut the period of service from three years to two. But the Kaiser was not content. " I shall never rest ", he declared, " until I have raised my navy to the same standard as my army ", and, from the turn of the century, Admiral Tirpitz was given the task of building a fleet to rival the British Royal Navy.

It was some time before Britain realised the danger. New developments—steel armour-plating, breech-loading guns, torpedoes—had made it essential to keep the fleet up to date so

* Persia was divided into two zones, the northern to be Russian, the southern British. Thus Britain succeeded in keeping Russia away from the Persian Gulf.

THE WAR LORDS: KAISER WILHELM II (CENTRE) WITH HIS CHIEF OF
GENERAL STAFF, GENERAL HELMUTH JOHANNES VON MOLTKE (FORE-
GROUND) AND PRUSSIAN OFFICERS

31

that building had gone on steadily under the eye of Admiral Fisher, the First Sea Lord, who was prepared to go to any lengths to modernise his beloved Navy. In 1906, H.M.S. *Dreadnought*,* a new type of battleship, was launched. Two of these great vessels were to be built in 1908 when it was learned

The Dreadnought Debate

that Tirpitz had laid down four battleships † of equal power. McKenna, First Lord of the Admiralty, and Fisher immediately asked for six dreadnoughts but were opposed by Lloyd George and, of all persons, Winston Churchill who, intent upon social reform, declared " Germany has nothing to fight about ". Fisher increased his demand to eight and, to obtain popular support, unscrupulously " leaked " naval secrets and Cabinet discussions to the Press.

Grey at the Foreign Office supported Fisher and, to avoid the resignation of Lloyd George and Churchill, Asquith settled the matter by promising four dreadnoughts at once and four more soon afterwards. In fact, Fisher contrived to have all eight laid down and Lloyd George had to find the unheard-of sum of £15 million extra taxation for his 1909 Budget. As we have seen, he used the opportunity in his own way. The other opponent of naval spending, Winston Churchill, was to become First Lord of the Admiralty by the time the dreadnoughts were ready for sea.

* She was armed with ten 12-inch guns, more than twice the number carried by any previous vessel and was the first battleship with steam turbines and she could burn oil as well as coal. She made all other battleships obsolete, including all of Britain's older ships, so the arrival of one new type made a huge building programme necessary.

† These German battleships, copies of the dreadnought, were too big to go through the Kiel Canal and the Germans set about widening it so that their fleet could operate in the Baltic against Russia and in the North Sea against Britain.

H.M.S. DREADNOUGHT, 1909

It was curious that the public which became so agitated about Britain's dreadnoughts took little interest in the Army reforms put through in 1907 by Haldane, who created the Territorial Force and an Expeditionary Force that could rapidly be mobilised for service overseas.

The dreadnought debate took place at a time when events in the Near East were causing international alarm. Turkey still ruled the greater part of the Balkans where Greeks, Slavs (Serbs and Croats) Rumanians and Bulgars were united only in hatred of a corrupt oppressor. As Turkey appeared ever more likely to crumble, Austria and Russia took an increasing interest in the fate of the Balkan principalities. Regarding herself as the champion of the Slav peoples, Russia saw the opportunity to secure an outlet to the sea via the Dardanelles. *The Balkans* For Austria, with Germany to the north and Italy to the south, this was the only area in which she could expand. However, in 1908 a revolution took place in Turkey where a group of ardent nationalists known as the Young Turks, forced the Sultan to bring in reforms which, if effective, would soon change Turkey into a vigorous power. Alarmed by this possibility, Austria promptly annexed two Balkan states, Bosnia and Herzegovina, and Bulgaria declared its own independence. Russia gained nothing and Serbia, seeing an end to her hopes of becoming the greatest of the Balkan countries, became bitterly hostile to Austria.

Having courted Turkish friendship for ten years,* Germany was annoyed with Austria but, putting the best face on the affair, Kaiser William bombastically declared that he stood by his ally " like a knight in shining armour ". For the time being the situation simmered down, so much so that Anglo-German relations became quite friendly and in May 1911 the Kaiser visited London for the unveiling of the Queen Victoria Memorial.

In that same year there was another crisis which shook Europe more than the Tangier affair or the seizure of Bosnia. French troops, claiming to protect European residents, occupied Fez,

---

* In the nineties, a German company had obtained permission to build railways in Turkey. The German dream was a line running from Berlin to Baghdad and on to the Persian Gulf, so that German influence would extend from the Baltic to the Indian Ocean. Thus, in her drive towards the East, Germany could not allow Russia to dominate the Balkans.

the capital of Morocco, whereupon Germany demanded
" compensation " in the Congo and reinforced this demand by
sending the gunboat *Panther* to the Moroccan port of Agadir.
This action not only incensed France, but Britain became
alarmed at the possibility of a German naval base on the
Atlantic coast of North Africa. A warship was sent to lie alongside the *Panther* and Lloyd George, hitherto known to be a
friend of Germany, made a speech in which he declared that
there were situations in which the price of peace would be " a
humiliation intolerable for a great country like ours to endure ".

The Germans took the hint or the threat. They were angry
but they were not quite ready for war, so they accepted two
slices of French Congo as compensation and the *Panther* sailed
away from Agadir.

The results of the crisis were deplorable. Certainly, France
and Britain were drawn closer together, but Germany now saw
Britain as the chief opponent to all her aims. " It cannot go
on," declared a German paper. " The conflict between us, far
from being settled, is now more than ever inevitable." Efforts
were made to ease the situation and Haldane, who knew the
country well, went to Germany to try to obtain an agreement.
But the Germans only insisted that " England will as a matter
of course remain neutral if war is forced on Germany ".

In 1912 the Balkans again burst into flames. Greece, Serbia,
Montenegro and Bulgaria formed the Balkan League to throw
off the Turkish yoke, and their armies were so completely
successful that Turkey lost all her European territory except
Constantinople and a strip of coast.* However, the victors soon
fell out over the spoils. In 1913, Bulgaria attacked Serbia and
Greece, but Rumania and Turkey fell upon the attacker with
the result that Bulgaria was defeated. Serbia emerged as the
strongest Balkan state. Her burning ambition was to wrest
Bosnia from Austria, and the Austrians, well aware of the fact,
were determined to crush Serbia at the first opportunity. That
opportunity arrived in the summer of 1914.

On 28th June the Archduke Francis Ferdinand, heir to the
thrones of Austria and Hungary, was shot dead as he sat in his
motor-car in Sarajevo, the capital of Bosnia. The assassin, a

---

* The Balkan League was able to strike when Turkey was already
in difficulties. Italy, taking advantage of the Agadir crisis, had sent
an army to North Africa to attack and seize the isolated Turkish
province of Tripoli. Like Germany, Italy wanted colonies in Africa.

THE BALKANS
IN 1914

nineteen-year-old Bosnian student, was undoubtedly assisted by
the Black Hand, a terrorist secret society whose activities were
known to the Serbian Government; the plot was hatched in
Serbia and the fatal revolver was purchased in Belgrade. The
Austrians could not have wished for a better case and the
Emperor Francis Joseph wrote to the Kaiser asking for approval
of measures to punish the Serbs. William II, about to leave for
his annual cruise with the fleet, replied with a promise of full
support and he briefly warned his Service chiefs of the possibility
of war with Russia and consequently with France.

Sarajevo

There was a pause until 23rd July when an Austrian ultimatum was delivered to Serbia. It demanded the virtual
extinction of Serbia as an independent country. On seeing a
copy of its harsh terms, the Russian Foreign Minister exclaimed,
" This means a European war ". Yet Serbia accepted all the
demands, apart from one or two which she offered to submit to
an international court. The Kaiser, who had now cooled down,
declared that " all grounds for war disappear ". But Austria
was not to be baulked of her prey. Pleas to extend the time-
limit were rejected and since Serbia had not accepted every
clause of the ultimatum, war was declared on 28th July. Within

35

a week, Russia, Germany, France, Belgium and Britain had all joined in.

Who was to blame and who were the men who, almost lightly, took the lead in bringing misery to a continent? Austria's monarch was the aged Emperor Francis Joseph, but his country's affairs were largely in the hands of Count von Berchtold and General Conrad, the army Chief of Staff. This aggressive pair were determined to crush Serbia and, to that extent, war was certain but it might still have remained a local conflict.

Responsibility for Russia's foreign policy lay with Sazonov, an excitable aristocrat too weak in times of crisis to resist the pressure of the Russian generals. Nor could Sazonov turn for support and wise guidance to the Tsar Nicholas, a troubled, obstinate man whose idealistic nature longed for peace while his feeble will could do little to restrain the forces of aggression abroad and of revolution at home. But, unless the Serbs were treated outrageously, Russia did not ·want war. The country was seething with internal unrest, the huge armies were ill-equipped and the railway system, essential to modern warfare, was not completed.

France, a country where governments and politicians were held in contempt, was in some ways the most civilised and reasonable of all the Great Powers and her government, whose leading politicians were Briand, Poincaré, Clemenceau and Viviani, showed more moderation and sense than the rest during the fateful days of July 1914. Certainly, she regarded Germany as her natural enemy and she had helped Russia with money to build factories and railways as part of her plan to contain the enemy, but her moves were defensive and, in the days when Grey refused to proclaim a positive alliance, France did not utter reproaches. The logic of events would bring Britain in by her side.

The German nation, obedient, industrious and highly organised, had been fed too long with tales of encirclement not to hate the British, to fear the French and to dread the Russian monster. Their monarch, Kaiser William II, was a vain, bombastic creature, as full of energy as he was devoid of common-sense, for his public utterances were usually silly and sometimes recklessly dangerous. Yet it is easy to exaggerate his responsibility for the war. Little as he would have agreed, neither he nor the Chancellor, Bethmann-Hollweg, was in control of Germany's destiny. The army and the navy, personified by

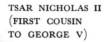

TSAR NICHOLAS II
(FIRST COUSIN
TO GEORGE V)

von Moltke, the Chief of Staff, and von Tirpitz at the Admiralty, were the real power in Germany. The generals had worked assiduously for the war which was to occur when they wanted it and it would be won according to the plan * that had been the basis of army training for years. Victory over France and Russia would solve all Germany's problems and Britain, a sea-power with a pitiful little army, would be unable to hinder their grand design. In a country where generals were not controlled by politicians, the power of the military was enormous: " Who gives the orders, Moltke or Bethmann? " exclaimed the Austrian minister when he received Moltke's telegram telling him to mobilise against Russia. Bethmann urged caution but the Austrians obeyed Moltke.

" Who gives the orders? "

In Britain the Cabinet which contained two great war-leaders of the future, Lloyd George and Churchill, was opposed to war up until the last moment. Domestic troubles and the Ulster crisis seemed more important than Balkan squabbles and, in general, the Liberals were ill-informed about European affairs. They tended to be anti-war, anti-Russian and pro-German, for Germany, with its social insurance, its trade unions and good educational system, seemed to be an enviable example of an enlightened nation, provided one chose to overlook the military aristocrats.

Thus Grey, the Foreign Secretary, refused to come into the open to proclaim Britain's support for France and Russia because he knew that only Asquith, Haldane and Churchill would support him. Instead, he proposed a London conference to settle the business of Serbia while warning Germany not to count on British neutrality and reminding France that the *entente* did not necessarily mean military and naval aid. Germany rejected the conference but, in a bid for Britain's neutrality, Bethmann-Hollweg promised that if Germany was

* This was the famous Schlieffen Plan prepared by General von Schlieffen, German Chief of Staff in 1905. In a war against France and Russia (and probably Britain) he proposed a scythe-like attack through Holland, Luxembourg and Belgium in order to by-pass French frontier defences and to sweep round towards Paris. The eastern front against Russia would be held defensively until France was beaten. The plan, regularly revised, was the key to German preparations. Vast military expansion occurred in 1913 so that the war machine would be at its peak by summer 1914. The Kiel Canal had been widened by June 1914.

"forced" to enter Belgium, that country's integrity would be respected "when war was over". Faced by this sinister suggestion, the Cabinet remembered that Britain was bound by treaty to guarantee Belgian neutrality and by tradition to prevent the Low Countries from falling into the grip of a Great Power. Even so, on 1st August, Asquith did no more than "regret" Germany's failure to relieve anxiety over the matter.

But Germany could not alter her plans at this late hour. The machine of war was wound up and no one could stop it.

Sazonov, angered to learn that Austrian guns were bombarding Belgrade while Austro-Russian talks were proceeding, prevailed upon the Tsar to order general mobilisation. The Kaiser, thoroughly frightened by now, sent frantic telegrams; the French advised caution; Russian mobilisation was put off and put on again; Germany demanded that Russian war preparations should cease within twelve hours and that France should hand over two key fortresses as guarantee of her neutrality. Both demands were ignored. On 2nd August Germany declared war upon Russia and, on the following day, upon France. Grey immediately informed France that the British Navy would not allow the German fleet to operate in the Channel * and on 4th August, when German troops marched into Belgium, Britain was at war with Germany.

" A scrap of paper "

In his last interview with the British Ambassador, the German Chancellor sourly observed that Britain was going to war "for a scrap of paper"—the treaty that guaranteed Belgium. The remark was cynical but true, for the Government that had refused to give France any firm promises of help, was suddenly united by the unprovoked attack on "brave little Belgium". Like magic, all dissension ceased. Cabinet, Parliament, trade unionists, suffragettes and even the Irish Nationalists were united in believing that Britain had no option but to fight.

* Since 1912 Britain and France had agreed that the French Navy should be concentrated in the Mediterranean and the British Navy should be responsible for the North Sea and the Channel.

"BRAVO,
BELGIUM!"
"PUNCH"
CARTOON,
12 AUGUST 1914

BELGIAN REFUGEES FLEEING FROM THE GERMAN ADVANCE, AUGUST 1914

4 The Great War

As the first units of the finest military machine the world had ever seen entered Belgium, the Belgian Army, led by King Albert, stood ready to make a brave but hopeless resistance.

As German Chief of Staff, it fell to von Moltke to carry out the prepared plan that would speedily overthrow France: " Remember, we can be in Paris in a fortnight ", the Kaiser had remarked. Two German armies would sweep through Belgium and across the lightly-held frontier into France, to thrust towards Paris, which would be captured or isolated, while two more German armies engaged the French centre and three others (one commanded by the Kaiser's son, the Crown Prince) pinned down the bulk of the French Army. This, the Germans rightly calculated, would be concentrated round the powerful defences of Verdun and Nancy. Like a boxer, von Moltke would engage his opponent's attention with his left but his right hook would deliver the knock-out blow. Fortunately, he did not put quite enough weight into his right.

The Belgian fortress towns of Liège and Namur stood in the way of the German advance. They were strongly defended but were not proof against the enormous howitzers that were *Belgium* brought up to smash their defences. However, this took time *overrun* and it was not until 23rd August that Namur fell and the remnant of the Belgian Army retreated to Antwerp. Von

Kluck (German 1st Army) and von Bülow (2nd Army) swept into France.

To their surprise, the Germans found that a small British Army was already in position alongside the hard-pressed French Army under Lanzerac. The Belgian resistance had given Haldane time to get two-thirds of the British Expeditionary Force across the Channel by 19th August and, at General Lanzerac's request, Sir John French, the British commander, *Mons* agreed to stand and fight at Mons. The rapid fire of the British regulars so impressed the Germans that they calculated that there were twenty-eight machine-guns to a battalion whereas in fact there were only two. Mons checked von Kluck and, like the Belgian resistance, upset the German timetable; but the outnumbered British and French forces had to fall back towards Paris. As they retreated they fought stubborn delaying battles at Le Cateau (26th August) and at Guise (29th August) and everything now depended upon the speed with which General Joffre, the French Commander-in-Chief, could bring help to his imperilled left.

Joffre, a stout imperturbable man, had always been aware of the German plan to attack through Belgium but he had underrated its strength and speed. His own plan was to make a fiery counter-attack into Lorraine in order to cut German communications and therefore to paralyse their right wing. But the French assault was repulsed with hideous losses and, by the time Belgium fell, Joffre had been obliged to pull back behind his own frontier. But he did not lose his head. Relying

BRITISH ARTILLERYMEN MOVING UP TO THE FRONT

GENERAL JOFFRE REVIEWING FRENCH INFANTRY

on the powerful defences in the east, he stealthily transferred troops from that area in order to save the situation near Paris.

By the end of August the British and French armies that had taken the blow of the German right hook had retreated south of the river Marne and Paris was so threatened that the French Government moved to Bordeaux on 4th September. It seemed as if the German plan had succeeded perfectly.

According to the Schlieffen Plan, Paris should have been encircled but von Kluck had not enough men for the task

and his siege howitzers were still outside Antwerp. Moreover,
even the best of troops cannot fight and advance indefinitely
and von Kluck's men were not only tired but they had out-
marched their supplies of food and ammunition. Thus, instead
of circling Paris, von Kluck decided, presumably on von
Moltke's orders, to turn south-east and to march across the
defences of the capital in order to join up with von Bülow and
smash the French centre. In doing so, he was bound to expose
his flank, and Joffre, who learned of the situation from the
reports of French aviators and from Gallieni, the energetic
Paris commandant, ordered a counter-attack.

The Germans had made two mistakes. They thought that
the British and French wing was battered beyond recovery,
and they had continued to hammer away at the French defences
in the east in the belief that they were holding down the bulk
of the French troops. Yet Joffre had amassed a new army
(the 6th) on the extreme left and another (the 9th), under
General Foch, to reinforce the centre.

Battle of the Marne 1914

Early in September the " beaten " British and French
armies actually began to advance north, driving the Germans back to the Marne and across it. On the 5th, a critical
situation was saved on the left when General Gallieni rushed
garrison troops out from Paris in taxis and motor-buses. As
German air-observers reported that fresh streams of motor-
vehicles were pouring out of Paris, von Kluck pulled back.
With Foch holding von Bülow's fierce assault and then counter-
attacking, the entire German line from Verdun westwards had
to fall back to positions north of the river Aisne. The " miracle
of the Marne " had saved France and her allies.

There was still a chance that the Germans might finish the
war quickly. If they could capture the Channel ports, the
alliance between France and Britain would be in peril. But
Sir John French, realising the danger, skilfully transferred the

THE WESTERN FRONT, AUGUST/SEPTEMBER 1914

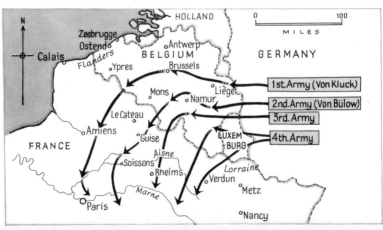

B.E.F. north-west and, in a series of desperate engagements that went on through the autumn in and around the town of Ypres, he defied all the German attempts to break through to the coast. Antwerp held on until October when most of the Belgian defenders managed to get away to join the Allies and to hold a strip of Belgian soil on the British left until the end of the war.

The Channel ports were saved and by the winter of 1914 the war in the west had reached a stage that no one had foreseen. Two huge determined armies had dug themselves into trenches that stretched from the Belgian coast to Switzerland and all the stock-in-trade of professional commanders—the use of cavalry, swift advances, outflanking movements and tactical withdrawals—had come to nought. Instead, there developed a long drawn out struggle between immovable armies who, in mud and slime, through the horrors of artillery bombardment, poison gas and massed assaults, tried to bleed each other to death.

A TRENCH IN THE FRENCH SECTOR OF THE LINE

The causes of the deadlock were not far to seek, though a solution defied the generals of both sides. Certainly some of them realised early on the dilemma of static warfare, as when Sir John French stated, " given forces fairly equally matched, you can bend but you cannot break your enemy's trench line ".

Military developments had given overwhelming advantages to defence. The magazine rifle and the belt-fed machine-gun provided infantry with a firepower so deadly that cavalry engagements and massed charges were doomed by the time the war was three months old, although it took the generals years to learn the facts of death. In the case of the senior British officers this was understandable for many had made their reputations in the cavalry and had never had the opportunity to command vast numbers of troops. Moreover, in military matters, the French were very much the " senior partners " of the alliance. In any case, the deployment of enormous civilian armies was a new aspect of war and behind the generals

43

were civilian governments pressing them to win battles, to get results, to solve the insoluble.

It was soon clear that whereas concentrated artillery-fire could blast defenders out of buildings and surface defences, it was far more difficult to shift troops who had dug themselves into narrow trenches. Heavy shell-fire made damp ground almost impassable for attacking infantry who invariably found that the enemy, far from being wiped out, was still able to deliver a murderous fire from behind barbed-wire entanglements. As the war proceeded, attempts were made to break the deadlock by giving even a temporary advantage to the attackers—there were " creeping barrages " of artillery fire that advanced just ahead of the infantry, poison gas, shells designed to destroy barbed wire and the British invention of the tank which could flatten wire and cross trenches. But new ideas, notably the convoy system at sea and the tank on land, were usually opposed by those in command. Generals on both sides tended to believe that the way to win the war was to break through the opposing defences by frontal assault and in the process to kill so many of the enemy that his ability and will to resist would be broken.

Deadlock

At the outbreak of war the British public did not share Grey's sorrow or Kitchener's realistic gloom. As in Berlin, cheering crowds gathered in the streets; the strain of waiting was over, the die was cast and eager young men queued up outside the recruiting offices hoping fervently to be granted the privilege of serving King and Country before it was all over. Wars between major powers (Germany and France in 1870, Russia and Japan in 1905) had been short and the civilians had no more idea than the professional soldiers what this war would develop into. So the ladies sang " We don't want to lose you but we think you ought to go " and soon they were handing out white feathers of cowardice to any likely looking man not in uniform. The best and bravest of the country's youth volunteered for service in a mood of heroic gaiety.

" They went with songs to the battle, they were young ",* and although they died and the mood of those who followed them changed from ironic jesting to grim acceptance of the horrors of trench life, the soldiers and the public never doubted that they must go on to the bitter end.

* From a poem by Laurence Binyon.

For this was the first war that involved whole nations. Professional soldiers were too few to fight a modern war and every country, Britain included, conscripted its soldiers from the civilian populace and all who stayed at home became involved in the struggle—making shells and uniforms, tucking up their skirts to hoe potatoes and drive buses, or merely standing in queues for their food rations. Both sides tried to starve the other into surrender, and there was little room for chivalry in this kind of contest when towns were bombed from the air and merchant ships were sunk without warning.

Among the few who did not greet the war with enthusiasm was the veteran general Lord Kitchener * who prophesied a war lasting three years, and called for 100,000 volunteers to start with, while making plans for an army of millions. Brought by Asquith into the Cabinet as Secretary of State for War, Kitchener served his country tirelessly, but he proved to be a most difficult colleague for the politicians and for anyone whose opinions differed from his own.

Kitchener

As always, Britain was unprepared for war. Even the Navy, ready for action at the beginning of August, thanks to Winston Churchill, was short of cruisers and destroyers and the Grand Fleet had to operate from the west coast of Scotland until the North Sea bases were completed. The Army lacked supplies of every kind. Shortage of shells and rifle ammunition became

* Horatio Herbert Kitchener, 1850–1916, b. in Ireland, entered Army 1871, served in Sudan 1883–85, became Sirdar or C.-in-C. Egyptian Army; 1898 won Sudan back by battle of Omdurman, became Lord Kitchener of Khartoum. 1900–02, C.-in-C. South Africa, finished Boer War; 1902–09 C.-in-C. India; 1911 Consul-General Egypt; 1914 Secretary of War; 1916 drowned in H.M.S. *Hampshire*.

1914. FRENCH TROOPS MOVE UP TO THE FRONT, WATCHED BY A VILLAGE PRIEST

a public scandal, and even Kitchener did not foresee the need to preserve experienced regulars to train the hordes of volunteers who flocked to join his new army. Thus, while Britain was creating its armies and manufacturing the supplies and munitions of war, the French had to bear the brunt of the fighting on the Western Front and they naturally resented their ally's aversion to conscription * when every Frenchman had to serve in the army for three years and on the reserve for another eighteen.

The Eastern Front, 1914

During the first weeks of the war, Russia had served France nobly by attacking East Prussia. Two Russian armies, under Rennenkampf and Samsonov, advanced so swiftly that the thoroughly alarmed German High Command brought out of retirement a Hanoverian general named von Hindenburg who had made a special study of the area. He was given as his Chief of Staff, Erich von Ludendorff, and by a series of brilliant manœuvres (in which they were helped by their enemy's uncoded wireless messages), these two generals defeated the Russians at Tannenberg (August) and the Masurian Lakes (September), killing or capturing three-quarters of the invading armies.

Further south, in Galicia, the Russians did much better against the Austrians whose armies contained many Czech and Slav conscripts who had no appetite for fighting in the service of their Hapsburg masters. After a rash Austrian advance had been smashed by the Grand Duke Nicholas, Galicia was overrun and the Germans had to rescue their ally by invading Poland. They took Lodz but the Russians held on to Warsaw, and in December the Serbs inflicted a severe defeat on the Austrians and recaptured Belgrade.

Thus, by the end of 1914, the Germans were faced by the war on two fronts that they had always dreaded. The knockout blow against France had failed and their armies were entrenched along the Aisne and held at Ypres; in the east they had repulsed the Russian " steam-roller " but Austria had suffered heavy defeats. At sea every German merchant ship had been captured or driven into harbour, the raiding cruiser *Emden* had been sunk and although the British had been defeated in the Pacific at Coronel (November), they had taken revenge by destroying all four German warships at the Falkland Islands a few weeks later.

* Introduced in Britain early in 1916.

On the other hand, France and Russia had suffered appalling losses, half the men of the B.E.F. were casualties and Kitchener's New Army was training with inadequate instructors and equipment. This meant that the French, who had already lost 850,000 killed, captured and wounded, had to hold 400 miles of front to the British 30 and were to shoulder a burden that reduced them to exhaustion by the time Britain was able to make her full war effort. Russia's position was especially alarming because her supply of shells was being used up far quicker than they could be replaced; a million rifles had been lost and every kind of war material was scarce. The Serbian successes were more than offset by the entry of Turkey into the war on the side of Germany.

By 1915 agile minds on both sides were considering ways to break the deadlock in France. The Germans thought of poison-gas and the British were experimenting with mobile forts (called " tanks " for security reasons) that could cross trenches and withstand machine-gun fire. Churchill, First Lord of the Admiralty, supported this work, even diverting Admiralty funds for the purpose but, in addition to technical difficulties, the tank enthusiasts had to overcome high-level opposition to a novel weapon.

Churchill and Lloyd George also supported the idea of a surprise attack in south-east Europe. While Lloyd George wished to mount the assault from Salonika in order to bring the Balkan states to the Allied side, Churchill preferred the advantages that would be gained by capturing Constantinople. With Turkey knocked out of the war, the Dardanelles would be open for sea-traffic and Russia could be supplied with the war materials that her armies needed so desperately. Moreover, success against Turkey would assuredly lead to an attack on Austria through the Balkans. *The Dardanelles plan*

The Dardanelles plan called for a combined operation between land and sea forces, since troops would have to be landed on a hostile shore and maintained there, but there was good reason to believe that the Turkish defences would not stand up to a strong well-directed attack. Unfortunately, Kitchener did not feel able to release troops from France. But instead of being abandoned or postponed, the project was still attempted. Churchill, passionately urging the expedition, believed that naval units could do the job alone, and the British Cabinet, without taking sufficient advice even upon the geography of the landing-places, agreed to go ahead. For this, Asquith and Kitchener must bear the major share of responsibility.

On 19th February 1915, British and French warships began a prolonged bombardment of the shore defences of the Dardanelles but, without troops or an efficient minesweeping force, this merely gave the Turks time to concentrate their defence forces and to dig in. By the time Kitchener was prevailed upon to release one division, the 29th, the Navy had failed to destroy the Turkish defences and the Army was faced with the task of landing on an enemy shore when every element of surprise had vanished. The Navy was against going on and even General Hamilton, commander of the landing force of British, Australian, New Zealand and French troops, expressed doubts, but *Gallipoli* Churchill fought obstinately for his plan. On 25th April 1915, *1915* more than two months after the Turks had had warning, Allied forces landed on the beaches of the Gallipoli peninsula and instead of the bold dash to Constantinople there was bloody, muddled fighting that resulted in the stalemate of trench warfare.

On 6th August, Hamilton landed a fresh assault force at Suvla. This was a complete surprise but the British commander, Stopford, was too slow to take advantage of the favourable situation and the beachhead was sealed off. By October, Hamilton was replaced by Monro who, to Churchill's dismay, immediately advised a total withdrawal. Kitchener reluctantly agreed and it fell to General Birdwood, the new commander, to evacuate his heroic troops. In the one well-managed operation of the whole affair, this was carried out brilliantly and almost without loss.

Altogether, 205,000 British Empire and 47,000 French troops were killed, wounded or evacuated sick. The Turks lost over 250,000 and were indeed so near to collapse that had this fact been known and fresh troops available, success might have been snatched at the last moment and the course of history altered.

The British have never ceased to regard Gallipoli as a brilliant plan that was tragically bungled but, although nothing excuses the dreadful mishandling of the operation itself, the reluctance of Allied generals to divert troops from the Western Front was understandable. If it was true that the war might be won in south-east Europe, it was equally true that it could be lost in France.

A CORNER OF ANZAC BEACH, GALLIPOLI, 1915

Whatever the might-have-beens, the effect of Gallipoli was calamitous. At home it wrecked Kitchener's reputation, halted Churchill's career, drove Fisher into retirement and Asquith out of the office of Prime Minister. In the Balkans, Bulgaria came into the war to help wipe out Serbia, Greece decided not to join the Allies * and although British and French troops were sent to Salonika, they were bottled up almost as effectively as if they had been in a prisoner-of-war camp and were unable to avert the defeat of Rumania in 1916. Meanwhile Turkey was still in the war on Germany's side and the route to Russia remained closed.

In France, Joffre made his expected attacks in Champagne *The Western* with little success and heavy casualties, while the British *Front, 1915* attacked at Neuve Chapelle (March) and Loos (September) without breaking the German lines. At Ypres, the Germans used poison-gas for the first time but failed to follow up the momentary success of this horrible weapon and, by September,

* In 1917 the pro-German King Constantine was forced to abdicate and Greece, led by Monsieur Venizelos, came into the war on the Allied side.

the French and British had suffered another half-million casualties.

By the beginning of 1916, Kitchener's armies had grown so that the B.E.F. numbered one million men and was able to extend its front to sixty miles. But there was much alarm about the shortage of munitions—*The Times* reported that " Men died in heaps upon the Aubers Ridge ten days ago because the field-guns were short . . . of high-explosive shells "— and bitter attacks were made on the Government, particularly on Asquith and Kitchener, though Lloyd George, the one-time temperance speaker, roundly accused the workers of drunkenness and slacking.

This situation, as well as rumours of deep disagreements in the Cabinet, at the War Office and the Admiralty, led to the formation of a Coalition Government in which the Conservatives joined the Liberals. Asquith remained Prime Minister. But as the price of co-operation, the Conservatives demanded the removal of Churchill from the Admiralty and Bonar Law took his post as First Lord, while Lloyd George went to the new Ministry of Munitions. As ever, his bounding energy achieved miracles and the flow of war supplies eventually became a torrent, though the high wages paid to munition workers caused bitter resentment among the soldiers at the front.

At the end of the year Sir John French, Commander-in-Chief of the B.E.F., was replaced by Sir Douglas Haig, a general whose reputation is still a subject for passionate argument. In some views, Haig was a heartless and incompetent commander who used his friendship with King George V to outmanœuvre the politicians who would have curbed his prodigal waste of men's lives in useless frontal attacks. Other opinions held that Haig was the dedicated soldier whose tenacity upheld a tottering ally and brought his country to final victory.

1916 was a momentous year. Falkenhayn, the German C.-in-C.,* decided to attack France at Verdun, the great fortress system which for patriotic and strategic reasons the French were bound to defend, regardless of cost. Having inflicted such heavy defeats on Russia during the autumn that there was little to fear from that quarter, the Germans

SIR
DOUGLAS HAIG

* Moltke had been removed after the Battle of the Marne. Falkenhayn was later replaced by Hindenburg with Ludendorff, his " quartermaster ", the active commander of the German armies.

were able to concentrate vast numbers of men and guns into
the area facing Verdun. For some time Joffre obstinately
refused to believe in the likelihood of a major attack there.

However, in February 1916 the German bombardment
started with two million shells on the first day. Two lines of
French trenches were taken and only by the most heroic
sacrifices did the French manage to hold on to the forts and to
construct new trenches. The Germans kept up a remorseless
hammering for five months but the French, inspired by General
Pétain's rallying cry " Ils ne passeront pas! " (They shall not
pass) did not break. For once defence was more costly than
attack and the French Army, bled almost to the death, was
never the same again.

To relieve the frightful pressure, Haig agreed to attack on
the Somme where the British and French armies joined. His
troops, all volunteers, were splendid fighting-men but lacking
in experience, and the munitions position, although improved,
was far from perfect. Since there was no bulge in the enemy
line (as at Ypres and Verdun), Haig was forced to make a
frontal assault on defences that now included deep bomb-
proof dug-outs, concrete " pill-boxes " and wide belts of barbed
wire. It was an attack in the wrong place and at the wrong
time but it had to be made.

On 1st July the British assault was launched and by the end
of the day 60,000 men were dead or wounded. With courageous
persistence, the attacks continued until the German positions
were seriously dented and, on the British right, the French
achieved marvels considering the losses they had suffered.
Thrusts and counter-thrusts went on until the autumn rains
stopped the offensive, by which time the Germans had suffered
severely in their attempt to recover lost ground.

The British suffered casualties of over 400,000 of their finest
men and the French lost another 200,000. But their sacrifices
were not in vain for the Germans had to abandon the attack
on Verdun, and Ludendorff declared that his men had been
fought to a standstill. The war was to last two more years but
from the German point of view the Somme was the turning
point.

One notable feature of the battle was the first use of tanks.

A TANK IN
ACTION

Only eighteen of these monsters got into action on 15th September, for on muddy, shell-cratered ground, they were soon bogged down. However, lumbering along at a walking-pace, flattening wire and lurching across trenches, they substantially helped in the capture of Thiepval (25th September). There were too few of them and insufficient reserves to exploit their success but they were a pointer to the future which the Germans failed to recognise.

Russia, 1916   During the summer of 1916, Russia's vast reserves of manpower and fresh supplies of material that came via the new Murmansk to St Petersburg railway and the trans-Siberian line, allowed her to make an astonishing recovery. The Russian soldiers, better equipped, as brave as ever and ably led by General Brusilov, made another smashing advance into Galicia where thousands of Czechs deserted to their side. Austria was near to collapse and only the hesitation of Rumania and an ill-considered attack on the Germans prevented complete success. In the autumn the tide turned, for Germany again rescued her ally and, with the help of the Bulgarians and Turks, completely defeated Rumania. The Russians reeled back. They had lost another million men and at home the government was tottering.

Meanwhile, the Italians (who had joined the Allies in 1915) were attacking the Austrians along the stony hills north-east of Venice with little success and, although a Turkish drive towards Egypt and the Canal was easily repulsed, there was a minor disaster further east in Mesopotamia. An attempt to capture Baghdad failed and 10,000 British troops, who retreated to Kut, were starved into surrender.*

Only in Africa did the Allies have any marked success during 1916. General Botha had already taken German South-West Africa and in East Africa, General Smuts, another former foe of Britain, met a worthy opponent in the German commander Lettow-Vorbeck, whose skilful defence could not prevent most of German East Africa from falling into Allied hands.

From the outset, the British and German navies had been playing a waiting game, and while both sides longed for an all-out sea battle, neither could afford defeat. Command of the sea was essential to Britain's existence for, without it, her armies

* The prisoners were so badly treated that only one-third survived. General Maude captured Kut in February and Baghdad in March 1917.

ADMIRAL
JELLICOE ON
BOARD THE
" IRON DUKE "

could not be maintained and her population would speedily starve. Thus Admiral Jellicoe, who in Churchill's words was " the one man on either side who could lose the war in an afternoon ", could take no risks that might reduce Britain's superiority in capital ships. On the other hand, he desired above all else to bring the German fleet to battle on his own terms for its destruction would free the Navy for vital tasks other than this perpetual watching and waiting. The German plan was to reduce the British fleet by torpedo attacks and by luring strong units into the minefields that protected the German coast and harbours.

In the first two years of the war, there was minor activity in the North Sea including the shelling of some east coast towns and a successful action off Heligoland when four German ships were sunk. But the subsequent loss of five British cruisers by torpedoes underlined the menace of submarines.

In 1916, Admiral Scheer, the German commander, prepared a trap for the British Fleet. He sent Admiral Hipper with five battle-cruisers and supporting vessels to show himself off the Norwegian coast in order to lure Admiral Beatty's battle squadron towards the German main fleet, which Scheer intended to keep out of sight. On 30th May, naval intelligence reported that the Germans were at sea and, at once, the British fleets put out from Scapa, Cromarty and Rosyth. Beatty's force of six fast battle-cruisers made contact with Hipper off Jutland on the Danish coast but his four dreadnoughts were not yet within range. Hipper turned to draw Beatty towards Scheer's battle-ships and in a sharp action the British cruisers suffered badly. Two blew up almost at once and two more were lost later, but Beatty scored some hits and Hipper turned away as Scheer approached. At this, Beatty swung north to meet Jellicoe who was racing down with the Grand Fleet in six columns.

Jutland 1916

Realising that he was outgunned and outnumbered, Scheer turned away and disappeared into the evening mist. Momentarily, the two great fleets made contact again but, aided by a smoke screen and Jellicoe's fear of torpedo attacks at night, Scheer escaped to the safety of his mine fields and the great opportunity was lost for ever.

Naturally, the Germans claimed Jutland as a victory. Their losses had been lighter than the British * but they had refused the major engagement and the High Seas Fleet never ventured out again in full strength. It spent the rest of the war in harbour, and, at the end, the German sailors mutinied rather than put to sea. However, the result of the battle was a bitter disappointment to the Navy and the nation, and the Fleet had to remain on watch.

A few days after Jutland, the cruiser *Hampshire*, bound for Russia with Lord Kitchener aboard, was sunk by a mine. Kitchener and nearly all the crew were drowned. This tragedy had a deeply depressing effect on the British people who still looked on the veteran field-marshal as a peerless leader set high above the politicians and the other generals.

At the end of the year, Asquith resigned the Premiership. His fall was brought about chiefly by intrigue and by a hostile Press campaign, but although he was an able politician he had never seemed fitted to the role of an energetic war-leader. His

* The British lost 14 ships and 6,784 men; the Germans, 11 ships and 3,039 men.

place was taken by the ambitious little Welshman Lloyd George, who at once created a War Cabinet of only five members—to be joined from time to time by the leaders of the Dominions. At the head of affairs there was now a man whom the nation felt had the driving determination to win the war, even though his lack of military knowledge and excess of self-confidence were sometimes a handicap to his colleagues. The manoeuvres that brought Lloyd George to power caused a split in the Liberal Party and a breach between himself and Asquith that was never healed. Moreover, Lloyd George found himself engaged in an intense, behind-the-scenes struggle with the generals * who, aided by powerful allies and the Press, wanted the Government to be placed under Army control.

Lloyd George, Prime Minister

The year 1917 was marked by three reverberating events. In February, Germany began unrestricted U-boat warfare; in March the Russian Revolution occurred; and in April the United States entered the war on the Allies' side.

So far, the Germans had made only moderate use of submarines against merchant-ships, partly because their submarine force was not large at the outbreak of the war and because the United States had made angry protests after the sinking of the liner *Lusitania* in May 1915. Apart from this brutal incident, the British practice of searching neutral ships caused more resentment in America than the activities of submarines and it seemed that nothing would induce President Wilson to change his policy of neutrality.

However, by 1917 Ludendorff decided to withdraw to the dense defences of the Hindenburg Line and to allow the British and French to continue with their costly attacks while an all-out submarine offensive brought Britain to her knees. In the seas round Britain, off the French coast and in the Mediterranean, all ships, neutral included, were to be sunk at sight and the risk of provoking the United States into war was taken in the belief that Britain would have surrendered before American troops could reach Europe.

Half-hearted opposition from the Kaiser and his Chancellor was overridden and on 1st February the catastrophic campaign began. Losses were appalling. 260 ships were sunk in

---

* Lloyd George's chief opponents were Haig, General Robertson, Chief of the Imperial General Staff, Admiral Jellicoe, Lord Northcliffe and King George V. Eventually, he was able to " sack " Robertson and Jellicoe and he dearly would have liked to be rid of Haig.

February, 338 in March and 430 in April, by which time Britain had only six weeks' supply of corn left. For this ruthless form of warfare in which the submarine destroyed its victims by torpedo and of necessity left the seamen to drown, a force of 90 to 100 submarines operated from bases on the German coast and from Ostend and Zeebrugge. For a time they even moved in and out of the Straits of Dover and their losses were no more than ten in the first three months. By June food rationing was introduced in Britain, and those in the know predicted that the country could not last beyond November.

The U-boat campaign

The answer to this dire threat was the convoy system which Lloyd George and Beatty pressed upon those who objected that merchantmen sailing in fleets would only present easier targets to the enemy. In practice, a convoy was as difficult to find in the ocean as a single ship and the escorting destroyers equipped with hydrophones and depth charges proved to be an effective protection. By October the number of sinkings had been halved, and Germany's submarine losses mounted as American destroyers and submarine-chasers provided additional assistance. Welcome as this help was, the credit for victory at sea belonged to the British Navy and to the Merchant Navy, whose seamen, some of them torpedoed two and three times, seldom failed to sign on for yet another voyage.

U.S.A. enters the war

In 1914 the Americans had seen no reason why they should take part in a European war. A great many of them had emigrated from Central Europe and were far more sympathetic towards Germany than towards France, Britain and Russia. However, opinion gradually swung towards the Allies owing to the sinking of the *Lusitania* and to the volume of Allied trade, especially in war-supplies, but President Wilson would have stuck to his resolve to play no active part if the German submarines had refrained from sinking American ships and if the German Government had not made a foolish bid for Mexican support. A message was intercepted from the German Foreign Secretary to his Minister in Mexico authorising him to offer Texas, New Mexico and Arizona in return for Mexican help if the U.S. entered the war. This plot, the terrible shipping losses and the collapse of Tsarist Russia were enough to decide the issue and on 2nd April 1917 the U.S. declared war on Germany.

The Tsar, Nicholas II, was a good husband and an affectionate father but, as a ruler, he was weak and exceptionally stupid, forever wavering between good intentions and old-fashioned tyranny. His country had long been on the verge of revolution,* for all sections of the populace, except the nobles and the Army officers, were sick of their feeble, corrupt government and the decadent court. However, when war came, most people put aside their resentment and the Russian soldiers, mostly peasants, were deeply loyal to their " little Father ", the Tsar of all the Russias.

The Russian Revolution

Under the best of their generals, notably Brusilov, Alexeieff and the Grand Duke Nicholas, the Russian armies achieved miracles of endurance and valour but, in 1915, the Tsar took the disastrous decision of assuming supreme command. He was no soldier but, worse, his departure for the front left home affairs largely in the hands of the Tsarina Alexandra, a hysterical, autocratic woman who was herself under the sinister influence of a so-called " holy man " named Rasputin. This lustful, arrogant hypnotist had apparently cured the Tsarina's son of haemophilia and for a short but crucial period he completely dominated the court. By his behaviour and ascendancy over the doting Tsarina, he wrecked the Tsar's prestige and paralysed the government by impudently dismissing and appointing ministers at will. To make matters worse, there were wide-spread rumours of treachery and of pro-German leanings by the Tsarina and her friends.

GRIGORY RASPUTIN, MURDERED 1916

In March 1917 † the Revolution began in St Petersburg (Petrograd) with what was mistaken for a riot. The garrison joined the revolt which spread like wildfire. Workers disarmed the police, soldiers refused to intervene and formed their own soviets (workers' councils). Within three days, the Tsar had abdicated in favour of his brother but the people had already decided for a republic.

A provisional government, supported by the middle and upper classes and led by Prince Lvov, failed to gain control, and a new government of moderate Socialists under Alexander

* After defeat by Japan in 1905, there had been near-revolution with a serious naval mutiny at Sevastopol. The Tsar granted some reforms including a Duma or parliament, but there was little improvement because Nicholas soon returned to his high-handed ways.

† February, according to the unreformed Russian calendar. Hence this was known to Russians as the " February Revolution " which was followed by the " October Revolution " of November 1917.

Kerensky tried to carry out two impossible tasks, to create a democratic state and to persuade the Army to go on fighting the Germans. Meanwhile, Vladimir Lenin, leader of the Bolsheviks, the most extreme Socialist party in Russia, was being brought in a sealed train across Germany from his Swiss exile. The Germans, aware of his anti-war views, rightly believed that he would weaken the Russian will to go on fighting.

Throughout the summer of 1917, utter confusion reigned in Russia where Lenin, Trotsky and other Bolshevik leaders were advocating government by the workers while Kerensky and the officers' leagues tried to keep the war going. A Russian offensive failed, Riga was lost and the ill-fed, ill-armed soldiers, already infected by Bolshevik propaganda, began streaming homewards. In November, Lenin, who had temporarily fled to Finland, came out of hiding to overthrow the Kerensky government. The Bolsheviks took control.

In order to consolidate their hold, the Bolsheviks wanted an end to the war and the Germans, delighted as they were at the prospect of being able to move vast forces to the West, imposed harsh terms. By the Treaty of Brest-Litovsk, Lenin surrendered huge expanses of Russian territory including the grainlands of the Ukraine, but he was willing to pay the price for power.

While the Russian Revolution, an event even more tremendous than the war itself, was pursuing its turbulent course, the British and French were preparing to launch great offensives. Both were now well equipped, the French being particularly strong in heavy artillery while the British had fifty squadrons of aircraft and a growing production of tanks. Joffre and Haig had agreed their plans for 1917 when Joffre was suddenly replaced by a junior general named Nivelle who had won a reputation at Verdun.

Nivelle's offensive 1917

Filled with boundless self-confidence and visions of an immortal victory, Nivelle succeeded in winning support for his plan of an immense offensive that would burst the enemy line asunder. Without sharing Nivelle's exuberant optimism, Haig promised full support while Lloyd George, who disliked Haig and would have dismissed him if that had been possible, was an enthusiastic convert to the plan.

The French offensive failed. At first all went well, for the British made a strong push from Arras and the Canadians captured Vimy Ridge by a magnificent feat of arms; but, to the south, between Soissons and Reims, Nivelle's troops were

CANADIAN ARTILLERYMEN USING A CAPTURED GERMAN HOWITZER,
VIMY RIDGE, APRIL 1917

horribly mauled. Copies of his vaunted plan had fallen into the
hands of the Germans whose machine-guns, sited in shell-proof
pill-boxes, mowed down the troops. Fighting with tremendous
courage, the French soldiers did no worse and indeed in some
places better than in many earlier offensives, but in the end the
disappointment, the sense of a gigantic let-down after such
glowing promises of success, cracked their morale.

Utterly weary, shaken by their terrifying losses and by
rumours of treachery in the rear, some French units refused to
obey orders. Mutiny is far more terrible to a commander than
defeat, for the comradeship that holds an army together at all
other times causes it to fall into complete collapse when men no
longer respond to military discipline. There were reasons to
fear that the revolutionary disease that had infected the Russians
might be about to destroy the French Army.

Nivelle was promptly sacked and Pétain, the hero of Verdun,
a brave, dour pessimist, pulled the Army together and succeeded
in keeping its shaky condition a secret from the Germans.
Indeed, when begging Haig to keep the Germans away from the
French front, he did not reveal even to his ally the true state of
his army. While he was healing its wounds, as Clemenceau
the Prime Minister later healed the national morale of France,

59

Britain had to take over the burden that their ally had borne for so long.

Haig was forced to continue the Spring attacks with the added incentive that success in Flanders could result in clearing the Germans off the Flemish coast and out of their submarine lairs at Ostend and Zeebrugge. A gigantic bombardment and a big mining operation led to the capture of the Messines Ridge (June) and this was followed, after an unfortunate delay of six weeks, by the main attack, called the Third Battle of Ypres, but better known to the troops as Passchendaele.

Passchendaele, 1917

Delay had given the Germans time to concentrate their defences and the British artillery destroyed the drainage system of the flat plain so that in an abnormally wet summer, the battle area became a quagmire in which tanks and guns were bogged and men could move only by using wooden planks known as duckboards. If they slipped or fell exhausted, they were likely to drown in the slime or die horribly in gas-filled craters. " Welcome rain, our strongest ally ", wrote a German and in these conditions, despite heroic efforts and some successes, as at Menin Road Ridge, little could be achieved and the final break-through was as far off as ever. The attacks, seemingly so senseless to the troops who could not be told the real reason for their continuation, went on for three months and, in October, further efforts had to be made to prevent the transfer of German divisions to Italy where the Italians had suffered a colossal defeat.

PASSCHENDAELE, OCTOBER 1917. LAYING DUCKBOARDS ACROSS DEVA-STATED COUNTRY. PRISONERS AND WOUNDED CAN BE SEEN IN THE BACKGROUND

At last, in November, with the capture of the village of Passchendaele, the drawn-out agony came to an end. For 300,000 casualties, twice the German losses, the British had won five miles of morass where the shell holes were lip to lip. One success was at Cambrai on 20th November when 381 tanks penetrated for six miles taking 10,000 prisoners and 200 guns, but there were insufficient reserves (owing to the Italian situation) to follow up the gain and the troops felt more embittered than ever.

Haig's generalship during the prolonged offensive of 1917 has been much criticised, so, in justice, it is worth stressing that his difficulties were much increased by the abnormal conditions in which his armies had to fight:

"The weather in August and still more in late October and early November is the chief factor in the horrible reputation that hangs about Third Ypres. The second is a belief that the offensive was mere blind bashing. This is not the case. Tactics were seldom more skilful . . . At the start the Germans often outfought the British. Towards the end the British could count on winning if they could get to close quarters. And it was largely the churning of the ground into a morass by their own artillery that held them up.

"Those who saw it will never forget that battlefield in the wet: as far as the eye could see, a vision of brown mud and water, with a mixture of both spouting to extraordinary heights when heavy shells exploded in the ground; patient men trudging along the duckboards, bent a little forward by the loads on their backs; equally patient horses and mules plodding and slipping under the weight of their pack-saddles. It called for nerve and endurance, which were not wanting." *

During the summer of 1917, Cadorna, the Italian commander, *Caporetto* battered away at the Austrian defences along the river Isonzo where, on rocky terrain, he continued to lose twice as many men as the defenders, though the Italian soldiers, badly led and harshly treated in the matters of pay and leave, did not deserve their poor reputation. They fought stubbornly, as did the Austrian armies whose Slav troops had far more taste for fighting the Italians than the Russians.

By the autumn, Ludendorff was able to reinforce the Austrians

* *The First World War*, Cyril Falls (1960)

with a German army and on 24th October, after a hurricane bombardment, the Austro-Germans smashed through the Italian front near the village of Caporetto. In wild confusion, the Italian Second Army fled towards the plains, and when the Third and Fourth Armies were forced to pull back, some of their soldiers joined in the headlong flight. However, thanks to the steadiness of loyal troops, the rout was checked and the enemy's triumphant advance came to a dead stop on the river Piave.

Good staff work had earlier made arrangements for troop-trains to reach Italy, and in November eleven French and British divisions arrived to stiffen the resistance. The new line did not break; the Italians, defending their own soil, repulsed all further attacks. But for the Allies the only gleam in a dismal year, apart from East Africa and the capture of Baghdad, was Allenby's success in Palestine, where he was assisted by the Arab Revolt in which Colonel Lawrence (Lawrence of Arabia) acted as go-between for the British and the Arabs. In December 1917 Jerusalem was taken from the Turks.

Even so, the divisions in Palestine, Italy, Mesopotamia and at Salonika, however well they performed, were engaged in side-shows at the expense of Haig's army in France where the vital struggle was about to take place. In 1918, the Cabinet was reluctant to supply Haig with all the drafts that he wanted. Lloyd George, in particular, feared that the men would be squandered in another Passchendaele. As it turned out, Haig had not enough troops to hold the German attack.

German offensive, 1918 In German eyes, the situation at the beginning of 1918 was clear. Their allies Austria and Turkey were almost exhausted, shortages of food and materials in Germany were becoming acute, the submarine campaign had not starved Britain into surrender, and the arrival of vast numbers of fresh American troops must be expected as the year advanced. One great chance of victory remained if it were taken quickly. The collapse of Russia allowed the transfer of a million men and thousands of guns to the Western Front so that, for the first and only time in the war, the Germans would possess a clear superiority over the tired French and British armies.

The knock-out blow was to fall on the British because they were thought to be in a desperate plight for food and the French were believed to be too weary to launch a counter-attack to save their ally. The first blow was aimed at the British right wing (Generals Gough and Byng) against whom

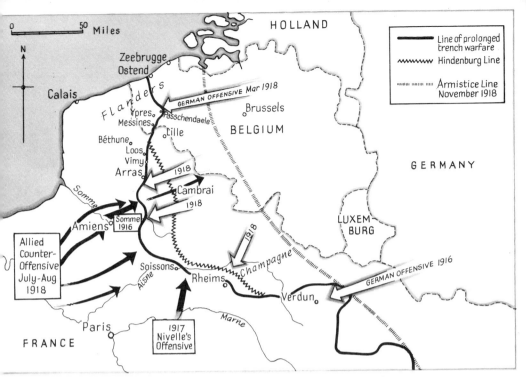

Ludendorff was able to concentrate 71 divisions and 2,500 heavy guns to 26 divisions and 976 guns. The second phase would be a breakthrough in Flanders.

The March offensive began on the 21st with a colossal bombardment of high explosives and gas shells followed by infantry attacks in dense fog which prevented the British machine-gunners from seeing the enemy. The Germans broke clean through the line into open country. Gough's Fifth Army took a fearful hammering and Haig had to pull back to avoid encirclement. An agonising lack of confidence existed between the Allied commanders, and this increased the danger of the Germans driving a wedge between the French and British armies. At this critical moment Marshal Foch, who had been given supreme command over both armies, flung in every unit he could scrape together to keep the line unbroken.

Meanwhile Arras held but the Germans pressed towards Amiens in a great bulge thirty miles wide. By now, the British were fighting hard and inflicting heavy casualties as the enemy advance slowed down. In places the German troops were disillusioned to find in the captured trenches food-dumps that showed that the British, who they had been told were starving, ate far better than they did.

On 9th April the second part of the German plan took effect when a fresh assault fell upon the British front further north

MARSHAL FOCH, 1918

63

between Ypres and Bethune. In morning mist the Germans broke through a single Portuguese division. Next day they recaptured Messines Ridge. As Ludendorff threw in all his reserves and the Channel ports were in danger, Haig normally, so taciturn, issued his famous Order of the Day:

" Backs to the wall "

"With our backs to the wall and believing in the justice of our cause, each one must fight on to the end."

The British Army, reinforced by seven French divisions, responded dourly. Ypres held fast and, by the end of April, the Germans had been halted. But Ludendorff had not finished. Attack was switched to the Aisne valley, the area of Nivelle's fiasco, a quiet sector where Foch had placed sixteen weary French and British divisions for a rest. Once again the Germans broke through and in three alarming days they were back on the Marne and within reach of Paris. Once again the offensive petered out because it had overrun itself, leaving yet another dangerous bulge in the German line.

All this time huge numbers of troops were arriving in France from the United States and although not very many had engaged the enemy so far, five American divisions acquitted themselves well in the Aisne battles. The presence of these fresh buoyant soldiers provided a tonic for the battle-scarred Allies and a gloomy prospect for the equally weary Germans, though, with infinite courage and resource, Ludendorff's soldiers wers still pressing hard enough for Clemenceau to think of getting rid of both Foch and Pétain.

On 18th July Foch hit back at the German bulge on the Marne. Pétain, pessimistic as ever, wanted to suspend the operation, but Foch exerted his generalissimo's authority and the counter-offensive was launched at the moment when Ludendorff was putting the final touches to his plan to crush the British in the north. Taken by surprise, assaulted by tanks and by ever-increasing numbers of aircraft, the Germans retreated, fighting strongly. For the moment Foch did not exploit this success. Instead, sensing that the miracle of victory might actually emerge from a situation so close to disaster, he delivered a new blow at the Amiens bulge where, on 8th August, General Rawlinson's 4th Army of British, French, Canadian and Australian troops, assisted by 450 tanks and the 1st French Army on the right advanced through thick mist and inflicted a severe defeat upon the enemy. The Germans went back,

A BRITISH
SOLDIER IN
ACTION DURING
THE GERMAN
OFFENSIVE

not in headlong flight but in grave disorder. To Ludendorff this was "the black day of the German army", not so much because his soldiers suffered a defeat but because, to his horror, he learned that retreating troops were jeering at units coming up to the relief, calling them "Strike-breakers" and "Pro-longers of the war".

By now Haig's losses in men, materials and guns had been more than made good and he could deliver punch upon punch in rapid succession. Elated by the speed of their advance, his troops kept up the pressure while the French and General Pershing's Americans joined in effectively on the Aisne and south of Verdun. Under these ceaseless attacks, the German Army began to crack. Its massive reserves had been used up, only boys and middle-aged men were coming into the ranks and in shells, guns, tanks and aircraft, the Allies had an ever-increasing superiority.

Above all, the tide of feeling had changed. The French *Allied* were filled with hope and the British were certain of victory. *Victory* At the end of September, undeterred by even Foch's doubts, the British burst through the Hindenburg Line while the Americans, under General Pershing, advanced steadily on the right and the French more cautiously in the centre. Suddenly, to the astonishment of the world, the whole front from Ypres to Verdun was moving forward, slowly, ponderously like an avalanche impelled by the immense weight behind. Checked here and there, the advance rolled on remorselessly and the Germans could not stop it. Seeing that they were beaten, their leaders wanted the war ended as suddenly as they had started it and on 4th October, Germany and Austria asked the President of the United States for an armistice. Wilson replied that they must accept his Fourteen Points, * evacuate all occupied territory

---

* Wilson's Fourteen Points, given in a speech to the U.S. Congress in January 1918 without consultation with the Allies, were: 1. No secret diplomacy. 2. Freedom of navigation at sea even in war. 3. Removal of economic barriers. 4. Reduction of armaments. 5. Adjustment of colonial claims. 6. Russian territory to be evacuated. 7. Restoration of Belgium. 8. Restoration of French territory including Alsace-Lorraine. 9. Readjustment of Italian frontiers. 10. People of Austria-Hungary to have opportunity for national development. 11. Balkan states to be evacuated—Serbia to have access to sea. 12. Non-Turkish peoples of Ottoman Empire to be freed. Dardanelles to be open to all shipping. 13. Poland to be independent. 14. An association of nations to be formed.

and accept the armistice conditions of the victorious governments. While they haggled and Ludendorff resigned, the Allies,
particularly Rawlinson's Army, kept at the enemy, driving him
from pillar to post and they were still hard at it when the war
ended on 11th November 1918.

Germany's allies had already collapsed, the Bulgarians on
30th September, the Turks on 31st October and the Austrians
on 3rd November after the Italians had avenged Caporetto by
the triumphant victory of Vittorio Veneto.

Adroitly, the Germans had avoided battle on their own soil,
for when they accepted terms they were still in eastern Belgium
and along the last fringe of French territory. At once they
started the legend that the German Army was never defeated
in the field; it was their allies and the civilians at home who had
let the fighting men down. This was absolutely untrue. They
were a beaten army, and both Ludendorff and Haig knew it.
In fact, the German people, hungry and ill-clad because of the
Allied sea-blockade, stood up very well to the strain of the war
and it was not until their armies were beaten and in rapid retreat
that riots broke out in many parts of Germany.

On 9th November the Kaiser abdicated and a German
republic was proclaimed. But although everything pointed to a
Bolshevik revolution, Germany was not Russia. There was a
strong middle class, a civil service and an army that was defeated
but not broken. Most important of all, the new Republic had
the support of the General Staff which promised to maintain
discipline and suppress Bolshevism.

ARMISTICE DAY,
11 NOVEMBER
1918

5 The Peace

THE reasons for which the war began were trivial compared with its cost. Eight to ten million men * died in battle or from wounds and many were the fittest and best of their country's youth. Millions more died from disease or dragged out the rest of their lives crippled, blind, permanently ill or insane.

Farms, factories, mines and railways were destroyed in wide areas of France, Belgium, Italy and Russia. A whole continent was short of food, raw materials and goods of every kind, for Europe's trade had been disrupted and world leadership in industry had passed to the United States.

Four empires collapsed and their crowned monarchs disappeared. The Kaiser fled to Holland, the Tsar and his family were murdered, the Emperor Carl of Austria was deposed and the Sultan of Turkey was soon to be ousted by a fierce dictator. The Great Powers declined in number from six to five, for Austria-Hungary vanished; but whereas before the war there had been twenty independent states in Europe, after the Peace Settlement there were twenty-six. Monarchy suffered badly, for all the new states, except Yugoslavia, were republics and only two of the five Great Powers retained their royal families.

Britain suffered none of the damage to her homeland that the French endured but her position as a world Power was permanently weakened. Her prosperity had been founded on trade and manufacture and these had well-nigh ceased. Many traditional markets were lost for ever, old customers were too poor to buy or had learned to make their own goods; the British merchant marine was seriously reduced, factories were old-fashioned and machinery worn out and Britain's debts were enormous. For much of the war she had acted as banker to the

* France lost 1 million dead, Austria-Hungary, 1 million; Italy, ½ million; United States, 81,000. German and Russian losses, not known exactly, were about 3 million each but possibly more. Total war deaths have been placed as high as 25 million.

The British Empire lost almost 1 million dead, of whom 750,000 were from the British Isles, 88% being battle deaths. In all 3,267,000 men and women of the Empire were killed, missing or wounded.

At sea 41,836 men of the Royal Navy and Merchant Service were drowned or killed.

67

Allies, raising heavy loans in America largely on their behalf, and when the war was ended the debtors could not or would not pay. But the Americans wanted their money, and when the next war came Britain was still handicapped by the cost of the first.

France suffered terribly in the war. Part of her land was in the hands of the enemy for four years, thousands of her people were forced to leave their homes and farms, many towns and villages were devastated and the mining and industrial area of the north-east was temporarily destroyed. Over a million Frenchmen died and this was a fearsome loss for the country with the lowest birth-rate of any of the leading Powers. Yet, despite defeatism in some quarters and a short-lived mutiny in the Army, France came through the war with great credit. Clemenceau, Foch, the common soldier and the stoical peasant all showed the traditional courage and perseverance of Frenchmen *Post-war* in defending their native soil, and even rival politicians and the *France* militant trade unionists had mostly sunk their differences when faced by the old enemy. This wartime unity lasted for some time after the war, since all Frenchmen believed that Germany's greater manpower and industrial strength would again threaten them unless she was shackled and held down. The French were united in their angry disappointment with the Treaty of Versailles and with Clemenceau's failure to obtain even more severe restrictions on Germany. In this mood they mercilessly caricatured President Wilson and became increasingly indignant with Britain's failure to understand and support the French viewpoint.

The post-war years in France were marked by financial

FRENCH TROOPS
PASSING
THROUGH A
RUINED TOWN,
1918

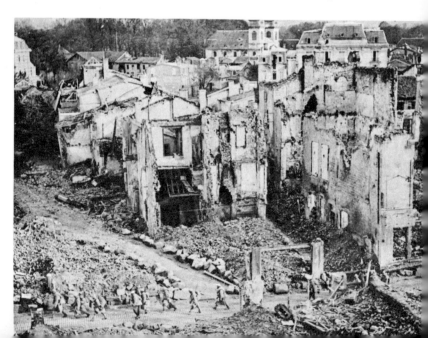

difficulties made worse by the expensive failure of the Ruhr adventure.* In 1924 the coalition government was replaced by Radicals and Socialists whose Foreign Secretary Briand did at least believe in the League of Nations. The value of the franc continued to fall and in 1926, Poincaré came back with another " national " government and emergency powers to rule by decree. Helped by increasing industrial output and improved conditions of world trade, Poincaré had brought about a general improvement by the time he retired in 1928 and was succeeded by Briand. This short period of comparative stability was the last that France was to know for many years. The arrival of the Depression from America and the menacing rise of the Nazis was soon to lead to the paralysis of successive governments and the spread of internal unrest.

The Peace Conference opened at Versailles in January 1919. During the two months' interval since the armistice, Britain had held what was known as the " Coupon Election " when Lloyd George and Bonar Law, appealing for a continuation of the Coalition Government, issued a certificate or " coupon " to those candidates who supported them. If Lloyd George wanted to discover the mood of the British people, he was left in no doubt. A newspaper campaign with the slogans " Hang the Kaiser " † and " Make Germany Pay " found ready acceptance and the Coalition stayed in power with an enormous majority over the Labour Party and the handful of Asquith Liberals.

The " Coupon Election "

Sir Eric Geddes' remark that he would squeeze Germany " until you can hear the pips squeak " has been condemned as a vengeful outburst against a brave enemy but, at the time when it was uttered, this was the view of the overwhelming majority of British and French citizens. All the victors, apart from the United States, had suffered enormous losses and they had no doubts who was to blame. After all, the Serbs had not attacked Austria nor had the Belgians invaded Germany and although the Kaiser had departed and the war lords had retired to the back of the stage, people had not forgotten the wanton damage committed right to the last moment by the retreating

* See p. 83
† Fortunately the Dutch Government refused to hand over the Kaiser who remained in exile at Doorn until his death in 1942. Execution would have turned him into a martyred hero whereas, by living on and publishing his Memoirs, he was seen to be a very ordinary man whose opinions were trivial.

German troops. January 1919 was too early for a spirit of forgiveness.

Thirty-two states sent diplomats to the conference but no German representatives were present. The full conference met rarely and real control was taken by France, Britain, the United States, Japan and Italy. Since Japan was concerned principally with her own interests and the Italian Prime Minister, Orlando, soon withdrew when he found that Italy was not going to receive all her demands, the vital decisions were taken by the " Big Three ", President Wilson, Lloyd George and Clemenceau.

The Big Three The key figure was Woodrow Wilson, who came to Europe like a Messiah bringing hope and justice to the Old World. It was he who, after preaching neutrality, had brought the United States into the war, had issued his Fourteen Points, had negotiated the armistice and was head of the state that was already feeding the starving peoples of Europe. The former professor arrived in Paris with enormous moral standing but he also possessed great shortcomings. Obstinate and self-righteous, he had no first-hand knowledge of Europe and its complicated problems; he lacked humour and earthy common sense and, worse, he lacked the support of the American Senate. Wilson was a Democrat and an idealist but the Republicans had just taken control and they disliked Wilson as much as they disliked getting entangled in European affairs.

PRESIDENT WOODROW WILSON ARRIVES IN PARIS, 1918

THE " BIG
THREE "
CLEMENCEAU,
WOODROW
WILSON AND
LLOYD GEORGE

Clemenceau, the " Tiger ", represented the unforgiving spirit of France. To this tough, clever old man, Wilson was a soft-headed missionary who could have his League of Nations and all his other lofty projects so long as France was made safe from German aggression. France had suffered twice in the Tiger's lifetime and he trusted no one when it came to the interests of his beloved country. Speaking of Wilson, he observed sourly: " He speaks like Jesus Christ but acts like Lloyd George ".

The British Prime Minister's position was far from easy. He was bound to try to extract every advantage for his own country and this he succeeded in doing, but he could not win the trust of either Wilson or Clemenceau. To the one, he appeared tricky and cynical; to the other, he was almost pro-German in his resistance to the extreme demands of France. Nor could he afford to be unmindful of the mood of his own electorate, who were determined to " Make Germany Pay ". In this atmosphere and with these three principals, the Peace Conference opened.

The Settlement * at Versailles was reached in a remarkably short time. It has been bitterly abused for being too mild to crush Germany and too harsh to bring her back into the European fold, yet, for all its weaknesses, it bore the marks of the justice and goodwill that Wilson tried so hard to achieve.

France recovered Alsace-Lorraine which the Germans had taken in 1870, but her demand for the creation of a separate

* The Treaty of Versailles made peace with Germany, the Treaty of St. Germain with Austria, the Treaty of Neuilly with Bulgaria, the Treaty of Trianon with Hungary and the Treaty of Sèvres (1920) with Turkey, whose revolutionary government under Kemal later rejected it for the Treaty of Lausanne (1923).

republic of the Rhineland and of permanent Allied control of the Rhine bridgeheads almost led to a breakdown of the conference. Wilson and Lloyd George argued that to detach the Rhineland from Germany was to sow the seeds for another war and they offered alternative suggestions to satisfy France. They promised that America and Britain would act together to defend her against aggression. In addition, the Allies would occupy the left bank of the Rhine for fifteen years.

Germany was forbidden to keep troops within thirty miles of the right bank. German conscription would cease and her army was restricted to a volunteer force of not more than 100,000 men, with no tanks, heavy guns or aircraft. The German Navy was to have no submarines nor any vessels larger than 10,000 tons (its Fleet had already been scuttled by its crews in Scapa Flow). To compensate France for the destruction of her coal-mines, the Germans were to hand over the Saar Valley coalfield until a plebiscite decided the area's future.

Altogether, Germany was to lose 28,000 square miles of territory (most of it recently acquired) and some 7 million inhabitants, though in terms of German-speaking people (excluding the Saar) the loss was under 3 per cent. Two small areas went to Belgium, northern Schleswig to Denmark, parts of West Prussia and Upper Silesia to Poland with a corridor through German territory to the sea, while the port of Danzig, under League of Nations' protection, was also to be controlled by Poland. Memel was to provide a port for the new state of Lithuania. The union of Germany and Austria was forbidden, and all the German colonies and Turkish possessions were shared among the Allies as mandates * of the League of Nations.

Although the conditions of the Versailles Treaty were mild compared with those that Germany had imposed upon Russia

* A mandate is a legal command. In this instance it was permission to govern the territories according to the principles of the League of Nations until they were ready for self-government. It was a means to seize Germany's colonies and yet to avoid contradicting Wilson's pledge that there would be no annexations. Britain received Palestine, Iraq and Transjordan from Turkey, German East Africa, parts of Togoland and the Cameroons from Germany. France received Syria and the Lebanon, and most of Togoland and the Cameroons. Belgium received a strip of German East Africa, the Union of South Africa took German West Africa. German islands in the Pacific were shared between Britain, Australia, New Zealand and Japan. Australia also received German New Guinea.

and Rumania in 1918, the Germans were outraged. The cabinet resigned rather than accept such terms but Ebert, the President, Hindenburg and Gröner, the Chief of Staff, knew that there was no choice. They wriggled for six weeks but on 28th June, two German delegates were led into the Hall of Mirrors at Versailles where, with hardly a word spoken, they signed the treaty and were marched out again.

Thus, the Germans were given the heaven-sent opportunity of complaining that they were deprived of all chance to negotiate but were forced to sign a " dictated " peace whose terms far exceeded the original Fourteen Points. Above all, they were deeply angered by the war-guilt clause and the demand for huge reparations.

Article 231 of the Treaty stated, " Germany accepts the responsibility of Germany and her allies for causing all the loss and damage to which the Allies and Associate Governments *Reparations* have been subjected as a consequence of the war imposed upon them by the aggression of Germany and her allies ". This statement, regarded in France and Britain as plain fact and by the Germans as lying hypocrisy, was inserted to give legal justification for the reparations claim.

From the Allies' point of view, the position was simple. The Germans had caused the war and they should pay for it. But what was the cost and how should it be paid? One estimate was £24,000 million, though more moderate opinions, including that of J. M. Keynes, the Cambridge economist, put the figure at £2,000 million and Keynes urged the cancellation of all other war debts. Neither Britain nor the U.S.A. would agree and France was only too happy at the prospect of Germany's economic ruin. Yet how could Germany pay such astronomic sums? Gold in itself would convey little benefit to people who had not earned it, and vast quantities of German goods (if and when they could produce them) would merely cause unemployment in the countries that received them. In the end, the Reparations Commission fixed the sum at £6,600 million and this was reduced to £2,000 million in 1929. Germany's calculations of what she paid included the value of the fleet scuttled by her own sailors, but, if foreign grants and loans were taken into account, Germany actually received more than she paid out! The question of reparations was never solved for the figures became meaningless. The only certain thing was that they caused a great deal of harm and did no one any good.

6 The League of Nations

THE economic side of the Peace Settlement did not interest
President Wilson half as much as the creation of the League of
Nations and of the new states which emerged from the ruins of
the Austro-Hungarian empire and the collapse of Russia. In
his opinion, dangerous rivalries would be ended by allowing
peoples speaking the same language to form separate independent states. By freeing those who had lived under alien rule and
by setting up an organised union of nations, he would bring
permanent peace to Europe.

But in Paris, Wilson found the problem more difficult than he
had imagined. Centuries of intermingling had made it virtually
impossible to draw new frontiers without including some
minority. However, the new countries were clamouring for
recognition and their existence had to be confirmed.

In this process, the Austro-Hungarian empire vanished and
the proud city of Vienna became the forlorn capital of a small
republic lacking almost every resource for its survival. The new
state of Czechoslovakia, founded by Masaryk and Dr Beneš, was
created from the old kingdom of Bohemia with Moravia and a
large portion of Hungary. It already included several races
when, in order to give it a defensible frontier, Wilson had to
agree to depart from the principle of self-determination.
Three million German-speaking people of the Sudetenland were
therefore included in Czechoslovakia.

Hungary, which had proclaimed itself a republic in 1918, lost
some more of her territory to Yugoslavia—the other new state
of central Europe. This was an enlarged Serbia which included
Serbs, Croats, Slovenes and some Magyars, Albanians and
Italians within its borders. Another miniature Austro-
Hungarian empire had been created.

Rumania gained some slices of territory from her neighbours,
including Transylvania from Hungary and Bessarabia from
Russia, but she had large Magyar and German minorities who
might prove troublesome. Bulgaria, having ended on the losing
side, was obliged to give land to Yugoslavia and to Greece but the
ancient kingdom of Poland that had been swallowed by her
powerful neighbours in the eighteenth century, came back into

existence.   However, the Poles were so dissatisfied with the
eastern frontier suggested by the Allies (the " Curzon Line "),
that, in 1920, led by Marshal Pilsudski, they attacked Russia
and pushed their frontier line some 200 miles farther east.

On the shores of the Baltic, Russia was obliged to accept the
independence of Finland that General Mannerheim had won in
1918, and the creation of three small states, Estonia, Latvia and
Lithuania, all of which had resentful minorities inside their
frontiers.

By the Treaty of Sèvres, Turkey was to keep Constantinople
but to lose all her Arab territories, which either became independent or were mandated to France and Britain.   Thanks to the
astute Venizelos, Greece appeared to do very well out of the
settlement, gaining Macedonia and Thrace on the mainland
and a considerable area round Smyrna in Asia Minor where
many Greeks had lived for centuries.

EUROPE IN 1921

MARSHAL
PILSUDSKI

The loss of Smyrna infuriated the Turks who found in Mustapha Kemal a leader far more able and vigorous than the Sultan whom he overthrew in 1921. When Kemal refused to accept the treaty, fighting broke out in which the Greeks were at first successful. However, in 1922, Kemal's forces overwhelmed the Greeks, captured Smyrna and forced a million Greeks from all parts of Asia Minor to flee to their homeland.

Italy was decidedly displeased with her gains from the war which amounted to the Southern Tyrol, Trieste and various islands in the Adriatic. Her other claims were overruled and her hopes of gaining colonies came to nothing.

Wilson's greatest achievement at Versailles was the creation of the League and it was through his insistence that the Covenant or solemn promise of the League was set at the head of all the peace treaties.

In twenty-six articles the Covenant stated that the purpose of the League was to achieve international peace and security. Membership was to be open to any self-governing state, dominion or colony that agreed to abide by the rules of the League, provided two-thirds of the Assembly approved its admission. Members promised to respect the territory and independence of others, to submit disputes to the League, and if this failed to provide a settlement after six months, to give three months' notice before declaring war. Armaments were to be reduced and any state that offended against the Covenant was liable to have " sanctions " imposed on it, that is, economic penalties or military action or both by the other Members. There were articles dealing with international agreements and with revision of treaties that became outdated or dangerous to peace.

The League worked through its Assembly and Council. The Assembly, composed of representatives of all the Member-states, met annually. The Council, composed of Permanent Members (the Great Powers) and of an agreed number of Non-Permanent Members, was to meet three times a year to discuss international problems and to inform the Assembly of its decisions. The intention was that the combined will of the Great Powers should prevail but that the voices of small nations should also be heard, though an obvious weakness was the rule that all decisions must be unanimous.

The League was many-sided; a permanent Court of International Justice was set up to deal with legal disputes between nations and there were committees and commissions that dealt

THE OPENING OF THE LEAGUE OF NATIONS AT GENEVA

with the Mandated Territories, the rights of minorities, disarmament, health, drugs, refugees, transport, communications
and conditions of labour.

Wilson and the supporters of the League believed that they
had built a system of security for great and small nations.
Peace would no longer depend upon the old treaties and
alliances but would be guarded by a permanent assembly of
nations at Geneva where, like civilised neighbours, they would
abide by the rule of law. In any case, it seemed that after
mankind's recent experience, no nation would be so rash as to
go to war again. For a few years the League was reasonably
successful and, in non-political affairs, it achieved a great deal.
But ultimately it failed to prevent the disaster of a Second World
War, because it had no army or police force to make its members
obey the rules.

Those who believed in the League suffered their most cruel
blow right at the beginning. On Wilson's return to America
he was faced by a hostile Congress, and to his utter dismay
the Senate refused to accept the Peace Treaties and therefore
the League of Nations. America had decided to turn its back
on Europe and although Wilson cried in anguish " The question
is whether we shall accept or reject the confidence of the world ",
his own people rejected him and his dream of a better world.*

Thus, although the League came into existence, it was always
a league of some nations and not the league of all nations.
Germany and Russia did not come in until 1926 and 1934 and

* Wilson, who lost the Presidency in 1920 to a Republican,
Warren Harding, set out on a nation-wide tour to win support for
his ideas but his health broke down and he died in 1924.

some of the principal Member-states left when it suited them, Germany and Japan in 1933, and Italy in 1936. The absence of the U.S.A. tended to give the League the appearance of an Anglo-French alliance but whereas Britain tried to base her foreign policy upon the principles of the League, France had little faith in its effectiveness. At Versailles, Clemenceau had dropped certain demands for security when given an agreement that the U.S.A. and Britain would come to France's aid if she were attacked. But America's refusal to ratify the Peace Treaties meant that this agreement was void and Britain rather shabbily backed out on the grounds that she was not obliged to act by herself.

France felt badly let down. Fearing a revival of German militarism, she sought security in the old manner, making alliances with Poland and the new states of south-east Europe. From 1930 she also began to spend vast sums on the never-completed Maginot Line that was to protect her eastern frontier.

But, despite its unfortunate start, the League did establish itself as an essential part of international relations. In the 1920's it settled a number of disputes between smaller nations, and in 1925 the Locarno Pact appeared to be a tremendous step towards permanent peace. France, Britain, Germany, Italy and Belgium signed agreements recognising the frontiers between Germany and her western neighbours and agreeing to go to war against anyone who violated them. This gave France satisfaction for the first time since 1919 and, since Germany signed the treaties voluntarily, her resentment at Versailles settlement seemed to be lessening.

In 1926 Germany was admitted to the League and in 1928 the Briand-Kellogg Pact renouncing war was eventually signed by sixty-three states. This was the high-water mark of confidence in the League but, in spite of endless discussions, no real advance was made in the vital matter of disarmament.

The trouble was that whereas most of the Great Powers were prepared to support the League as a kind of welfare club that met at Geneva, they knew that it was powerless to prevent war if a major Power was determined to wage war. So they made alliances, kept up their armaments and ignored events that seemed to be too far away or too inconvenient to be part of their business.

7 Europe after 1918

ALTHOUGH the Armistice of 1918 brought an end to the war against Germany, lesser fires of violence continued to burn for several years.

The new Baltic republics, Estonia and Latvia, suffered invasion by Bolshevik forces and by German troops who carried on fighting well into 1919 until Allied intervention established more settled conditions. As we have seen, Greece and Turkey fought a savage war that ended in 1922 with the triumph of Kemal. Hungary's Government was overthrown by a Communist named Bela Kun and civil war broke out in which Bela Kun was defeated by Admiral Horthy. Poland, having attacked Russia, was almost overwhelmed by the Red Army. With French assistance, Pilsudski drove the enemy back from Warsaw and forced Lenin to grant a new frontier, though it made Poland no safer than before.

The most savage violence occurred in Russia where a pitiless civil war was waged between Lenin's supporters, the Reds, and his opponents, the White Russians.

To this day, Lenin's name is venerated in Russia, his tomb is a place of pilgrimage and, as other people speak of God or Allah, Russian citizens say reverently " Lenin is always with us ". For it was Lenin who made the Revolution and preserved it against all its enemies. He had able and ruthless comrades in Trotsky, Stalin, Kamenev, Zinoviev and others, but it was the driving genius of this fanatical conspirator who had spent most of his life in Siberian prisons and in cheap lodgings in England and Switzerland, that established Communism in the empire of the Tsars.

VLADIMIR LENIN

Born in 1870 in a provincial town on the banks of the Volga, Lenin came not from a peasant's shack but from an educated middle-class home. His father was a schools' inspector. When he was seventeen, Lenin's older brother was hanged for his part in a conspiracy to assassinate the Tsar, and Lenin himself was expelled from Kazan University after a students' riot. He was, however, allowed to take his law examinations at St Petersburg where he came top in every subject. By this time Lenin had made a thorough study of the writings of Karl Marx, the

79

Lenin

German Jew whose theories as to how the working classes of the world ("the proletariat") should overthrow their employers ("the capitalists") became the handbook of Communism. For publishing an illegal newspaper, Lenin was sentenced to three years in Siberia and, after his release in 1900, he went into exile with his wife Krupskaya, a young revolutionary as devoted to the cause as he was. Living in poverty, Lenin and Leon Trotsky, a brilliant Jew who was part-friend and part-enemy, kept in constant touch with their revolutionary supporters. They both returned to Russia for the 1905 uprising but had to flee again. However, by the outbreak of war in 1914, they had formed the tightly-knit Bolshevik Party and were ready to organise revolution at the first opportunity. It came, as we have seen, in 1917 when the German General Staff decided to bring Lenin back from Switzerland to his homeland.

By his compelling personality and demonic energy, together with an unswerving grasp of the aims of the Revolution, Lenin became undisputed leader of the Bolsheviks. Once he had overthrown the Kerensky Government in November 1918, Lenin had no intention of sharing power with the other Socialist parties, the Mensheviks and Social Revolutionaries, whose more moderate and woolly aims he despised. Having bested them, he formed the Council of People's Commissars with himself at the head, Trotsky as Commissar for foreign affairs and Stalin as Commissar for nationalities. They would set up the proletarian state of his dreams. The people were won over by the promise of an immediate peace and a share-out of the great estates among the peasants.

Germany's terms were so harsh that even Trotsky could not accept them at first, but in March 1918 the Treaty of Brest-Litovsk was signed and, for a huge price, the peace was bought. But the Bolsheviks were only rid of their chief enemy. Other opponents speedily took up arms against them. With no common aim or policy, the anti-revolutionaries were a mixed collection of army officers, Conservatives, indignant Mensheviks and Social Revolutionaries and Czech ex-prisoners of war who had originally formed an army corps to help the Allies and who now stayed to fight the Revolution. General Kornilov led the White Russians in the south until his death, when Denikin succeeded him; another army under Chernov operated on the lower Volga, a third led by General Horvat took control of Manchuria and Admiral Kolchak commanded the counter-revolutionary forces in Siberia where the Czechs held the railway that ran to Vladivostok.

After Germany's defeat, the Allies unwisely decided to inter-vene on the side of the White Russians. French and British troops were landed at Murmansk and Archangel in the north, while Japanese and American soldiers entered Siberia through Vladivostok, but these armies were not large and the troops had no enthusiasm for their task. Indeed, the presence of foreigners hardened the determination of the Reds to win at all cost and, by the Second World War, the Russians had still not forgotten that Britain and America—and Mr Churchill in particular—had once tried to overthrow the people's cause.

For the Revolution was the cause of the common people. Westerners often pointed to the diabolical skill with which Lenin and a handful of dedicated Communists obtained complete power over an entire nation, but, in 1919, Lenin could not have succeeded unless he had given his people the faith to wage and to win a most bloody war that lasted more than two years. The peasants were fighting for their newly-acquired land and they knew that the White Russians stood for a return of the landlords. So, although Denikin made a great thrust through the Ukraine towards Moscow and an attack from the north threatened St Petersburg, Trotsky, commander of the Red Army, who sud-denly displayed a genius for war, contested every inch of ground and organised his reserves and a street-by-street defence of St Petersburg until the White Russians were repulsed. By 1920, Denikin had been driven from his base in the Crimea and Kolchak had surrendered in the east. The Allied forces were

ENG. BK. V—6

LEON TROTSKY

withdrawn and the last flickers of opposition to the Bolshevik régime died away.

Lenin had triumphed but, in the darkness of civil war, the nobler aims of the Revolution vanished. The workers lost their political liberties, for the leaders who had set out to build a new Russia without police, bureaucrats and a standing army turned their country into a one-party police state little different from Tsarist Russia except that it was more efficiently directed.

The Weimar Republic

At the end of the war, Germany became a republic with a National Assembly at Weimar, a university city some 120 miles south-east of Berlin. The President, a Social Democrat named Ebert, and his colleagues did their best to make a working success of Liberal democracy, a form of government that was a new experience for Germans; but from the outset the Weimar Republic had enemies to the left and to the right. The Spartacists or German Communist Party tried to overthrow the Republic by force and were defeated by the Social Democrats because of army support; in Bavaria, Munich was the scene of a brutal struggle between extreme Socialists and right-wing nationalists. Again the Social Democrats had to call on the Army to restore order but Munich remained the centre of opposition to the Republic and of the anti-Jewish agitation that was beginning to find favour with all who wanted a scapegoat for Germany's defeat.

In 1920 there was a minor revolution known as the Kapp Putsch when naval units, disbanded by order of the Allied Military Commission, seized Berlin and declared for a new government headed by a royalist named Kapp who was supported by General Ludendorff. The workers came out on strike and the revolt collapsed with Kapp's arrest, but, as always in Germany, the ex-Army officers were dealt with leniently.

The wobbly foundations of Ebert's government were further shaken by the report of the Reparations Commission that Germany must pay £100 million a year. After half-hearted

FRENCH CAVALRY
ENTER ESSEN
IN THE RUHR,
JANUARY 1923

SOME OF THE LEADING NAZIS: (LEFT TO RIGHT) HIMMLER, FRICK, GOEBBELS, HITLER, VON EPP, GOERING

efforts to comply, the Germans declared that they could not pay, whereupon, in 1923, Poincaré, the French Prime Minister, sent the French Army into the Ruhr. The Germans resisted the occupiers with strikes and sabotage, and their financial experts decided to evade their debts by adopting inflation, a huge increase in the amount of money in circulation so that, whereas in 1918, 20 marks were equal to the value of £1, by the end of 1923 the rate of exchange was 22,000,000,000 to the pound. Money ceased to have any value and a workman who took a suitcase to collect his wages would find on reaching the shops that the value of all those millions of paper notes had dropped since the morning. People on fixed incomes, civil servants, pensioners, the upper and middle classes were ruined, savings became worthless and the bitterness of the German people increased.

Adolf Hitler

Among the unhappy results of Poincaré's action was the arrival on the political scene of Adolf Hitler. This thirty-four-year-old son of an Austrian customs official had idled away his youth in Vienna before enlisting for war-service in a Bavarian regiment. He reached the rank of corporal and was awarded the Iron Cross. In Munich he joined an obscure political party that was to become the National Socialist German Workers' Party, the Nazis. At meetings in cellars and dingy halls, the insignificant little man with lank black hair, a scrubby moustache and burning eyes became transformed when he stood up to speak. In raving tones he attacked democracy, Communism, Socialism, Capitalism, the Weimar Government, the Treaty of Versailles and, above all, the Jews. People came to listen to this torrent of hatred for it fitted their mood of angry self-pity and, among the ex-officers, the failed journalists,

83

impoverished clerks and genuine patriots were Rudolph Hess, Hermann Goering, a hero of the Air Force, Joseph Goebbels, a warped, Satanic cripple and Ludendorff himself.

Disorder in Bavaria prompted Hitler and Ludendorff to organise a march of the Nazis through the streets of Munich to proclaim a new nationalist government for Germany. The hastily prepared plot failed miserably when police rifle-fire scattered the marchers and the two principals were arrested. But Hitler's trial brought him to the notice of the general public when from the dock he was allowed to make long ranting speeches that were printed in all the newspapers. He received only a light sentence and was soon at liberty to resume his self-appointed mission of building up a party to restore Germany's " greatness ". Funds began to come in from industrialists who feared Communism. A party newspaper poured out abusive hatred, and brown-shirted thugs with swastika badges on their arms broke into opponents' meetings and beat up Jews in the streets. Hitler's star was beginning to rise.

Stresemann   Meanwhile, Gustav Stresemann became Chancellor and Foreign Secretary of the Weimar Republic, and under his guidance Germany's fortunes improved. He called off the campaign of sabotage in the Ruhr and agreed to pay reparations in accordance with the Dawes Plan of 1924 which provided for payments as German recovery increased. France withdrew from the Ruhr, German inflation was checked and, with the aid of huge American loans, the republic seemed to be on the road to stability. However, there were still those who were working for its overthrow.

When Ebert died in 1925 the election of old Hindenburg as President gave heart to the militarists and nationalists. Under the skilful direction of General von Seeckt, Germany began to rebuild her armed forces whilst appearing to keep to the terms of the Versailles treaty. The army, restricted to 100,000 men, was composed of picked volunteers who were trained, not as private soldiers, but as officers of the future. Research into the use of armoured vehicles and aircraft went on, tank and flying schools were set up in Russia, while gliding clubs, civil flying, labour battalions and police-forces were organised so that they could be swiftly expanded into essential parts of the military machine.

The weakness of parliamentary democracy was not confined to Germany. Rising prices, unemployment, the closing of war industries and the spread of Communism added to the difficulties of government in many countries. In nearly all parliaments, apart from Britain's, the electoral system invited confusion. British voters could vote for any one of several candidates and the one who received most votes was elected, irrespective of whether he had an absolute majority over the others. This voting system led inevitably to a two-party parliament but on the continent most countries preferred the French second ballot * system, or the Belgium system of proportional representation or a Dutch version of the latter. These electoral methods (one or another of which was adopted by Germany, Austria, Poland, Czechoslovakia and the new Baltic states) produced parliaments containing a variety of parties with barely distinguishable aims and no hope of forming a government except through alliance with some of the other parties. Usually there were six or seven parties but the German Reichstag came to have forty!

Thus, most of the post-war countries of Europe tended to have governments which were weak and short-lived. Ministers came and went with bewildering rapidity and politics became notorious for jobbery and corruption. When the many-party system had reduced democracy to a farce, people were inclined to accept anyone who offered " strong government " in the place of bickering inactivity.

The first country to take this step was Italy. Poverty, high taxation and corrupt politics had been commonplace for years and now, after the sufferings of the war, came the disappointments at Versailles and the unrest caused by Communist *Mussolini* agitation. One of the most violent figures in Italian politics was Benito Mussolini, a blacksmith's son who had been an ardent Socialist and editor of a Marxist newspaper. When he

* Briefly, in the Second Ballot system, if a candidate does not receive an overall majority in the first ballot, a second is held in which voters decide between the leading candidates. There are several systems of Proportional Representation; the elector may vote by using numbers 1, 2, 3, 4, 5, 6 in order of preference for the various candidates, who are then elected according to the number of first-preference votes, second preference votes, etc. that they receive. The counting is obviously complicated. Electors may vote on a party list and if a party does not obtain enough votes in one constituency to gain a successful candidate, the votes go into a " pool " from which further candidates are elected in proportion to the total number of votes cast.

BENITO
MUSSOLINI

founded the Fascist Party in 1919, he hoped to be the Socialist
leader of Italy, but failure in the elections convinced him that
his best chance of success lay outside parliament.

With help from nationalists, who despised the feeble government, and industrialists who feared the Communists, Mussolini
organised gangs of black-shirted hooligans who virtually took
command of Milan and several northern cities. In October
1922, when the Fascists were threatening to march on Rome,
the government at last decided to call upon the Italian Army
to put down these lawless elements. But King Victor Emmanuel
refused to sign the proclamation of martial law. Instead, he
sent a telegram to Mussolini, inviting him to form a government,
and the triumphant march on Rome duly took place with
Mussolini himself travelling comfortably by train.

As Prime Minister, Mussolini demanded and was granted
full powers which he used to crush all opposition in parliament
and outside. Copying the Bolsheviks, he took control of all the
channels of information, newspapers, books, theatre, films and
radio when it came into everyday use. Schools, universities and
official text-books were made to obey the party line. The
Fascist gangs were welded into one party which, like the

Communists in Russia, formed an élite to direct and safeguard the régime everywhere. Local elections were abolished and towns were run by government, i.e. Fascist, officials. The unions were dealt with by the formation of " corporations ", supposedly representing workers and employers, but strikes were forbidden and disputes were settled by compulsory arbitration. The King, Prime Minister, Cabinet and Parliament were all retained as a façade but the real executive was the Fascist Grand Council. Mussolini, known as Il Duce (the leader), held absolute power.

How did the Italian people and the statesmen of the world come to take this fat blue-jowled dictator seriously? All his promises and threats are now seen to be the melodramatic posturings of a " sawdust Caesar ". But in the twenties and thirties, people did not know that there was so little real substance behind the braggart's talk, that his vaunted legions would fail miserably when put to the test and that he himself would come to an abject end. For Mussolini knew his people and how to talk to them. He injected a new vigour and discipline into the country, tackled unemployment with a huge programme of public works, drained marshes, encouraged farming and gave state aid to new industries. Observers noted cleanliness and order never seen before in Italy, splendid new roads and sports arenas, majestic railway stations and trains that actually ran on time. Mussolini impressed them, as he impressed Hitler—and Churchill—at first. Although he could not really solve Italy's economic problems, he put on such a show of bravado that other countries followed his example.

In Spain, de Rivera replaced the parliament with a military dictatorship, a forerunner of Franco's régime; in Portugal, *Dictatorship* General Carmona became ruler of the republic with Dr Salazar as his financial minister; in Poland during the same year, 1926, Pilsudski became an unwilling dictator, while the constant quarrelling of Croats and Serbs in Yugoslavia led King Alexander to set up what was virtually a royal dictatorship. It must be said, however, that in these four countries that accepted dictatorship because of the failure of their parliaments, there was little of the cruel despotism that was characteristic of the régimes in Russia and, presently, in Germany, where the torture-chamber, the firing squad and the concentration camp replaced the rule of law and the rights of citizens. In Italy there was less brutality but the tyranny was very much the same.

Lenin died in 1924 at the age of fifty-three from, it was said, " excessive brain activity ", but, before his death, he had made extraordinary changes in the state that he had brought into being. He had always believed that revolution in Russia would be the signal for proletarian risings all over Europe and the eventual establishment of world Communism, but this did not happen; and although Trotsky continued to preach world revolution, Lenin found himself grappling with the appalling problems created by war, revolution and civil war. Devastation, collapse of industry and communications and the refusal of the peasants to co-operate led to famine in the cities and the government was compelled to seize the peasants' hoarded grain. The peasants replied by producing no more than for their own needs. The food situation grew worse until Lenin allowed some private trading, especially in farming. This was the New Economic Policy. Foreign loans were obtained to build up industry, and a class of well-to-do peasants, the Kulaks, began to thrive.

Lenin's death brought a decisive change to this somewhat mild version of Communism for, out of the triumvirate who took the reins, Stalin, Zinoviev and Kamenev, Josef Stalin emerged as Russia's strong man. This impassive, heavily-moustached Georgian, a life-long conspirator and one of the architects of the Revolution, was General Secretary of the Party, a position which enabled him to know everything that was going on. Having manœuvred his two colleagues out of office and dismissed Trotsky (who was subsequently exiled and murdered), Stalin proceeded to bring all Russia under his own iron rule.

JOSEF STALIN

Nothing was allowed to stand in the way of economic progress. The N.E.P. was abandoned and five million Kulaks were killed, starved and imprisoned to impose collective farming upon a peasantry that did not want it. Industry was given its first Five Year Plan (1928) to create new towns and factories at staggering speed, and since machines, tractors and power-stations were more vital than consumer-goods, the people were forced to work for little visible reward. Later, good workers were rewarded with extra payment and such decorations as " Hero of Socialist Labour ", but, for the time being, the nation was ruthlessly drilled to bring " Socialism to one country ". Not for nothing had Josef Djugashvili taken the name of Stalin for it meant " Man of Steel ", and the Russian people accepted his oppressive rule because, as never in the days of the Tsar, they had hopes of the future.

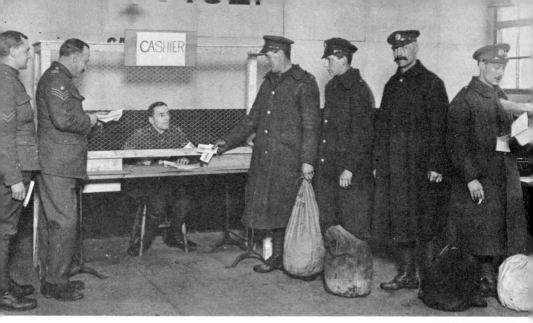

8 Lloyd George's Decline

ON Armistice Night 1918, the streets of London were filled
with hysterical cheering crowds. Victory, so dearly bought, had
come at last—the victory that would end all wars. There
would never be another. For this ideal a million men had
fought and died and soon the survivors would be coming home
to a land fit for heroes. But when they came, the soldiers were
in no mood for rejoicing or revenge. They left the flag-waving
and the talk of " Hang the Kaiser " to the civilians, for all that
they wanted was a job, a house and an end to being ordered
about.

Although it was natural for the soldiers to think that the
country owed them a decent living after all they had suffered, it
was not easy to resettle four million ex-servicemen when business
and industry were trying to adjust themselves to peacetime
conditions. Muddles over demobilisation caused one or two
riots and a mutiny at Calais. There was a desperate shortage
of houses and, although the Government's Addison Scheme to
build 350,000 homes was a well-intentioned project, the houses
were not yet up and they eventually proved to be too few and
too expensive.

The mood of the ex-serviceman became resentful. His faith
in authority and in his social betters had been shaken by the
waste and muddle he had seen in Flanders. Out there he had
learned that class-differences meant little when all men were in

danger. As a private soldier said to his mates just before an attack:

Disillusionment

" They're all in it wi' us an' one man's no better nor another . . . we all stan' the same chance now." *

Homecoming did not lessen his disillusionment. After a short boom, when war-gratuities and workers' savings vanished in a spending spree, there came a slump and the Government that had found millions of pounds a day for the war, seemed powerless to keep the wheels of industry turning. As for a land fit for heroes and a world made safe for democracy, those promises were found to be as empty as the rest of the politicians' talk.

The workers who had stayed at home in essential occupations were equally sour in their outlook. Most of them, the miners and railwaymen in particular, had known better wages and conditions than ever before and they were not going to return to pre-war standards without a struggle. So, as prices began to rise and wages failed to keep pace, they came out on strike and in 1919, thirty-two million days' work were lost. 1920 saw unemployment rise to a million and for the next twenty years the number of workless never fell below this figure.

The Government that came in after the 1918 " Coupon " Election was a Liberal-Conservative coalition, but since the Conservatives were in the majority Lloyd George was their prisoner. By overthrowing Asquith in 1916 he had lost the support of nearly all the leading Liberals and by now he was a Prime Minister without a party. However, he was " the man who won the war ". Bonar Law, the Conservative leader, liked and supported him and he went off to the Peace Conference unhampered by any doubts about his own future. He knew perfectly well that everyone, including those, like George V and Haig, who had previously detested him, now recognised him as the country's irreplaceable leader. " He can be Prime Minister for life if he likes ", observed Bonar Law.

Civil war

Among those elected to Parliament were seventy-three Irish Members. By now they were no longer John Redmond's moderate Irish Nationalists supporting Home Rule but members of Sinn Fein, the extremist party bent upon nothing less than complete independence. Instead of coming to Westminster, they made themselves into an Irish Parliament (Dail Eireann) at Dublin and declared Ireland to be an independent republic.

* *Her Privates We*, Manning (1930)

This was no more than a continuation of the events of 1916 when, on Easter Monday, the Irish Volunteers, Sinn Fein's " army ", had staged an unsuccessful rebellion. Defeat and the execution of Sir Roger Casement had merely postponed the struggle.

The problem of Lloyd George's Government was that Home Rule, passed by the Liberals in 1914 but suspended for the duration of the war, was no longer acceptable. John Redmond was dead and so was moderation. Ulster would fight rather than accept rule from Dublin and the Sinn Feiners, led by Eamon De Valera, Michael Collins and Arthur Griffith, were determined to win complete independence by force.

In 1919 all but seven members of the Dail were arrested but De Valera escaped from prison to the United States where he raised a fighting fund of 600,000 dollars from Irish-American sympathisers. Meanwhile, Michael Collins' Irish Volunteers, now called the I.R.A. (Irish Republican Army), began a campaign of violence against the English Government's forces, chiefly the Royal Irish Constabulary.

By 1920 there was civil war in Ireland. Barracks and Government buildings were attacked, post offices robbed, property looted and policemen, soldiers and civilians murdered. The Government's reply was to reinforce the Constabulary with troops recruited from English ex-servicemen (the " Black and Tans ") who were ordered to put down terror by counter-terror. While fighting went on with the savagery peculiar to civil wars, an effort was made to placate both sides. The Government of Ireland Act, 1920, offered separate parliaments in Dublin and Belfast with an all-Ireland Council composed of twenty members from each. Ulster accepted but the Sinn Feiners would have nothing to do with partition. In June 1921, when George V opened the Northern Parliament at Belfast, his earnest appeal to " all Irishmen . . . to forgive and forget " led to a truce. At this, Lloyd George invited De Valera and Sir James Craig (Prime Minister of Northern Ireland) to attend a conference in London.

" BLACK AND
TANS " ARREST
A SINN FEINER

After long negotiation, De Valera withdrew but he was persuaded to send Collins and Griffith in his place, and it was they who approved a treaty giving Ireland the status of a Dominion and the title of the Irish Free State. If it wished, Northern Ireland could stay out.

The Dail ratified the Treaty by 64 votes to 57 but the tragedy was not ended, for De Valera changed his mind and decided to oppose the agreement which his lieutenants had accepted. So the moderates, headed by Collins, and the extremists led by De Valera fought among themselves and in the struggle Collins was murdered and Griffith died of heart failure. Eventually W. T. Cosgrove became President of the Irish Free State and De Valera decided to call off his republican gunmen and to await his own hour. It came in 1932 when he succeeded Cosgrove as President and began the process of breaking all links with England. This was completed by 1949 when Eire left the Commonwealth.

Post-war slump

Although the Irish Treaty was in some ways a triumph for Lloyd George, the little Welshman's reputation was beginning to slide downhill. Trade was bad, taxation stood at wartime levels and, as unemployment soared, Lloyd George's Unemployment Insurance scheme was found to be inadequate. No one had foreseen a situation when huge numbers of men would be out of work for long periods. When the time limit for drawing unemployment pay (known as " the Dole ") ran out, men were given relief out of the rates. This meant that in areas where there was much unemployment—the East End of London, South Wales and Durham, for instance,—local boroughs got heavily into debt and the Government did nothing to help.

The greatest discontent was in the coal industry which had been taken out of private hands during the war. Owing to the loss of continental production, British coal fetched high prices and the miners earned reasonably good wages. For a short time after the war, while European pits were still out of action, there was a brisk export trade but in 1920 the price fell from 115s a ton to 85s and in 1921 to 24s a ton. Since the pit-head price was 39s a ton, the Government hastily returned the mines to the owners, who immediately declared that they could not sell coal at a loss. The miners must therefore work longer hours for less pay. The miners refused point-blank and the situation was made worse by the Sankey Report.

In 1919 a Royal Commission, under Lord Justice Sankey, was set up to consider the coal industry. Its members consisted of three miners and three supporters, and three coal-owners and three industrialists. Thus, the sides for and against nationalisation were equal and everything turned on the Chairman. Lord Sankey was known to have Socialist sympathies so, in promising to abide by the Commission's report, Lloyd George was apparently agreeing to nationalise the coalmines.

Sure enough, when the Report appeared in 1920, it recommended nationalisation but, in spite of Lloyd George's promises which were backed by Bonar Law, this was not carried out and the miners, more aggrieved than ever, looked for help to their partners in the Triple Alliance (see page 25). Neither the railwaymen, led by J. H. Thomas, nor the transport workers, led by Ernest Bevin, were keen to strike and when it appeared that the miners were hesitating about their demands, the other unions backed out. On Friday, 15th April 1921, J. H. Thomas announced that there would be no general strike in support of the miners and this became known as " Black Friday " by the workers. Left to go it alone, the miners remained on strike until June 1921, when Parliament voted £10 million to ease the situation. At this the miners gave in and accepted local settlements at lower wages. In one industry after another, in shipbuilding, engineering and textiles, wages—and unemployment benefit—came down sharply. This painful process was due to the fact that British exports had to compete with goods from other countries where wages and standards of living were lower and, since the Government was paying its debts abroad, taxes had to remain high. Unfortunately, high taxes and low wages meant that people had little to spend and this led to a declining home market. Factories closed, more people became unemployed and still fewer goods were produced.

A MINERS'
MEETING AT
WIGAN DURING
THE 1921 COAL
STRIKE

Certainly, prices fell but this was not much consolation to those on short time or out of work. As George V observed, " It is impossible to expect people to subsist upon the unemployment benefit of 15s. for men and 12s for women ", but just as anyone in financial difficulties tries to cut his expenses, so the Government decided to reduce public expenditure. Dr Addison's Housing Scheme was virtually ended, the Agricultural Wages Board, set up to assist farm workers' pay, was abolished and Sir Eric Geddes was given the task of applying the " Geddes Axe " wherever he could: it fell mainly on the cost of defence and education.

Yet there was no real effort to tackle the stagnation of heavy industry or the position of the unemployed. Although the King suggested that " emergency works such as road-making, land reclamation, light railways, forestation, although unremunerative, will nevertheless be doing some good, and meet the claim of those who demand work and not charity ", his ministers and the unions seemed to be opposed to the idea of creating work by direct Government action.

In such times, it was not surprising that the Coalition Government lost popularity and Lloyd George, whose fertile brain might well have devised schemes to benefit his crippled homeland, was constantly abroad and unable to dominate the Cabinet in his old style. Nor could he claim credit for any outstanding successes in foreign affairs. In 1919 Indian relations suffered when British troops opened fire on a rioting crowd at Amritsar; the intervention of British troops in Russia and Ireland had been neither successful nor popular and all the rushing round to international conferences seemed to achieve nothing more than bad feeling with France over the German reparations.

In July 1922 the World Reconstruction Conference met at Genoa and Lloyd George invited the United States, Russia and Germany to join the other nations for discussions. Germany and Russia both sent representatives but, in the face of French obstinacy, the conference broke down and the Russians and Germans went off to sign a treaty of their own. Thus, Lloyd George was blamed for provoking the French and for throwing the Russians and Germans into each other's arms. But if in many ways he was dogged by bad luck, his last fiasco was his own fault.

In the quarrel between Greece and Turkey, Lloyd George was

LLOYD GEORGE, DURING A POLITICAL TOUR SHORTLY AFTER HIS FALL
FROM OFFICE

decidedly pro-Greek and, in August 1922, when Greek and
Turkish armies were facing each other in Asia Minor, he made
an unwise speech in the House of Commons. He spoke so
strongly in favour of Greece that Mustapha Kemal, the Turkish
commander, expecting that this would provoke attack, decided
to strike the first blow. The Greeks were swept clean out of
Asia Minor and Kemal's army advanced to the Allied neutral
zone south of the Dardanelles at Chanak. The French and
Italians withdrew and only six battalions of British soldiers faced *Chanak crisis*
the victorious Turks. Fortunately nothing happened, but a
totally unnecessary war was avoided only by a hair's-breadth.

The Chanak crisis was the last straw for those Conservatives
who had been longing to bring the Coalition to an end. They
had been restrained by Bonar Law, a most loyal admirer of
Lloyd George's genius, but Bonar Law had now retired from
the Cabinet because of ill-health, and Lord Curzon, exasperated by the Prime Minister's criticism and interference,
resigned from the Foreign Office. This in itself showed that
Lloyd George's fall was imminent, for Curzon was an adept at
backing the winning side, but there were other reasons for the
Prime Minister's decline in power and popularity.

His series of foreign conferences had led, not to glowing
success, but to a worsening of the situation in Europe and this at
a time when people considered that Lloyd George should have
given the utmost attention to the problems and difficulties at
home. With his colleagues in the Cabinet, he had become
sharp-tempered to the point of rudeness and even his admirer
Churchill had felt the sting of his rebukes. But a Prime Minister
without a party could not afford to bully his associates. A
dictator needs power and, by now, Lloyd George had nothing

95

to call upon, not even popularity. There was much scandal, too, about the sale of titles in the Honours List and the collection of a Lloyd George Party Fund, all of which was damaging to his reputation.

On 19th October 1922 a meeting of rank-and-file Conservatives was held at the Carlton Club where Bonar Law and Stanley Baldwin made the decisive speeches that led to the Party's withdrawal from the Coalition. Lloyd George immediately resigned and Bonar Law became Prime Minister with Curzon back as Foreign Secretary and, to the surprise of many, Stanley Baldwin as Chancellor of the Exchequer.

Fall of Lloyd George

Lloyd George was out but at the time no one would have believed that the Welsh wizard's effective career was ended. The statesman who had played a dominating part in home and world affairs since 1906 would never hold office again. Churchill said of him,

" He was the greatest master of the art of getting things done and of putting things through that I ever knew; in fact no British politician in my day possessed half his competence."

Lloyd George was as brilliant as ever but by now his triumphs were over and hardly anyone in politics trusted him. He had always been too clever and too ambitious for most of the others and he gave himself away when he described Bonar Law as " honest to the point of simplicity ". He did not realise that people had come to prefer an honest man to one who was clever to the point of duplicity. Yet it was a tragedy that the ablest man in politics should have been relegated to the sidelines all through the twenties when Britain stood in such need of leadership.

The country soon found its honest man in Stanley Baldwin, the quiet, middle-class millionaire who, virtually unknown until the previous year, became Prime Minister in May 1923 when Bonar Law's health finally collapsed. Baldwin was extraordinarily lucky. As Chancellor of the Exchequer, he had just made a disastrous agreement to pay the British debt to America at the rate of £34 million a year irrespective of whether Britain's European debtors paid up. Any man who had mishandled negotiations as badly as Baldwin would have expected to be ruined, yet in some curious way he actually gained prestige when it seemed that no matter what the continental dodgers did, Britain would pay up honourably. Even so, Lord Curzon was a far more experienced statesman and he fully expected to become Prime Minister. But Curzon, apart from his haughty manner

Stanley Baldwin Prime Minister

and unlovable character, suffered the inescapable handicap of being a peer and since there was apparently no one else in the Party, the post went to Baldwin. In the first blaze of indignation, Curzon described his rival as " a man of the utmost insignificance ".

The description was unjust. Baldwin has been harshly criticised for his failure to deal more determinedly with unemployment and to understand the threat of Fascism, but he was a far shrewder party-man than Curzon and he made real efforts to " heal the nation ". He spoke from the heart when he said,

" There is only one thing which I feel is worth giving one's strength to, and that is the binding together of all classes of our people in an effort to make life in this country better in every sense of the word."

Baldwin's first premiership lasted only seven months. At the end of 1923, he called for a General Election because he had come to feel that unemployment could be relieved by Protection, i.e. by protecting home industries from foreign competition by tariffs on imported goods. The British public, still loyal to Free Trade, did not agree with him, and returned a Parliament consisting of 258 Conservatives, 191 Labour M.P.'s and 159 Liberals, who were temporarily united in the name of Free Trade. There was, however, no real reconciliation between Asquith and Lloyd George.

No Party had a clear majority and Baldwin resumed office. However, when Asquith led nearly all his followers into the opposition lobby in support of a Labour amendment, the Government was defeated and Baldwin resigned. The way was clear for the first Labour Government and Ramsay MacDonald was summoned to Buckingham Palace to kiss hands as Prime Minister. On 22nd January 1924, George V, who accepted the Socialists with a good grace and became particularly fond of J. H. Thomas's broad jokes, wrote in his diary, " Today 23 years ago dear Grandmama died. I wonder what she would have thought of a Labour Government ! "

STANLEY BALDWIN WITH J. H. THOMAS (LEFT) AND NEVILLE CHAMBERLAIN

RAMSAY MACDONALD, 1924. TO HIS LEFT, MARGARET BONDFIELD, J. H. THOMAS, ROBERT SMILLIE

9 MacDonald and Baldwin, 1924–29

JAMES RAMSAY MACDONALD, brought up in poverty at Lossie-mouth on the Moray Firth, had made his way to London where as a young man he worked as a clerk and educated himself until he became a well-known writer on Socialism and economics. Devoted to building up a Labour Parliamentary Party, he was Chairman of the Party in 1911 but had to resign in 1914 owing to his opposition to the war. By 1922 he had regained the leadership and now, at the age of fifty-seven, handsome, eloquent, the picture of dignified statesmanship, he was the first Labour Prime Minister of Britain. Those who *The first* feared a sudden onrush of Socialism did not realise that *Labour* MacDonald's primary aim was to prove that Labour was as *Government* respectable and as fit to govern as either of the other parties.

His task in forming a Government was not easy. Apart from Arthur Henderson, who had served in Lloyd George's War Cabinet, none of his colleagues had been in office and there was not much talent to call upon. Philip Snowden * was the natural choice for Chancellor of the Exchequer, and J. H. Thomas, † the former engine-driver, breezy, vulgar and openly

* Philip Snowden, 1864–1937, b. Keighley, Yorks; civil servant, crippled in cycling accident; 1903–06, Chairman I.L.P.; 1906, M.P.; 1924 and 1929–32, Chancellor of Exchequer. Became Lord Snowden.

† James Henry Thomas, 1874–1949, b. Newport, Mon.; 1910, M.P.; formed National Union of Railwaymen, became its general secretary; 1924, Colonial Secretary; 1926, leading role in General Strike; 1929, Lord Privy Seal; 1930–35, Dominions Secretary. Deprived of union secretaryship on joining National Government. Career ended when found to have disclosed Budget secrets.

delighted to find himself in office, became Colonial Secretary. Both were men of moderate, even conservative outlook. Only five members of the Cabinet were trade unionists and the one left-winger of note was John Wheatley, Minister of Health, a leading member of the Independent Labour Party (I.L.P.) which acted as the " ginger " group, urging thorough-going Socialism upon the cautious moderates.

MacDonald took the Foreign Office himself and did remarkably well. Fortunate in finding that the French, with a Socialist premier, M. Herriot, were less violently anti-German than usual, he managed to persuade them to accept the Dawes Plan, which allowed Germany to pay reduced reparations. He recognised the Bolshevik Government and opened trade talks, though he soon found that it was far from easy to negotiate with the suspicious Russians. MacDonald's greatest triumph could have been the Geneva Protocol which he worked out with the aid of Henderson and Herriot. This was a scheme by which nations were to agree to use their armies and navies to enforce decisions of the League of Nations, and nine nations, including France, had signed the Protocol when Labour fell from office.

At home, MacDonald's Government did less well. Despite obvious sympathy for the unemployed, shown by raising the Dole a few shillings, nothing was done to tackle unemployment itself and Snowden's Budget was disappointingly timid. The one real achievement was Wheatley's Housing Act of 1924 which gave bigger subsidies and rate-aid for building working-class homes, so that, in the next fifteen years, the building industry was able to put up half a million " council houses ".

After nine months, the Labour Government was defeated, not because of its failures at home but because of public alarm about " Bolshevism " aroused by MacDonald's efforts to come to friendlier terms with Russia. When the Conservatives accused the Government of dropping a prosecution against J. R. Campbell, editor of a Communist paper, a vote of censure was carried and Parliament was dissolved.

The 1924 election

The General Election that followed in October 1924 was remarkable, not only for being the first in which " wireless " was used for election broadcasts, but for the Zinoviev Letter. This was supposed to have been sent by the Russian Bolshevik Zinoviev to the British Communist Party instructing them how to control the Labour movement and bring about a workers' revolt. The Foreign Office published the text of the letter and protested to Russia. MacDonald handled the matter clumsily and the Press let itself go in hysterical attempts to discover Communism in the British Labour Party. In the election, Labour lost 42 seats, a setback naturally ascribed to the dishonest behaviour of its opponents but, in fact, Labour's vote actually increased and the real sufferer from the " Red Letter " scare was the Liberal Party, which lost 118 seats. *

Conservatives in office 1924–29

Thus, when Baldwin came back in 1924, a large part of the nation sighed with relief. For Prime Minister, they now had the plain man of politics, not clever perhaps but straight, a pig-loving countryman who would give the people the quiet government they wanted. Actually, Baldwin was an able politician, but he was also a sensitive, rather lazy man who reacted to events only when they pressed so hard that something had to be done. Then, having behaved in a way that was often foreign to his real nature, he would let things slide as before and hope for the best.

The leading men in Baldwin's Cabinet were Austen Chamberlain (Foreign Secretary), his half-brother, Neville Chamberlain (Minister of Health) and Winston Churchill who, having rejoined the Conservatives because he opposed Liberal support for the Labour government, was given the post of Chancellor of the Exchequer. While the Prime Minister presided over affairs with indolent good-humour—" he would sniff and snuff at problems like an elderly spaniel ", wrote Sir Harold Nicolson—these three attempted to solve the country's problems.

Austen Chamberlain promptly scrapped the Russian treaties and the Geneva Protocol but he followed MacDonald's policy of working for a better understanding with France and Germany. The Locarno Pact, signed in 1925 by Britain, France, Germany, Italy and Belgium, was hailed as the British Foreign Secretary's personal triumph.

CHURCHILL,
CHANCELLOR
OF THE
EXCHEQUER

Meanwhile, at the Treasury, Churchill's advisers persuaded him that Britain should return to the Gold Standard, giving the £ its pre-war value to enable it " to look the dollar in the face " and to make Britain once again the financial centre of the world. This certainly reduced the burden of the American debt but, as

* The 1924 Election results were: Conservatives, 415 seats; Labour, 152; Liberals, 42. The Conservatives obtained 7.4 million votes, Labour 5.5 million, Liberals 3 million.

J. M. Keynes pointed out in a pamphlet called *The Economic Consequences of Mr. Churchill*, it also made it more difficult to sell British goods abroad. Foreign buyers found that an article which previously cost, say, 18s was now priced at 20s, so that British industry was handicapped and unemployment remained high.

Neville Chamberlain, true to the memory of his father, " Radical Joe ", whom he had followed as Lord Mayor of Birmingham, diligently applied himself to a great programme of social reform which, between 1924 and 1929, he put through often in the teeth of opposition from Left and Right. In twenty-five Acts of Parliament he expanded the work of local authorities and won his place as a founder of the Welfare State by reforming the Poor Law and the National Insurance and Rating systems. The Widows', Orphans' and Old Age Pensioners' Act of 1925 granted pensions of 10s a week to all persons over sixty-five and to widows, who also received allowances for dependent children. Tremendous changes were brought about by the Local Government Act of 1929, for it put Poor Relief (now renamed " Public Assistance ") and the work of the Guardians into the hands of county and borough councils which were also given much wider powers to deal with public health, hospitals, child welfare, roads, town and country planning. To assist the councils to carry out their responsibilities, the Treasury made " block grants " calculated more or less according to local needs. This was an improvement on the former practice of giving percentage grants, i.e. a proportion of the local authority's expenditure, because it had had the effect of giving more help to a prosperous area than to a poor one.

In 1925 there was some improvement in trade. Production went up and unemployment fell from about 2 million to 1,300,000. There had even been a rise in coal exports owing to the shut-down of German mines during the Ruhr occupation. Industrial unrest was less noticeable and people were beginning to hope that the " Locarno spirit " of goodwill would spread in all directions, when there occurred the General Strike of 1926, the first and only strike of its kind in British history.

The General Strike 1926

The root cause of the General Strike was yet another crisis in the coal industry, caused partly by the reopening of German mines and partly by the return to the Gold Standard. Coal exports fell badly and there was a loss of £2 million for the first half of 1925. With the £ dearer abroad, British goods were hard to sell and prices had to be reduced somehow. Since the price of coal affected the cost of all manufactures, economies were considered absolutely essential. But the only way to produce cheaper coal, apart from wholesale modernisation of the pits, was to cut wages and to lengthen the miners' working day. This was what the mine-owners proposed to do in 1925. The Miners' Federation refused to agree. Their secretary, a fiery Communist named A. J. Cook, passionately denounced the injustice of cutting wages rather than profits and he coined the defiant cry of " Not a penny off the pay, not a minute on the day! ". The Miners' President, Herbert Smith, was less voluble. His stock reply to every proposal was " Nowt doin' " and, for their stubborn attitude, he and the other miners' leaders were much criticised.

But what else could they say? Every miner knew that one enquiry after another had shown that the industry was old-fashioned and badly-run; they had not forgotten that the Government broke its word over the Sankey Report and they knew all too well that they were earning a bare living for hard and dangerous work. On both sides there was hostility and suspicion. Lord Birkenhead observed that he would have thought the miners' leaders the stupidest men in the kingdom if he had not met their employers!

In the summer of 1925, when the mine-owners announced an end to existing wage-agreements, Baldwin declared that the Government would not provide any subsidy. The miners appealed for help to the General Council of the Trades Union Congress which offered to stop all movement of coal throughout the country. This threat caused Baldwin to perform a back-somersault for, on 31st July, he announced that a £10 million subsidy would help out wages while a Royal Commission headed by Sir Herbert Samuel examined the coal industry.

The Samuel Report   The Samuel Report came out in March 1926. It offered the miners much that they wanted for the industry's future * (though not nationalisation) but it also recommended an end to the subsidy on 30th April and cuts in wages for the time being. The miners rejected this clause and, in reply to the owners' final offer of a national wage even lower than Samuel's figure, they declared a coal strike to begin on 1st May.

* The recommendations included profit-sharing and an end to mining royalties. There were to be better working conditions, pit-head baths, family allowances and amalgamations of small pits.

Meanwhile the General Council of the T.U.C., reinforced by Ramsay MacDonald, continued talks with Baldwin on behalf of the miners, but negotiations broke down when the miners refused to accept wage reductions without knowing the plans to modernise the industry. " I want to see the horse I am going to mount," said Herbert Smith. On 1st May, therefore, a meeting of union officials authorised the General Council to carry on the dispute and to call upon certain trades to cease work " as and when required ". It was agreed that all workers in transport, heavy industry, printing, building, gas and electricity would come out first and that other unions would be held in reserve.

By this time, some of the union leaders were beginning to have second thoughts. Men like J. H. Thomas did not really want a head-on clash with the Government nor a situation in which extremists might easily take over leadership of the workers. All they wanted was a fair deal for the miners and an end to the old talk about betraying fellow-workers. Beyond this, the T.U.C. had no clear aims or plan of campaign. Perhaps the Government would again give way to threats.

But the Government already had a plan to deal with the situation. Known as O.M.S. (Organisation for the Maintenance of Supplies), it divided the country into regions each under a Civil Commissioner who had wide powers to call upon the armed services and to enrol special constables and volunteers who would act as drivers, porters and dockers. Trade unionists viewed these amateur preparations with amusement until, with the strike a certainty, they suddenly realised they had no organisation of their own. Ernest Bevin,* a man of massive frame and equally massive ability, was given the task of making up for lost time and, by working night and day, he created a strike organisation to keep in touch with the " Councils of Action " that were set up all over the country.

At the last minute, when all the miners' leaders except Cook had gone home, the General Council made another approach to Baldwin, and the Cabinet was going over the familiar ground when news arrived that printers of the *Daily Mail* had gone

* Ernest Bevin, 1881-1951, b. Winsford, Somerset, of poor parents. Orphaned, became van-boy, driver and official in dockers' union, Bristol. Known as " the Dockers' K.C." from brilliant handling of their claims. Built up Transport and General Workers' Union; its general secretary, 1921-40. Minister of Labour in Churchill's wartime government; 1945-51, Foreign Secretary.

HERBERT SMITH
AND A. J. COOK,
THE MINERS'
LEADERS

on strike rather than set up an article hostile to the workers. This decided Baldwin to negotiate no longer. The meeting broke up and the strike was on.

The Strike

On 4th May 1926 Britain came near to a complete standstill. Buses, trams and trains ceased to run, no newspapers appeared, all building stopped, the docks, pits, furnaces and power-stations were shut and in the place of the familiar noise of industry and transport, a strange silence fell upon London and every sizeable town. Almost at once, the Government's emergency plans came into operation, with the B.B.C. putting out news and volunteers trying their hand at loading lorries and driving buses and trains. An official newspaper, the *British Gazette*, * was produced in the offices of the *Morning Post* where Baldwin wisely placed Winston Churchill in the editor's chair and thus kept his most pugnacious minister busy but out of harm's way. Hyde Park was turned into a huge food depot, the Navy was used to man power-stations, warships took station at the principal ports and troops were moved into London.

For a day or two all went well. The unions, well-satisfied by the almost 100 per cent response of their members, were confident of success, and the novelty of the situation and the fine weather created a holiday spirit in which the public good-humouredly cheered the appearance of an occasional bus erratically driven by an undergraduate and chortled over the story of a chief constable's wife kicking off at a football match between strikers and police. But, as days went by and more volunteers enrolled, this gala mood changed. Stones were thrown, buses and trams were overturned and some of their drivers received rough handling. In Scotland and the North, violent clashes and baton-charges took place while, from the London docks, a hundred food lorries were escorted to Hyde Park by twenty armoured cars and detachments of the Guards.

By the end of a week, the Government showed no sign of weakening. Sir Herbert Samuel was making unofficial efforts to work out a settlement of the miners' dispute with a Negotiating Committee of the T.U.C. but Baldwin made no peace offer. On 6th May he declared " the General Strike is a challenge to Parliament " and there was much talk that the strike was

* The General Council of the T.U.C. published the *British Worker* as an answer to the Government's news sheet. The Government also had control of the B.B.C. and would not allow the Archbishop of Canterbury to broadcast a plea for peace and moderation.

GENERAL STRIKE, FIFTH DAY—AN ARMOURED CAR IN OXFORD STREET

illegal, though this could only have been true if it was a conspiracy against the state. It was really no more than a sympathetic strike for industrial purposes but the union leaders became increasingly nervous.

The Government made it clear that there would be no talks about the mines until the strike was called off, so if the unions went on, they might be inviting further violence and perhaps even revolution. There was nothing for it but to go back and Samuel's revised plan for settling the miners' dispute seemed to be the life-line that was needed. But in accepting the Samuel Memorandum, as it was called, the General Council of the T.U.C. ignored two inconvenient facts. Samuel had no official standing and his proposals had not been accepted by Baldwin or the miners.

For some strange reason, the miners were not represented on the Negotiating Committee and when they saw the Samuel Memorandum they rejected it out of hand. But Thomas and his supporters still felt entitled to go ahead and they persuaded the General Council to call off the strike. A deputation was sent to announce this decision to the Prime Minister. Although Thomas pleaded that he had done " the big thing " and Bevin did his best to obtain an undertaking favourable to the miners, Baldwin's reply was so vague that, as he left Downing Street, it dawned on Bevin, if not upon the others, that they had taken part in a complete surrender.

The General Strike ended on 12th May, after lasting for nine days. Local Strike Committees could hardly believe the telegrams telling them to resume work, and puzzled workers who returned to their jobs were soon out on strike again when they discovered that there was not only no " square deal " for the miners but that, in many cases, they themselves were offered work only " as the situation permitted " and then at lower wage-rates. In some cases, men regarded as ringleaders failed to get their jobs back and, ironically, among the worst sufferers were Thomas's own railwaymen.

The whole episode, so often supposed to be a shining instance of British patience and good humour, ended in angry bitterness. Meanwhile the miners, abandoned by friend and foe alike, stayed stubbornly and logically on strike all through the summer and autumn, but, in the end, beaten all along the line by the owners, they drifted back to work on worse terms than ever. For some of them there was never to be any regular work again and all through the inter-war years, even when prosperity returned to much of the country, the mining communities, especially of Durham and South Wales, remained the hardest hit of the " distressed areas ".

The General Strike humiliated the workers and so discredited their leaders that union membership suffered a sharp drop. *Trades* Not content with these results, however, the Tory extremists *Disputes Act* pressed for a measure of revenge that provided Labour with a *1927* grievance for the next twenty years. The Trade Disputes Act of 1927 made sympathetic strikes illegal, forbade civil servants to belong to a union connected with the T.U.C. and compelled all union members to give in written notice if they wished to contribute to the union's political fund: i.e. they must " contract in " and not, as previously, " contract out " of paying the levy.

Thus, instead of healing the nation's wounds as he had promised, Baldwin ranged himself and his party alongside the coal-owners and no amount of social reform could undo the impression that Conservatives were the natural enemies of organised labour.

Curiously enough, having passed this unpleasant Act and cancelled the trade agreement with Russia, the Government accepted social reforms that Chamberlain was putting through with the active assistance of Winston Churchill. They also agreed to two measures of nationalisation, the Electricity Act (1926) which set up the Central Electricity Board to distribute power by the national grid, and the granting of a charter to the B.B.C. as a public corporation.

One last reform was the Equal Franchise Act (1928) giving women the same right as men to vote at the age of twenty-one. At this time, young women were jocularly known as " flappers " and the " Flapper Vote " was much ridiculed by the Rothermere Press and in more serious quarters it was attacked because the Government seemed to have brought off a smart manœuvre to win additional votes.

During the three years following the Strike, business and trade picked up, except in heavy industry, and abroad the scene was quieter and more hopeful than anyone could remember. At Geneva there was much talk of disarmament and if Britain, alone of the Powers, reduced her Navy and Air Force to dangerously low levels whilst managing to quarrel with the U.S.A. over cruiser strengths, there was still the Briand-Kellogg Pact. Named after the French Foreign Minister and the American Secretary of State, this was an agreement signed by more than sixty nations that they would renounce war as an instrument of policy. It would have been uncharitable to point out that since wars of self-defence were excluded and nothing definite was laid down, the Pact was really no more than a statement of pious hopes.

Briand-Kellogg Pact

In the affairs of the British Empire, the great event was the Imperial Conference of 1926, when Lord Balfour's Committee produced its definition that Britain and the Dominions were " autonomous Communities within the British Commonwealth, equal in status . . . united by a common allegiance to the Crown, and freely associated as members of the British Commonwealth of Nations ". The principal result was the passing of the Statute of Westminster in 1931 which gave legal recognition to what was already accepted in practice, namely the equality of all the Dominions.

Imperial Conference

FLAPPERS, ON THEIR WAY TO VOTE FOR THE FIRST TIME

10 The Second Labour Government

WHEN it came to the General Election of May 1929, if the Conservatives thought that the bitter feelings aroused by the General Strike and the Trade Disputes Act had vanished or that the seven million " flappers " and other new voters were impressed by the Government's record, they were heading for disappointment. Their campaign amounted to little more than placarding the country with photographs of Baldwin bearing the dismal legend " Safety First ", whereas the most positive programme was put forward by the Liberals. In a bid to regain office, Lloyd George produced a pamphlet called " We Can Conquer Unemployment " in which he advocated building a national system of trunk roads, more houses, generating stations and telephone exchanges, besides improving land drainage and the railways.

These schemes would not only provide work for the un-employed but by injecting new life into the entire economy, would pay for themselves without extra taxation. It was a worthy bid and it failed. Labour, who claimed to be able to do the job better than the Liberals, returned 287 M.P.'s; the Conservatives won 261 seats and the Liberals, for all their efforts and over five million votes, had only 59 seats. Thus, for the second time, a Labour Government took office without a clear majority and Ramsay MacDonald was again Prime Minister. As was to be expected, he chose a Cabinet of moderates, with Snowden, Thomas, Henderson and J. R. Clynes in the key posts as well as Margaret Bondfield, Minister of Labour, who achieved fame (and presently unpopularity) as the first woman in the Cabinet. But there were no jobs for the ardent Socialists of the Left, not even for John Wheatley.

Since MacDonald could remain in office only by permission of the Liberals, it could be argued that he had to proceed cautiously but, with his view that Socialism should come gradually and respectably, it was doubtful if he would ever have embarked upon the out-and-out Socialism that the I.L.P. was demanding. As it was, a Labour Government could do no more than tinker with the existing system and the result was described by one of its own members:

"The Second Labour Government's record abroad is a moderate success story, not lacking in courage and skill. Its record at home is a hard-luck story, with failure almost unredeemed either by courage or skill." *

As Foreign Secretary, Arthur Henderson spent much of his time at Geneva where his goodwill and sincere belief in the ideals of the League made him the most respected figure in the endless talks on disarmament. He reopened diplomatic relations with Russia and was a leading supporter of the evacuation of the Rhineland in 1930, when the occupying forces, including British troops, were withdrawn. MacDonald himself was responsible for clearing away the bad feeling about cruiser strengths that had existed between Britain and U.S.A. since 1927. Democratically-minded Americans took a liking to the Scot who had risen from humble beginnings, and during his visit to President Hoover MacDonald achieved a popularity he never knew at home. This cordial success led to the London Naval Conference of 1930 when Britain, America and Japan agreed to accept various restrictions to the tonnage of armament of their navies which would keep roughly to a 5:5:3 ratio, and Britain scaled down her cruiser needs from seventy to fifty.

Labour's Foreign policy

Labour's good intentions towards Palestine and Egypt made little progress in face of the implacable hostility between Arabs and incoming Jews and the Egyptian refusal to give up claim to the Sudan. In India there was unrest and violence. When, in 1930, the Simon Report appeared, the result of a Commission led by Sir John Simon to enquire into the future government of India, its recommendations for gradual progress towards Dominion Status were rejected by the Congress Party. But the report was a masterly survey of the situation, and its recommendations led to a marked advance in self-government in the Provinces. Britain's reluctance to meet all the demands of Congress was due not to a refusal to let go the reins of power, but to three major difficulties: enmity between Hindus and Muslims; the position of the Indian States to whose rulers Britain was bound by treaties so that they could not be handed over, even to an Indian Government, against their will; and the state of the armed forces in which training of Indian officers was still at an early stage. Disorders led to the imprisonment of Gandhi, Nehru and other Indian leaders, but MacDonald

MAHATMA GANDHI, 1931

* *Call Back Yesterday*, Hugh Dalton (1953)

still pursued conciliation and at a Round Table Conference in London (boycotted by Congress), some progress was made to which the Conservatives gave approval.   Churchill, whose views on India were doubtless coloured by the memory of his subaltern days there in Queen Victoria's reign, was aghast at the " wanton recklessness " of making concessions to nationalism. He resigned from the " Shadow Cabinet " and thereby not only condemned himself to the wilderness all through the thirties, but left the way clear for Neville Chamberlain to succeed Baldwin.

" A hard-luck story, with failure almost unredeemed by courage and skill " ; it was certainly Labour's misfortune to take office just before the collapse of the American stock market ushered in the Great Depression.

The Wall
Street crash
For half a century America had been the land of opportunity. Vast natural resources, the absence of old-fashioned attitudes and the get-ahead zest of a people who relished the rewards of commercial success, had produced wealth at an astounding rate. When the industrial countries of Europe set about ruining themselves in 1914, Americans did not neglect their opportunities and at the end of the war America emerged as the richest country in the world with the machines and methods to go on getting still richer.   She had lent enormous sums to Europe and although these war debts were not cancelled, she went on exporting her surplus wealth in the form of further loans.

Germany was financed by American money and the Germans formed the habit of paying their reparations and the interest on earlier loans by fresh borrowings.   Since Germany's creditors relied on German reparations for their own recovery, Europe became dangerously dependent upon American loans.

By 1928 this help was drying up as American investors poured their money into their own stocks and shares.   Demand for shares always puts up the price and, as the mania for share-buying grew, with everyone from Texan millionaires to Detroit car-assembly hands talking of nothing but their investments, so the prices soared up and up.   Fortunes were made by those who bought cheap and sold at a higher price but most people went on buying, often on borrowed money.   It was like a game in which all were winners and no one could lose.

One day, in October 1929, for no particular reason, the bubble burst.   At Wall Street, the home of the New York Stock

Exchange, there was some selling of shares. Perhaps at long last it occurred to someone that his one-dollar shares could not really be worth the seven dollars a share that he had paid. So he sold while the going was good; so did someone else and word began to get round that prices were falling. The rush to sell became a panic as thousands of investors tried to unload their shares on a market where there were now no buyers. Men who had believed themselves rich, suddenly found that they possessed only a handful of share certificates that no one wanted and a list of debts they could not pay. There were suicides and bankruptcies; companies failed and factories closed their doors, yet the real wealth of America was unchanged. The oil wells, the mines, the meat, the corn and the superb industrial equipment were still there. What had happened was that confidence and buying power had suddenly vanished and the effects of the crash spread across the Atlantic.

Europe's fragile economy was too closely linked with America's to be able to withstand the shock, though the full effects were not felt until 1931. Dismay and a falling-off of trade led to increased unemployment; then, as the depression deepened, a kind of vicious circle set in that baffled the politicians and economists.

World-wide unemployment meant that millions of people could buy only the bare necessities of life, so the industries making consumer goods, such as clothes, furniture, cars and domestic equipment, were hard hit and many of their workers became unemployed too. Governments put up tariffs to protect their home industries but this restricted world trade still further. As people became poorer, revenue from taxation fell just when governments had to find huge sums for " dole " or relief for the workless, so economies were made that affected government

The Great Depression

employees and those who were engaged on government contracts. There was a world slump in agriculture caused not by shortage but by a glut of food which nevertheless could not reach the undernourished millions. New fertilisers and machinery had produced bigger crops so that prices fell and to try to make a living, farmers produced still bigger crops and prices fell lower still. Thus the food-producing countries could not afford to buy machinery and consumer goods from the industrial nations and the vicious circle continued until it reached a stage of tragic absurdity when crops were burnt and wheat and coffee were dumped into the sea.

In Britain the task of dealing with unemployment had been taken on by J. H. Thomas whose assistants included Sir Oswald Mosley, an ambitious young man from Birmingham. Thomas had plenty of ideas, most of them taken from Lloyd George's pamphlet, but he achieved next to nothing because a major programme of public works required large-scale spending of Government money which Philip Snowden, the economy-minded Chancellor, would not allow. The Dole was raised, tests by which men had to prove that they were " genuinely seeking work " were abolished and more persons were able to draw " transitional benefits ", i.e. unemployment pay despite not having made the minimum number of insurance payments. But these measures only made the lives of the unemployed slightly less wretched. They did nothing to lessen unemployment and any improvement brought about by a few schemes of public works was swallowed up by the worsening trade position. Exports fell from £839 million in 1929 to £666 million in 1930 and £461 million in 1931.

Exasperated by this lack of progress, Mosley put forward his own plan that included earlier retirement of workers, tariffs, *Fascism* import restrictions, bulk buying agreements with foreign *in Britain* producers, and control of industry and banking. This was much too drastic for Mr. Snowden and the Cabinet. In disgust Mosley resigned and formed a Labour " ginger " group which attracted young men like Aneurin Bevan and John Strachey. Influenced by Fascist ideas which were now prevalent on the continent, Mosley became so extreme that genuine socialists soon left him. After expulsion from the Labour Party, he founded the British Union of Fascists, an organisation whose unpleasant ideas fortunately made little headway in Britain. However, the violence of Mosley's speeches and his followers'

behaviour did cause the Labour Party to disregard the positive measures that he had earlier suggested for tackling unemployment.

MacDonald and his Ministers, apparently incapable of taking any action by themselves, pushed their problems on to the shoulders of a business man, named Sir George May who was made chairman of an Economy Committee which was to report upon the situation. MacDonald himself had no constructive ideas and Snowden, who was by now under the influence of Montagu Norman, Governor of the Bank of England, clung obstinately to the Gold Standard and Free Trade. The I.L.P., formerly so influential, had by this time lost its power to invigorate Labour policies.

Meanwhile, unemployment went on growing like a monstrous fungus that no one could control. From just over a million in June 1929, it reached 2 million in the following year and almost 3 million in 1931. This meant that out of every hundred workers, more than twenty had nothing to do. In some industries, the position was worse; in shipbuilding, every other man was out of work; in coalmining, one man in three and in cotton manufacture, one person in four. A great part of the nation, 7 or 8 million men, women and children, were living in want, not eating well enough to keep healthy and deprived by some strange accident which few could understand and none could put right, of almost all the pleasures and decencies of life.

Mass unemployment

The unemployed man with a wife and three children received 29s 3d a week (increased to about 36s in 1936). By laying out every halfpenny with the utmost care the wife could just feed her family, and by patching and darning she somehow kept them clothed. With luck, she managed to give her man an occasional 3d to bet on a horse or 2d for five cigarettes. The Dole was just enough to stop him becoming a revolutionary and it was in any case more than he would have got in, say, Canada or the U.S.A.

The astonishing thing about the unemployed was their good behaviour, which could be called patience or apathy. The Means Test made them bitter but it did not provoke riots or crime. When a man ran out of his right to insurance benefit, he went on to " transitional benefit " which took into consideration any savings, pension or other earnings coming into the household. Thus, if a son or daughter found work at 15s a week, the father's unemployment pay was reduced by that amount and this could lead to ill-feeling in the family and to a further abasement of a man's pride.

Boys would leave school at fourteen and find a " blind alley " job for a couple of years but, at sixteen, when they would have qualified for a man's wage, they joined their fathers at the street corner and in the queue at the Labour Exchange. Some of them kicked a football about on vacant land near the closed pit; some of them joined a club or an occupational centre; there were those who studied for examinations or banded together to level ground for a football pitch or a recreation ground. Many got married on the Dole and settled down to a life without work. Perhaps the saddest of all were the " long unemployed ", usually older men who had been out of work for more than a year, who came to realise that they would never get another job for the rest of their lives. In 1936 there were 205,000 who had been out of work for two years or longer; in Crook, Durham, 71 per cent of the unemployed had been " out " for over five years; in the Rhondda Valley, 45 per cent.

This is what the wife of one of these men said about unemployment:

" If only he had work "

" If only he had work. Just imagine what it would be like. On the whole, my husband has worked about one year out of twelve and a half . . . He fell out of work about four months after I was married, so I've hardly known what a week's wage was . . . there's no enjoyment, no pictures, no papers, no sports. Everything's patched and mended in our house . . . but with all the struggling, you can't manage. All the struggling is just for food. Still, we're happier than some . . .

UNEMPLOYMEN
A DURHAM FAMI
GOING HOME. BY 19
THE FATHER, A MINE
HAD BEEN OUT OF WO
FOR 14 YEA

we all help. The kids wash the dishes and so on. Everyone does something. The only hope we have got is the hope to come . . . Perhaps, after all, it's worse for the men. The women have their work and their home. I have no hope my husband will ever work again." *

In a roundabout way, the world slump put the Labour Government out of office. Germany and Austria, badly affected by the withdrawal of American loans, had been kept going by Britain and France, for the latter, less dependent than most countries on world trade, was in a good financial position. However, when the Paris bankers heard of a proposed customs union between Germany and Austria, they withdrew their money to force Austria to abandon the union. In May 1931 the chief bank in Vienna collapsed and this was followed by bank failures in Germany.

The crisis was felt in London whose banks had lent large sums to Germany and Austria, and the situation was made worse by *The crisis of 1931* the appearance of the report of Sir George May's committee. Calling for severe economies, the May Report painted such an alarming picture of Britain's financial plight that foreign investors made panic withdrawals of their money and the Bank of England itself was in grave danger. An American loan could save the situation but it was alleged that the New York bankers insisted that the British Government should balance its budget. In any case, every financial expert said the same thing: Britain must take steps to restore confidence abroad; unless this was done, there would be a complete financial collapse and ruin.

The Labour Government was face to face with a dilemma. In order to balance the budget, severe economies had to be made and the cost of the Dole must be reduced. In order to get anywhere near the required figure, a cut of 10 per cent (the May Committee said 20 per cent) had to be made in unemployment pay. But how could a Labour Government do this to the poorest members of the community, the very people whom they longed to help above all others? Moreover, it was surely absurd to reduce the purchasing power of the masses at a time when the great problem was a world-wide excess of goods which people could not afford to buy.

MacDonald and Snowden felt that the cuts were inevitable and they carried with them a bare majority of the Cabinet, but Henderson, Clynes, Lansbury and several others were absolutely

* *Time to Spare*, Felix Greene (1935)

opposed to the cuts.   Rather than betray what they felt was
their duty to the working class, they would resign and, after
long and painful discussion, MacDonald wearily accepted their
view.   There was no question of re-forming the Cabinet and he
went to Buckingham Palace to inform the King that the Labour
Government was at an end.   His Majesty said that he would
meet the three Party leaders, MacDonald, Baldwin and Samuel
(Lloyd George was ill) the next day and the Labour ministers
went home believing that a Conservative or Conservative-
Liberal Government would take office.

Later on, most of them declared that they were " stupefied "
to learn that MacDonald had agreed to lead a National Government.   The actual request was made to him by King George V
but the suggestion came first from Sir Herbert Samuel;   Baldwin
agreed, feeling that economies affecting the working class would
be best put forward by a government containing Labour
members.   So MacDonald accepted the invitation and formed
a Cabinet of four Conservatives, two Liberals (Samuel and
Lord Reading) and three Labour men, Snowden, J. H. Thomas
and Lord Sankey.   But for his illness, Lloyd George would
almost certainly have joined them.

Labour's reply was to expel MacDonald from the Party and *MacDonald*
to denounce his betrayal of the working-class movement.   What *expelled*
made him take the decision that earned him the name of traitor?
His enemies declared that he had never been a true Socialist;
that, bedazzled by the company of society hostesses, he had long
planned to ditch his own party in order to retain power.   But
MacDonald had spent his life working to build up the Labour
Party and to prove its fitness to govern.   He had wrestled hard to
keep the Government intact and had persuaded a majority of
the Cabinet to agree to the cuts in unemployment pay.   How
could he know that the King would ask him to form a National
Government?   But, when he did, was it not his duty to put
country before party?   He said himself, " Any man in my
position at the time, knowing all that I did, would have acted as
I acted ".   However, even Snowden, who had convinced
MacDonald of the need for the economies and had followed him
into the new Cabinet, turned on him in the end and the Labour
Party never forgave him.   Indeed, by the time Parliament re-
assembled, many of them had convinced themselves that the
whole crisis was nothing more than a sinister plot by the
financiers—a " Bankers' Ramp ", they called it.

11 The National Government

AT the General Election in October 1931, the country returned a National Government by a huge majority and the Labour Party sustained the most crushing defeat in its history. From 287 M.P.s in 1929, Labour was reduced to 46. Henderson, and all the former Cabinet Ministers except Lansbury, were defeated. In the National Government MacDonald remained Prime Minister but, despite the presence of some Liberal and Labour members, this was really a Conservative Government and, with a smaller majority after the 1935 election, it remained in office until the Second World War. Baldwin succeeded MacDonald in 1935 and was himself succeeded by Neville Chamberlain in 1937. Thus, throughout the fateful period of the thirties, Britain was led by three of the most bitterly abused politicians of her entire history, whose reputations have collapsed under a deluge of hostile criticism. But none of them was the villain he has since been made out to be; indeed, each was a decent, reasonable man and each had very much more ability than almost all their critics. None was a great leader but it may be said that, until disaster came, each was the kind of man the country wanted and deserved.

Remedies Once the Labour Government was out, the accepted remedies for the slump were economy and Protection. Snowden's Budget imposed extra taxation and reduced unemployment pay from 17s a week to 15s 3d for men and from 15s to 13s 6d for women, besides limiting benefits to twenty-six weeks per year, with a Means Test to reduce public assistance payments if there was any other income in the family. Salaries of civil servants and teachers were cut and so was the pay of the police and the armed services, thus causing a minor " mutiny " in the fleet at Invergordon. Even before the October election, the Gold Standard was abandoned without the fearsome results that had been predicted. With the £ worth 3.49 dollars instead of 4.86, British exporters found it easier to sell their goods when foreigners saw that these were now cheaper to buy. Free Trade was the next to go when Neville Chamberlain (who had taken over the Exchequer from Snowden) put tariffs of 10 per cent on all

THE JARRO
MARCHERS, L
BY ELL
WILKINSON,
THEIR WAY
LONDON 19

imports except food and raw materials. Again, the effects were not disastrous.

Farmers were given protection in the form of subsidies on certain crops, a Milk Marketing Board was set up to ensure regular prices and markets, and foreign imports of food were limited by quota. An Imperial Conference met at Ottawa to try to arrange a system of Empire Free Trade, but it was far from easy to satisfy the requirements of Dominions such as Canada and Australia that wished to export food to Britain while protecting their own infant industries. The result was a tangle of tariff agreements within the Commonwealth and the resignations of Snowden and Samuel, both unrepentant Free-traders.

By 1933 economic recovery was beginning to stir, for, although *Partial* British exports did not greatly improve, the cost of imports was *recovery* less, owing to the world slump in prices of food and raw materials. Thus, the balance of trade was better and unemployment came down slowly until, in July 1935, it was below two million. But, like the recovery, it was unevenly spread.

In the Midlands and the south-east, in towns and cities such as Watford, Luton, Oxford, Coventry, Birmingham and London, unemployment was low (5 to 8.6 per cent), but in the older industrial areas, dependent mainly upon exports of coal, steel and ships, the figures were appallingly high. In Greenock, Workington, Motherwell, Gateshead, Abertillery and Merthyr Tydfil, between 36 and 61.9 per cent of workers were unemployed in 1934; at West Auckland, a Durham mining village, only 100 men out of 1,000 had had work in a period of seven years.

These were the places where the legend of " the hungry thirties " was to haunt the memories of all who lived through

this period, and among the worst, or the best, known was Jarrow, " the town that was murdered ".   Here, in 1934, 67.8 per cent of insured workers, mostly shipyard men, were out of a job and in September 1935, 72.9 per cent.   Led by Ellen Wilkinson, their fiery little M.P., 200 Jarrow men made a " hunger march " to London to draw attention to the town's plight, and this helped towards the founding of new industries in the area and elsewhere.

By the late thirties the steel industry was expanding, with new steel works opened at Workington, Ebbw Vale and Corby, Northamptonshire, whose workers were recruited from the steel towns of Lanarkshire.   The Special Areas Act (1934) enabled grants to be made for developments in the worst-hit areas but on too small a scale to have much effect, apart from building a few social centres and children's swings.   However, a similar Act of 1937 offered advantages, such as remission of rent and rates, to firms opening up in distressed areas and this led to the setting up of light industries on trading estates near Glasgow, Gateshead and in South Wales.   Even so, most of the new jobs were for women, and unemployment remained higher than in the rest of the country.   It was only rearmament from 1936 onwards that brought real relief to the areas in which the Industrial Revolution had been born.

Output of coal rose from 207 million tons in 1933 to 241 million tons in 1937 and, although exports were still far lower than in earlier years (50 million tons in 1936 as against 80 million in 1907), there was some improvement for the miners.   They received a wage increase of a shilling a shift.   Despite the mine-owners' opposition to every form of Government " interference ", they were obliged to swallow the abolition of mining royalties in 1938 for which, by the Coal Act, they received £66 million compensation.   This step was taken, it should be noted, not by a Labour Government but by a Conservative-dominated National Government.

Broadly speaking, recovery in the late thirties took place in new industries such as chemicals, soap and vegetable oils, radio, motor-cars, rayon and furniture, and in the building trade which erected more than $2\frac{1}{2}$ million houses between 1930 and 1939.   Altogether about 4 million new houses were built between the wars, of which over a quarter in England and Wales and two-thirds in Scotland were provided by local authorities.

The new working-class home had three bedrooms, sitting-room, kitchen, bath, electric light and gas or electric cooker. There was a sizeable garden at the back and front (twelve houses to the acre was the recommended density) and the house stood with hundreds of others on an estate at the edge of an older town whose shops, pubs and cinemas could be reached only by bus or cycle. Some of these estates were huge; Becontree, near Dagenham, Essex, had over 100,000 inhabitants and Kingstanding, Birmingham, about 30,000. People grew accustomed to travelling considerable distances to work and to their pleasures, not only from these estates but also from the suburbs of Outer London which grew at a terrific rate during the thirties.

Low building costs and enterprise by thriving building societies were responsible for the erection of hundreds of thousands of houses which, though frequently ill-sited and unlovely to look upon, realised the dreams of innumerable clerks, factory-hands and businessmen. A non-parlour council house cost barely £300 in the mid-thirties, a privately-owned bungalow £400 to £600 and a semi-detached three-bedroomed house from £500 to £850, though it has to be remembered that in 1934 three-quarters of all the families in Britain had incomes of £4 a week or less. The average wage for workers in main industries was about 50s a week but farm wages ranged from barely 30s to 38s a week. Middle-class families, one-fifth of the total, had incomes of between £4 and £10 a week and only one family in twenty earned more than £10 weekly.

The cost of living fell so that workers in, say, Luton or Wembley, were able to enjoy a better standard of life than ever before. In many cases, they had no knowledge or understanding of the plight of the unemployed in Abertillery and Clydeside.

The New Deal

In the United States of America, where the Great Depression had started, recovery took a dramatic course. President Hoover who had succeeded Coolidge in 1928, had had great experience of dealing with poverty in post-war Europe but he was head of the Republican Party which had no patience with government " interference ". Things would get better of their own accord, prosperity was just around the corner. In the meantime, unemployment rose to twelve millions and the nation's income was halved. There was no system of unemployment benefit and this was the time of the " breadlines " and soup kitchens when hungry men and women queued up for a few mouthfuls of food. In 1932 Hoover was defeated and the Democratic candidate became President. He was Franklin D. Roosevelt.

A lawyer, crippled by polio so that he could not walk or stand unaided, Roosevelt possessed the style of a great man and the precious gift of being able to match his ideals with words that appealed directly to the ordinary citizen. He promised to overcome the slump with a " New Deal " that would put America back on her feet.

In a country devoted to rugged capitalism, Roosevelt's plans were fiercely resisted but opposition in Congress and in the Supreme Court only intensified his determination to succeed. In essence, his plan was the same as Lloyd George's: to spend rather than to cut down and, by creating work and therefore purchasing-power, to inject new life into the stagnant economy. Huge government loans were made for housing, roads, bridges and parks; subsidies were given to farmers (in some cases, alas, to reduce production) and in special areas vast projects were carried out to restore fertility to the land.

ROOSEVELT IN 1920, A YEAR BEFORE HE BECAME CRIPPLED

The New Deal's most famous achievement was the formation of the Tennessee Valley Authority to tackle the destitution caused by overcropping and cutting down trees in a great area stretching across half a dozen states where three million people were living in poverty. Afforestation, dam-building, power-stations and new farming methods produced miracles of recovery. The cost was enormous and many Americans were deeply offended by higher taxes and by controls upon working hours, conditions, child-labour and free enterprise. However, Roosevelt had shown that the country was rich enough to finance its own recovery and he remained in office as President until his death.

12 Between the Wars

It would be a mistake to regard the years between the wars as a period of unrelieved gloom and stagnation. Certainly, from some points of view these were the " wasted years " when such slogans as " Safety First " and " Back to Normal " expressed the outlook of a harassed people and their spineless leaders. But, besides unemployment and social distress, there was a good deal of enjoyment, progress and hope for the future.

The almost revolutionary change in the status of women was not due to the pre-war activities of Mrs Pankhurst's Suffragettes nor even to possession of the vote, but to the fact that women were now needed in business and industry. A girl at a typewriter was cheaper to employ than a male clerk, and in the new factories that made electrical and domestic goods, women's wages were lower and their fingers more nimble than men's. Girls at school sat for the same examinations as boys; Oxford, London and the newer universities allowed women to take degrees, though Cambridge did not yield until 1948. Thus a whole new range of occupations was opened up for women, but it was unusual to continue working after marriage because, with much unemployment and a surplus of women over men, it was considered unfair for a woman to occupy a job when she had a husband to keep her.

There was no returning to the pre-war days when a young woman could scarcely go anywhere without a chaperon. Women who had done war-work and were now earning their own living gained freedoms more delightful than the vote. Their clothes became lighter and more colourful; they wore rayon stockings instead of the older wool or cotton and they refused to allow their skirts to go back to ground-level. Even grandmothers yielded to the fashion of cutting off their hair and, after the ultra-short " Eton crop " went out, permanent waves came to stay. The " Bright Young Things " of the twenties with their wild parties and night-clubs created a legend of frantic gaiety which was no part of the lives of the vast majority; nevertheless, the antics of a small set did reflect the general desire for pleasure and entertainment.

123

The gramophone and the wireless brought light music, jazz and popular singers known as " crooners " to a much wider public than the old music-halls. Dancing became a craze with a succession of new dances, the fox-trot, the charleston, the quick-step, so that hotels and restaurants provided dance-floors and, in the suburbs and the provinces, new dance-halls, The Locarno and The Palais, were crowded with enthusiasts.

Dancing

Cinema-going was even more popular. The British film industry had been almost snuffed out by the war, and American films, made now in Hollywood, had the field practically to themselves. Rudolph Valentino, Mary Pickford, Greta Garbo and above all Charlie Chaplin were the greatest stars of the silent screen. But it was not until the arrival of the " talkies " in 1928 that the cinema became the most popular of all forms of amusement yet invented.

Throughout Britain, vast new cinemas, eclipsing church and town-hall in size and opulence, provided entertainment in a style never known before. Programmes lasting three or four hours cost less than a shilling, so that even the unemployed could sometimes escape from their drab lives into an atmosphere of luxury and make-believe.

The Quota Act of 1927 compelled cinemas to show a small proportion of British films and this led to the production of some of the worst films ever made. Gradually, however, a more reputable film industry emerged in Britain where its leading director, Alfred Hitchcock, showed, as did René Clair in France, that successful films need not be devoid of artistic qualities.

CHARLIE CHAPLIN

The all-conquering appeal of the cinema threatened to destroy the live theatre, for nearly all the music-halls, the palaces of variety and the local theatres had to close down and serious drama seemed unable to compete with the sophisticated comedies and musicals of Noel Coward and Ivor Novello. However, in a shabby district of South London, a masterful woman named Lilian Baylis kept alive the notion of a national theatre and persisted in producing Shakespeare's plays at the Old Vic.

Thanks largely to broadcasting, the British, supposedly an unmusical race, took an increasing interest in music during this period when Sir Thomas Beecham and Sir Henry Wood were the most celebrated conductors and Vaughan Williams and William Walton the leading composers. By the thirties,

Music

Benjamin Britten was already displaying the genius that was later to make him the most widely acclaimed British composer of the century.

Broadcasting began from the Marconi Company's station in London in 1922 and, by the end of the year, the British Broadcasting Company was putting out programmes from eight stations. A committee of enquiry recommended that when the company's licence expired, broadcasting should be carried out solely by a public corporation for whom the Postmaster General should be answerable to Parliament. Thus, in December 1926, the British Broadcasting Corporation came into existence with *Broadcasting* a board of five governors appointed by the Prime Minister and a director-general to take charge of the day-to-day running. This post was held until 1938 by John Reith, manager of the original company. Thus, throughout the years when the wireless-set changed from being a novelty to an essential piece of furniture in almost every home, the tone and policy of the B.B.C. were directed by a high-principled Scot who believed that it was his duty to provide not merely entertainment but education, culture and good moral standards.

Experiments in television began in the twenties, and in 1936 the world's first public television service was started from Alexandra Palace in North London. Programmes and audience were still very limited at the outbreak of the Second World War when the service was closed down until 1946.

Drunkenness, so commonplace in earlier days that a powerful temperance movement had grown up, became much less prevalent after 1918. Standards of behaviour improved, the hours and numbers of public-houses were reduced and, most effective of all, steep taxes were put on drink, particularly spirits, so that a bottle of whisky rose from its pre-war price of 3s 6d to 25s. Curiously enough, the "drink trade" was not *Drink* ruined, for as public houses became more respectable, they attracted a wider custom and, mostly in southern England, numbers of smart "roadhouses" were built to cater for motorists. Village inns and country hotels began to recover some of their former prosperity when people who could afford motor-cars discovered the pleasure of touring along the comparatively uncongested roads.

Although drunkenness declined, gambling increased, despite a law that permitted a man to bet by letter, telephone or on a racecourse but scarcely anywhere else. However, the law was

Gambling cheerfully flouted and horse-race betting alone was estimated to amount to £230 million in 1929. Totalisator betting, a system whereby nearly all the money staked is shared between the winners, was legalised in 1928 by which date greyhound racing (begun at Manchester in 1926) had captured a large following in most of the bigger towns and cities of Britain. Betting on football matches began in a small way with newspaper competitions but, by the thirties, the " pools " had become an industry employing thousands of people to deal with the millions of " investors " who lived in perpetual hope of winning a fortune.

Sport held a tremendous appeal for all classes, though most people could only watch it or read about it rather than play games themselves. The National Playing Fields Association was founded in 1925 to provide more sports grounds. Local authorities began to lay out recreation grounds and to permit wider use of parks but there was an overall shortage of sporting facilities of every kind, from football pitches to tennis courts and swimming baths. Elementary schools, even in country districts, rarely had their own playing fields and only a minority of the large industrial firms, such as motor manufacturers, had begun to organise sports facilities for their employees.

Association Football enjoyed a tremendous boom after the war when soldiers came home full of enthusiasm for the game they had been able to play more often in the Army than in civilian life. The English League was extended to four divisions of professional clubs. The first Cup Final at Wembley Stadium in 1923 attracted so huge a crowd, estimated at over 120,000, that disaster was only narrowly averted, but in Scotland, where *Football* enthusiasm for football was probably higher still, Hampden Park, Glasgow, could hold 150,000 spectators. Scotland and England were still the supreme soccer nations of the world and the visits of foreign teams provided nothing more than light entertainment compared with the stern encounters of League and Cup. The triumphs of such teams as Bolton Wanderers and Sheffield Wednesday were eclipsed by those of the Arsenal in the thirties, when Herbert Chapman, a manager with a flair for publicity, built up a team of star players, for one of whom he paid the then outrageous transfer fee of £10,000.

Rugby Football did not attract the huge crowds drawn by soccer, except in South Wales where rugby was passionately supported by all classes, and in the North of England where

Rugby League football, the professional version of the game, was played.

Sports in which only a small minority of the public took part, golf and tennis in particular, attracted enormous interest, as did the Boat Race, the Derby and the Grand National. Already, British supremacy in sport was vanishing and American golfers won every British Open Championship between 1923 and 1934, when Henry Cotton put a temporary end to the success of overseas players. In lawn tennis this tendency was even more marked, for, between the wars, Fred Perry and W. M. Johnson were the only home players to win the men's singles at Wimbledon. At cricket, the Australians were immensely powerful, producing not only a number of outstanding bowlers, but a succession of brilliant batsmen including Bradman, the greatest run-scorer of all. England had some fine cricketers in Hobbs, Sutcliffe and Hammond, but even in the thirties, when Larwood's " bodyline " bowling almost brought about a Commonwealth crisis and Hutton scored 364 runs at the Oval, success in the Test Matches was all too rare.

JACK HOBBS

During Edwardian days, motoring was a diversion that belonged, like field sports, sailing and foreign travel, to the rich. The motor industry, such as it was, consisted of a number of small firms which built their vehicles from components obtained from engineering works and manufacturers who were willing to supply them as a side-line. However, in 1914 an Oxford cycle-maker, William Morris, who was already producing fifty Morris cars a week, paid a visit to America to discover how Henry Ford turned out his " tin lizzies " by the thousand. The war delayed Morris's plans but in the twenties he established a line-assembly system at his Oxford works to bring out a succession of Morris cars designed and priced to attract the motorist

BABY AUSTIN
WITH
SUNSHINE ROOF
1930

of moderate means. A four-seater Morris Cowley cost about
£340 (Morris was constantly cutting prices in order to sell cars
even during the worst years of the Depression), and the 8 h.p.
Morris Minor was produced for no more than £125, though this
was a figure far beyond the reach of working men. Meanwhile,
from Birmingham, Herbert Austin turned out a similar range
of cars, including the 7 h.p. " Baby Austin " which, until the
advent of the " Mini ", was the most popular small car ever
made. Britain also made some of the finest luxury motor-cars,
Rolls-Royces and Bentleys, which already possessed such refine-
ments as self-starters and radios.

The number of private cars advanced from 242,000 in 1921 to
just over 1 million in 1930 when goods vehicles totalled barely
a third of this number,* but long-distance lorries with diesel
engines were beginning to challenge the railways' monopoly of
goods traffic. Motor-coaches enabled people to make long
journeys by road and regular bus services broke the isolation of
Public innumerable villages. Numbers of buses and coaches showed
transport surprisingly little increase (40,000 in 1928, 53,000 in 1938) but
their size and comfort improved and double-deckers with
covered tops appeared in 1923. Clattering wooden-seated trams
had their peak year in 1927 when over 14,000 were in use but,
by the thirties, a number of towns began to scrap trams in
favour of more manœuvrable buses and trolleybuses. Problems
of transporting millions of people in the capital led to the
creation of the London Passenger Transport Board in 1933.

More vehicles and faster speeds caused a tremendous number

* The numbers of vehicles in use were (to nearest thousand):

	Total Vehicles	Cars	Goods Vehicles
1921	846,000	242,000	128,000
1930	2,274,000	1,056,000	348,000
1939	3,149,000	2,034,000	488,000
1964	12,369,000	8,247,000	1,576,000

TRAMCARS IN
BIRMINGHAM
1938

of accidents, though fortunately these did not rise in proportion to the increasing number of vehicles. It took time for children and old people to become accustomed to the dangers of the roads, for more pedestrians were killed in 1928 than in 1964 when traffic was six times as great.* The Road Traffic Act of 1930 did away with the long-ignored speed limit of 20 m.p.h., but four years later a 30 m.p.h. limit in built-up areas had to be introduced. The Highway Code and compulsory third-party insurance appeared and every year saw some new device to reduce accidents. These included driving tests (1934), round-abouts, traffic signs and lights, one-way streets, road-markings, " cat's eyes " and pedestrian crossings with " Belisha Beacons ", named after Mr Hore-Belisha, Minister of Transport.

A half-hearted programme of road-building was launched, partly to cope with the increasing traffic and partly to provide work for the unemployed. The first British roads with dual *Roads* carriageways, the Mersey Tunnel and some new highways in Scotland and Lancashire were built; the Great West Road was completed and there were improvements to the Great North Road. Round London and a few towns such as Watford, Croydon, Kingston and Ipswich, by-passes and circular routes

*	Persons killed	Pedestrians	Cyclists	Vehicles in use
1928	6,138	(3,255)	(691)	2,039,000
1934	7,343	(3,529)	(1,536)	2,405,000
1938	6,648	(3,046)	(1,401)	3,085,000
1964	7,820	(2,986)	(583)	12,369,000

It is estimated that in the first sixty years of this century, there were nearly 9,000,000 casualties on the roads of Britain, of whom 260,000 were killed.

were constructed but most were two- or three-lane roads soon to be flanked by rows of houses. Barely adequate for the traffic which then existed, the new roads were designed with little regard to what other countries were doing or to the needs of the future. The fault lay with successive governments. Between 1915 and 1920, part of the Road Fund was diverted into the Exchequer and in 1926, Churchill, who did not wish to see motor transport advance at the expense of the railways, took £7 million out of the Fund. When he became Chancellor of the Exchequer, Neville Chamberlain followed the same course so that, from 1937, the pretence of taxing motorists in order to build roads was dropped and, apart from improvements to their surfaces, British highways remained much as they had been in the days of horse-drawn traffic.

Railways   Until 1921 there were many separate railway companies, each with its separate colours and loyalties. These vanished when four groups were formed—the Great Western, the London, Midland & Scottish, the London and North Eastern and the Southern. This led to greater efficiency and standardisation of locomotives, rolling stock and signals. Apart from a few shunting engines, diesel engines were not yet in use. Steam was still paramount and some express trains averaged over 70 m.p.h. on long runs, while in 1938 *Mallard* achieved the record speed of 126 m.p.h. No new railways were built other than extensions to the London Underground. The chief progress was in electrifying stretches of line in Lancashire, in the north-east, in the London suburbs and to such towns as Brighton, Portsmouth and Maidstone. In spite of huge increases in the numbers of daily travellers in London (the term " commuter " was not yet in use), the railways steadily lost money and, by the thirties, branch lines were beginning to be closed down.

Flying   Flying had made great advances during the war and there were plenty of pilots and mechanics ready to devote their skills to building up civil air services. In 1919, using a Vickers Vimy Bomber, two R.A.F. airmen, Alcock and Brown, made the first flight across the Atlantic, and in the same year another Vimy, piloted by the brothers Ross and Keith Smith, reached Australia in just under twenty-eight days. An adventurous pair of airmen survived two crashes before reaching Capetown in forty-five days in 1920. Throughout the twenties, flyers such as Alan Cobham, Lindbergh (who made the first solo crossing of the Atlantic in 1927), Kingsford Smith, Hinkler and Wiley Post

displayed great courage and endurance in pioneering new routes across areas where landing-grounds, fuel and skilled servicing were practically non-existent. The public followed their exploits with breathless excitement and when Amy Johnson, on a solo flight to Australia, finally landed on 24th May 1930, newspaper placards all over the world said simply " She's there! ". Aeroplanes did not affect the life of the ordinary man, but, like space travel in the sixties, they stirred his imagination.

AN EARLY AIRLINER: THE ARMSTRONG-WHITWORTH ' ARGOSY ', 1929

The work of the pioneer fliers led to the establishment of regular air routes. The first was the London–Paris service started in 1919; then came services to Amsterdam, Brussels, Manchester, Belfast and the Channel Islands, but passengers were few and the competing companies were soon in financial difficulties. With government assistance, a single company named Imperial Airways was formed in 1924. Regular flights were made to European capitals and there were continuous efforts to establish a long-distance airline to India. By 1929 there was a weekly service from London which, by means of aeroplanes, train and flying-boat, carried passengers to Karachi in eight days; Delhi was the next point to be reached, then Singapore and, in 1934 (for mails only), Brisbane. The passenger service to Australia commenced in 1935 and regular flights had been made from Cairo to Capetown since 1932. The great expanse of the Atlantic presented special problems of safety and refuelling and it was not until May 1939 that the *Yankee Clipper*, a Pan American Airways flying-boat, inaugurated a regular mail service. A month later, the *Dixie Clipper* carried twenty-two passengers across the Atlantic.

A form of air transport which had a brief and eventful career was the airship. In imitation of the German zeppelins, Britain built the airship R 34 which flew the Atlantic in 1919 and, ten years later, the German *Graf Zeppelin* made an air voyage round the world. This monstrous aircraft, over 700 feet long, required a crew of forty and, since it travelled at only about 60 m.p.h.

131

and carried but twenty passengers, it is surprising that anyone believed that airships had a useful future. Two more were built in Britain but the loss of the R 101 which crashed in France on its way to India in 1930, and the destruction by fire of the *Hindenburg* in 1937 put an end to the commercial use of airships.

Public interest in flying, sport, film-stars and, to a lesser extent, politicians was continuously fanned by the popular newspapers, among which the *Daily Mail*, founded in 1896 by Alfred Harmsworth (Lord Northcliffe), was still the pace-setter. Northcliffe acquired many other publications, including the *Daily Mirror* (1903) " the first newspaper for women ", and *The Times*, but after his death in 1922 most of his " empire " passed to his brother, Lord Rothermere. *The Times* was disposed of and some new figures came on the scene to challenge the supremacy of the *Mail*. The Berry brothers (later Lords Camrose and Kemsley) bought the *Daily Sketch* and the *Daily*

Newspapers   *Telegraph* (1927), while a dynamic Canadian named Max Aitken, who had become Lord Beaverbrook during the war, stormed into Fleet Street to make the *Daily Express* the most widely-read daily in the world. By 1930 the popular newspapers, which now included the Liberal *News Chronicle* and Labour's successful paper the *Daily Herald*, were engaged in a circulation war during which they offered all kinds of free gifts to new readers. In this competitive struggle, a number of evening and daily papers vanished, including the country's oldest daily newspaper, the *Morning Post*. Provincial and Scottish papers (though not the *Manchester Guardian* or the *Scotsman*) began to be threatened by the London Press which was increasingly controlled by a handful of powerful Press " barons ".

The " Fisher " Education Act * of 1918 brought some overdue improvements to the system of public education in England and Wales. Fees at elementary schools were abolished (a charge of a few pennies a week had persisted in some areas) and the

Education   leaving age was fixed at 14 to put an end to the pitiful business of little " part-timers " starting work at 11 or 12. Local authorities were encouraged to provide better opportunities for older pupils and also for the very young, though few of them did this and by 1920 there were only twenty nursery schools in the country. There were to be day-continuation schools

* So-called because H. A. L. Fisher was President of the Board of Education.

providing additional education up to 16 but, since attendance was not compulsory (except in Rugby), this part of the Act was a failure.

The bulk of the nation still received an education all too short and meagre for a major industrial Power. Nine children out of ten attended an elementary school from about the age of 5 until 14 and, in many cases, their entire schooling took place in one building. The youngest went through a doorway marked " INFANTS " to spend two years or so at their alphabets and numbers before proceeding as a rule upstairs to " Standard One " on the first floor and then through the " Standards ", literally " going up " until they reached the top of the barrack-like building that was so familiar in most large towns. In villages the whole school was usually housed in one long room sub-divided by curtains or partitions. Almost everyone left at 14, for only one pupil in a hundred stayed at elementary school for another year.

Elementary education tended to be formal and lacking in opportunity for creative work, science, domestic arts and physical exercise. But, if limited, the teaching was usually thorough and work of a high standard was achieved by talented children who were unable to obtain a secondary education. Attending only one school in their lives, they frequently retained a lasting affection for " Denbigh Road " or " Rishton Wesleyan Day School " and, in country districts, the village schoolmaster was a figure of considerable stature.

This one-school system was condemned by the Hadow Report of 1926 which recommended that at 11 years children should be sorted out and sent to secondary, i.e. grammar-type schools, or to senior elementary schools. In some areas there were also " central " schools which were a kind of half-way house between the other two types. " Reorganisation ", as it was called, took a long time to complete. New senior schools had to be built and the cost was heavy for local authorities and particularly for the churches which had pioneered public education and, in 1920, still had 12,000 " voluntary " schools while council schools numbered 8,700. However, by 1939, most authorities had reorganised elementary education into two main stages.

Secondary education was a privilege enjoyed by the few. In 1920, out of 6,291,000 children at State schools, only 308,000 were in secondary schools, with a further 10,000 in junior technical schools, * that is, one child in 21 had the chance of receiving more than the bare essentials of learning. About a third of those in secondary schools had won free places by means of the " scholarship " examination and the parents of the others paid fees usually of between one and four guineas a term. The position was slightly better by 1938 when out of $5\frac{1}{2}$ million children, half a million were receiving a secondary education and 48 per cent of them paid no fees; but the chances of winning a free place varied widely in different parts of the country.

A university education was unattainable by any except a fortunate handful of the population. The first 200 State scholarships were offered in 1920 and some local authorities made student grants which, curiously enough, were more liberal in the poorest parts of Britain, so that a miner's son in Scotland, South Wales or Northern England stood a better chance of entering a university than a labourer's son from the wealthier southern counties. It was calculated that the number of ex-elementary school pupils reaching a university was 4 in 1,000 † and, in any case, university places themselves were few, 32,000 in the English and Welsh universities and 10,000 in Scotland.

Altogether, education during the inter-war years presented a depressing picture of half-hearted measures which did little to remedy the lack of progress since the century opened. The vast majority of the nation's children continued to receive an education which in length and quality was unworthy of their abilities and inadequate for Britain's needs.

* There were between 300,000 and 400,000 at independent schools.
† *Britain Between the Wars*, C. L. Mowat (1955)

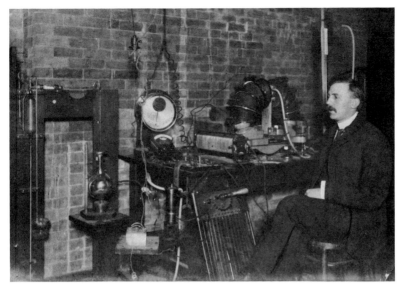

Despite defects in the educational system, Britain did not lack ability and achievement in science and medicine. At the universities, principally at Manchester and Cambridge, a group of gifted men were inspired first by J. J. Thomson and later by the New Zealander, Ernest Rutherford. These scientists were the founders of modern nuclear physics and when in 1919 *Science* Rutherford published his account of splitting the atom, he and his colleagues had brought mankind to the threshold of the Atomic Age. Thanks to them, the world's first nuclear power-station was to be a British one—opened in 1956 at Calder Hall in Cumberland. They also carried out research in radio-physics and this led to the discovery of radar by Robert Watson-Watt, whose work in the thirties enabled the R.A.F. to track Goering's bomber forces during the Second World War.

One discovery leads to another and developments in radar helped Bernard Lovell, who worked with Watson-Watt and with P. M. S. Blackett, to develop the new science of radio-astronomy. Their work at Jodrell Bank since the war has produced increasing knowledge of space and the universe.

The principle of jet-propulsion was known long before aircraft construction could cope with speeds of over 400 m.p.h. Even so, in 1930 a young R.A.F. officer, Frank Whittle, patented a jet-engine that used a gas-turbine for propulsion. Lack of money meant that little could be done until war came but Whittle's inventive persistence heralded the jet air-liners of the future.

The progress of medical science was equally exciting. Diseases, such as smallpox, diabetes and diphtheria, were almost conquered during the twenties and thirties by the use of new

serums. An anti-tetanus injection had saved thousands of lives during the First World War. A Scot, Alexander Fleming, who was an army doctor engaged in that work, continued his career in bacteriology and in 1929 discovered penicillin, a drug which proved to be a most powerful destroyer of bacteria. Howard Florey and others continued and developed Fleming's work. Another example of the application of chemistry to medicine was the production of the sulphonamide drugs such as " M & B 693 " which was in use in the thirties. By this time, there was increasing knowledge of food values and preventive medicine.

Parallel with these advances went the progress of surgery. Improved antiseptics and anaesthetics, together with technical innovations such as air-conditioning, steam-sterilisers and fine-quality surgical equipment, made operating theatres safer and more efficient. Just before the war a National Blood Transfusion Service was formed, and in plastic surgery Harold Gillies and Archibald MacIndoe developed techniques which restored so many disfigured servicemen and civilians. One of the outstanding differences between the present time and the period described at the beginning of this book is the modern rarity of cripples, especially crippled children. This increase in human happiness and usefulness was due to advances in orthopædic surgery.

In general, the health of the nation improved between the wars—deaths from tuberculosis, for instance, dropped from 1,066 per million in England and Wales in 1922–24 to 657 in 1937—but a report published in 1936 by Sir John Boyd Orr *

* *Food, Health and Income: A Survey of Adequacy of Diet in Relation to Income.*

made gloomy reading. He found that 4½ million persons, 10 per cent of the population, were very badly fed (average weekly expenditure on food was 4s each) and half the nation could be considered ill-fed. His findings were of course open to doubt, for standards of nutrition could be queried and his critics could point out that in most respects eating habits had improved. Consumption of eggs, butter, vegetables and fruit had increased by from 46 to 88 per cent per head since the days of Lloyd George's " People's Budget ". However, as Booth and Rowntree had shown, standards of life were shockingly low among the Edwardian poor so that the improvement which undoubtedly existed was still too little.

Malnutrition

Ill nourishment and its effects were obviously most widespread in the areas of chronic unemployment. In Durham and South Wales, the death-rate from tuberculosis was higher than average; infant mortality was higher in Scotland (76.8 per 1,000 live births in 1935), in Sunderland (92) and in Jarrow (114) than in Surrey (41) or the Midlands (59). There was improvement in the cleanliness and well-being of children for, whereas in 1912, 39.5 per cent of London school children were found to be verminous, in 1937 the figure was 7.9 per cent. Even so, during the Second World War, many people were shocked by the habits and uncleanliness of some of the slum families which were evacuated to safe areas.

A striking difference between the inter-war years and the present time was the decline in the birth-rate. In Victorian times families of ten and more were commonplace; by the twenties a family usually consisted of father, mother and two children. In 1903, 948,000 babies had been born in England and Wales but in 1925 the number was 711,000 and in 1933, 580,000. In Scotland, the live birth-rate fell from 25.4 per thousand in 1911–15 to 17.6 in 1933. The population was still rising but more slowly than before. The proportion of old people was increasing and it was expected that after a period when births and deaths were about equal, the population would decline so rapidly that by about the end of the century there would be only about 5 million persons in the whole of Great Britain. Less alarming estimates put the figure for the year 2047 at between 29 and 52 million. No one expected the population " explosion " which has, in fact, occurred since 1947.

The birth-rate

13 The End of Security

LOCARNO, the Kellogg Pact and the efforts of Mac-Donald, Austen Chamberlain, Briand and Stresemann led to a brief period of tranquillity during which the League's reputation stood high. People had begun to hope that disarmament and collective security would abolish war when their hopes were shattered by events in the Far East.

CHINESE PEASANTS AT A TIME OF FAMINE

For many years, China had been plagued by banditry and the greed of Japan and the major Western Powers. Taking advantage of the weak and corrupt Manchu dynasty, the foreigners had acquired ports and trading rights while the Chinese people lived for the most part in ignorance and poverty. In 1912 a revolution destroyed the old régime, but the hopes of Dr Sun Yat-sen, who had worked incessantly for the revolution, were soon dashed. A Christian and an admirer of Britain, he had hoped that his People's National Party (the Kuomintang) would establish a democracy. However, an army general seized power and Sun Yat-sen became head of a government at Canton in the south while a rival government ruled at Peking in the north. Some provinces fell into the grip of " war lords " who, to the misery of the people, plundered the country like bandit chiefs.

Chinese revolution 1912

Meanwhile, a young officer named Chiang Kai-shek had distinguished himself by Sun Yat-sen's side in the Kuomintang, and a number of Communists had also attained positions of power. Among these were Chou En-lai and Mao Tse-tung, an assistant librarian at Peking University who became an avid admirer of Marx and Lenin. Mao, son of a well-to-do peasant, had seen a great deal of the bitter poverty in which most Chinese lived, and he recognised the way in which power might be won: " Whoever wins the peasants will win China ", he said.

In 1925, Sun Yat-sen died and was succeeded, as head of the Kuomintang, by General Chiang Kai-shek who, with Chou En-lai and Mao Tse-tung in his armies, crushed the " war lords " in the north and began to bring some order to the country. However, he was disturbed by the spread of Communist ideas and by the way in which the peasants seized the land wherever his armies liberated a province. Chiang and many of his followers came from the landed classes and they therefore turned upon their Communist supporters and tried to destroy them. Mao fled to the south-east to set up a local Soviet government among the mountains where, despite all that Chiang could do, he held out for several years. Eventually, Mao and 100,000 of his followers undertook the " Long March " to Northern China, in order to be nearer to the Russian border where the chances of survival were better. This was in 1934. By then Chiang Kai-shek, the acknowledged ruler of China, had troubles that seemed even worse than the Communists.

Since the beginning of the century, Japan's leaders had been westernising their country's industry and armed forces with tremendous zest. Japan itself had few resources; the country was overcrowded and, although her leaders had taken the Chinese peninsula of Korea and had invested a good deal of money in the northern province of Manchuria, they still felt the need to expand. In addition, they knew that if Chiang Kai-shek succeeded in becoming really strong, they would lose the gains they had made.

MAO TSE-TUNG

Thus, in 1931, claiming that their trading rights in Manchuria had been violated, the Japanese Government sent an army to take over the entire province. Chiang appealed to the League of Nations which condemned Japan's action and asked her to withdraw her forces. The reply was polite but unrepentant. What Japan did was to turn Manchuria into a nominally independent state called Manchukuo with a puppet-emperor (the last of the Manchus) on the throne.

Manchuria 1931

This defiance of the League's authority was recognised as a threat to peace everywhere but hopes rested solely on Britain and America. They were the only Powers that possessed strong naval forces in the Far East.

Although not a member of the League, the U.S.A. was angered by the Japanese invasion and the American Secretary of State offered to discuss combined action with Britain. This approach was frigidly declined by Sir John Simon, the Foreign Secretary. Nothing was done to hinder renewed aggression in 1933, the year when Japan resigned from the League. A major conflict, called the Sino-Japanese War, broke out in 1937 and continued to ravage China for the next eight years. It led directly to the triumph of Mao and the Communists.

The Japanese invasion stirred the patriotism of the Chinese

people and alarmed Stalin. He therefore told Mao that he and his followers must come to terms with Chiang Kai-shek. This they did and although neither leader had anything but detestation for the other, they joined forces to confront the powerful Japanese armies which for a time appeared to be invincible. However, China is a vast country. It absorbed armies and money like a sponge. The resistance of its people, inured to centuries of hardship, was indestructible, and it was in a desperate attempt to solve the problem of the China War that Japan attacked Pearl Harbour in 1941.

CHIANG KAI-SHEK

The attack on Manchuria was a mortal blow to the League and much blame was laid upon all the member-states, especially Britain. Certainly, some joint action should have been taken, but it is difficult to see what could have been done to deter Japan from embarking upon a war on her own doorstep. Even if the League had possessed an army or could have raised the huge forces necessary to restrain the aggressor, the problems of transport alone were insuperable at this time. No Western nation felt threatened by the conflict and there was a good deal of sympathy for Japan, who appeared to be merely protecting her economic interests against Chinese anarchy. China was a great way off and, in any case, with rising unemployment and world depression, there was enough to worry about nearer home.

An additional anxiety was the pugnacious attitude of Germany and Italy. The Slump had brought Germany to the verge of ruin. Her dollar-aided recovery came crashing down and by 1931 more than six million Germans were out of work. The Government tottered, no party could command a majority in the

Germany:
Rise of the
Nazis

Reichstag and the Nazis began to come into their own. In 1928 they had had only 12 seats, but two years later they held 107 and, by 1932, when 230 of Hitler's followers were elected, their ranting leader had become a major figure in German politics. In that same year, the Nazis lost 34 seats in the November elections, but Hitler turned this setback into an advantage that brought him to power.

Von Papen, a Catholic aristocrat whose Nationalist Party was backed by the big industrialists, proposed that the Nationalists and the Nazis should join forces under Hitler as Chancellor and Papen as Vice-Chancellor. This would give them a majority in Parliament to confound the growing Communist Party. Privately, Papen and Hindenburg, the aged, doddering President, despised Hitler as an ill-bred upstart but they

believed that they and the ruling class would be able to use him
as a puppet once they had put him in office. Thus, in January
1933, Hitler became Chancellor of Germany. He had his own
ideas about puppets.

At once he demanded new elections, and in February the
Reichstag building was mysteriously destroyed by fire. Although
the Nazis blamed this on to the Communists and did everything
to foment public alarm, they polled only 43.9 per cent of the
votes. However, with the Nationalists' support, this was all that
Hitler needed. A two-thirds majority in the Reichstag was
required to change the Weimar Constitution and, with Goering's
storm-troopers patrolling the streets, the Communists and others
who would have voted against Hitler either went into hiding or
were arrested. The Government therefore obtained power for
four years to pass laws without the Reichstag; all laws were
to be drafted by the Chancellor and to come into immediate
effect. Overnight and apparently legally, the Weimar Republic
was closed down.

The various states of Germany lost their separate parliaments
and came under the central Government. Nazis were appointed
to all key positions, trade union officials were arrested and taken
to concentration camps and all political parties except the
Nazis were abolished. In a campaign of terror, Communists,
Socialists and Jews were publicly beaten up or were suddenly
arrested, often at dead of night, so that they disappeared
completely and were sometimes never heard of again.

Even so, Hitler was not yet quite master of Germany. Hindenburg was too old to bother about, Papen was contemptuously
put into the background but the S.A., the brownshirted storm-
troops, were likely to prove troublesome. Useful since the early
days for street-fighting and battering opponents, the S.A. was
an unruly organisation with various aims, including social

revolution. Hitler had no intention of granting this and he much preferred the S.S., a picked body of fanatical Nazis, disciplined, efficient and utterly devoted to the Führer (the Leader), as Hitler was now called. By Hitler's order, the S.A. was destroyed on 30th June 1934, " the Night of the Long Knives ", when some 400 of his old friends and supporters were savagely done to death. In August, Hindenburg died and

Hitler in power

Hitler declared himself President, Chancellor and Commander-in-Chief of the Army, which took an oath of loyalty to the Führer. His position in Germany was now unassailable for, in a plebiscite, 89.9 per cent of the German people gave approval to his actions. Only a military or diplomatic defeat by foreign powers could now unseat him.

This possibility existed. The tone of the Nazis was very disturbing to France and Britain. Germany's re-arming was now well known and had aroused considerable alarm at Geneva where a Disarmament Conference was in progress. Hitler soothed this disquiet by declaring that war would be " madness " and that Germany was ready to disarm completely if other nations would do the same. Sir John Simon and the French then put forward a plan whereby, after a five-year pause, general disarmament would bring all countries down to equality with Germany. In October, Hitler withdrew his representative from the Conference and announced Germany's resignation from the League. He expected that the French would march into the Ruhr and the Poles into East Prussia. Nothing happened. The first of his gambles had come off.

His next step was to make a non-aggression pact with Poland, an ally of France. Then, in 1934, the Austrian Chancellor, Dr Dollfuss, was murdered by Nazis, a premature crime because Hitler was not yet strong enough to unite Austria to Germany. However, in the following year, he introduced military conscription and openly announced the formation of a German Army.

The League protested and, at Stresa, France, Britain and Italy met to condemn German action; but the only results were a pact between Russia and France and the astounding fact of the Anglo-German Naval Treaty (June 1935). Germany agreed to build not more than 35 per cent of Britain's naval strength (not including submarines however) but, by obviously

accepting the German right to rearm, Britain had made nonsense of the League and the Versailles Treaty.

These events were watched with growing satisfaction by Mussolini, who at this time was Europe's No. 1 dictator and who, like most of that breed, desired military glory to bolster up his power. In East Africa, next door to Italian Somaliland and Eritrea (an Italian colony since 1885), lay Abyssinia, a mountainous country, independent and semi-barbaric, whose people adhered to an ancient form of the Christian religion. Italy had long coveted this unpromising land but in 1896 had suffered a humiliating defeat at Adowa, which Mussolini now proposed to avenge. In December 1934 a convenient clash occurred on the border between Abyssinian and Italian territory. Italy demanded compensation and Abyssinia appealed to the League. It was an unfortunate moment, for the League was much more concerned about Germany. Moreover, while neither Britain nor France favoured Mussolini's designs on Abyssinia, neither wanted a serious breach with Italy. Laval, the French Foreign Minister, was particularly anxious to win Italian friendship in the hope that Italy would guarantee Austria's independence, and Britain had by now disarmed to such a level that she could not contemplate military action against anyone. Thus, when Mussolini promised to negotiate, both Powers hoped that things might be smoothed over.

Abyssinia

There was some delay during which the British people voiced their support for the principles of the League. In October 1935 Italian armies invaded Abyssinia where, with modern equipment, they did remarkably badly against the Emperor Haile Selassie's ill-armed defenders. The League imposed sanctions against Italy but since these did not include oil and coal, the two most vital commodities, they merely angered Mussolini into denouncing the Stresa agreement without hindering his war. The French and British therefore tried to find some other way of stopping Italy and retaining her friendship. Sir Samuel Hoare and Pierre Laval concocted a plan whereby about two-thirds of Abyssinia should be handed over to Italy and the remaining third should be given a small outlet to the sea which *The Times* described as " a corridor for camels ".

Hoare-Laval Pact

An outburst of indignation in Britain brought the Hoare-Laval pact to nought. Hoare had to resign and Baldwin, full of lame excuses, appointed Anthony Eden in his place. In any case, Mussolini would not have settled for two-thirds of Abyssinia. In 1936 a new commander, Badoglio, used aircraft and poison gas to take Addis Ababa, the capital, and to force the Emperor to flee. Abyssinia became part of Italian East Africa and, with the ending of sanctions in July, the world accepted the situation and altered the map of Africa accordingly.

The Abyssinian episode had frightening consequences. It revealed the weakness of France and Britain, the helplessness of the League and the failure of collective security. Worse, it threw Mussolini and Hitler into each other's arms, exulting over their own cleverness and the feebleness of all who opposed them. By a treaty of October 1936, they agreed to co-operate in foreign policy and, a year later, Mussolini joined the Anti-Comintern Pact which Germany and Japan had already formed to oppose Communism.

The Rhineland   It was during the Abyssinian campaign that Hitler took perhaps his biggest gamble. When he decided to march into

GERMAN TROOPS REOCCUPY THE RHINELAND, 1936

the Rhineland his generals were appalled by the risk, since France and her Polish and Czech allies could have put forces into the field that would have annihilated the then puny German Army. The French were prepared to act, but not alone, and Britain, which could offer only two divisions if it came to fighting, took the attitude that it was unreasonable to prevent Germany from doing as she liked inside her own frontiers. There were protests but no action. Hitler himself knew that it was touch and go: " the forty-eight hours after the march into the Rhineland were the most nerve-wracking in my whole life ", he said afterwards. Once again he triumphed. The generals were proved wrong and to the German people Adolf Hitler was now a miracle-man.

By this time, Hitler was a complete dictator. There was no opposition to him in the Reichstag, the Press or the trade unions. Even the General Staff, which had called the tune in the Kaiser's day, obeyed every command of the corporal who had become their Commander-in-Chief. His word was law. If he disliked a picture it was removed from the art gallery; if music did not please him, it was banned; books by Jewish or " decadent " authors were taken from the libraries and publicly burnt. Jews were excluded from business, the professions and the arts; suspicion that a man's great-grandmother was a Jewess was enough to ruin him. Every aspect of life in Germany, from trade to sport, was controlled by Hitler and his henchmen.

The leading figures of the inner circle that surrounded the Führer were, in their different ways, as evil and demented as their master. Hermann Goering, apparently the most normal, had been an air ace in the First World War; brave, good-humoured and capable as far as the German Air Force was concerned, he was the only one of the gang who seemed able to retain his own popularity and a few shreds of independence. He was nevertheless a fat, swaggering bully who helped himself greedily to the riches that came within his grasp. At least in his greed and showmanship, Goering was human. The others did not want money but power.

The Nazi leaders

Goebbels, his rival, was a clever little cripple with a piercing insight into the weaknesses and follies of his fellow-men. His raving oratory, second only to Hitler's, and his political sharpness brought him the post of Minister of Propaganda in which, through Press, radio, theatre, books and schools, he controlled and moulded the minds of the German people. Of the two,

Goebbels was probably closer to Hitler than Goering. As fanatical as his leader, he was utterly loyal and, at the end, he killed his family and himself when he knew that his master was dead in the Berlin bunker. Among the others were Rudolph Hess, Hitler's deputy and a co-founder of the Party, who flew to Scotland in 1941 to try to make peace and became completely insane; Heinrich Himmler, commander of the S.S., and chief of the Gestapo or secret police, whose mild appearance concealed a ruthless dedication to the Nazi creed; and Julius Streicher, the Jew-hater in chief, who was the cruellest and most filthy-minded creature of them all.

The Spanish Civil War   In many parts of Europe the struggle between Right and Left was becoming more intense, and in Spain the conflict burst into flames. Since King Alfonso's abdication in 1931, the republic had known many changes of government and, in the elections of February 1936, the Right (the Falange) gained slightly more votes than the Left which, nevertheless, owing to the Spanish electoral system, still had a majority in the Assembly (Cortes). When disorders broke out, the Right, chiefly the business and land-owning classes, the Roman Catholic Church and Army officers, supported a military uprising that had already occurred in Spanish Morocco under General Franco. By November, Franco's forces, " the Nationalists ", had control of most of the south, west and north of Spain and had set up a government at Burgos. The Republicans or " Loyalists " who included Communists, Socialists, Syndicalists and Anarchists, held Madrid, central and eastern Spain where Barcelona became their seat of government.

The Spanish Civil War had immense significance for the rest of the world. People who had been apparently unmoved by the fate of German Jews or of Italian and German trade unionists, now took sides. They attended public meetings, denounced the atrocities and raised money for arms, ambulances and food, mostly to support the Republicans. The British and French Governments supported a policy of non-intervention, for many Conservatives regarded Franco as the upholder of law and order; but Léon Blum, the French Premier, was in a difficult position. A Socialist, he would have preferred to help the Spanish Republicans, but with appeasers and Fascists on one side and Communists on the other, this clever charming man had all his work cut out to hold the French Left together and to stay in office as head of a " Popular Front " government.

REPUBLICAN OR 'LOYALIST' FIGHTERS IN BARCELONA DURING THE
CIVIL WAR

But "non-intervention" (also agreed to by Germany, Italy
and Russia) did not allow the Spaniards to fight out their
quarrel among themselves. Foreign troops and equipment
poured into Spain, and by 1937 Franco was supported by an
Italian army numbering between 40,000 and 80,000 and by
thousands of Germans, many of them pilots and technicians,
who came to try out new tactics with the aircraft and tanks
which they brought with them. Russian help to the Republicans
was on a less lavish scale but volunteers from many countries
formed the International Brigade to help fight the Fascists.

The rest of the world looked on with fascinated horror at the
appalling struggle that took place. Terrible atrocities were
committed by both sides, though Franco's forces tended to earn
the worse reputation, partly because his troops were usually
advancing and their policy was to wipe out all opposition in
captured districts. One of the greatest horrors—because it was
an act as yet unfamiliar to the world—was the deliberate
destruction by bombers of the Basque town of Guernica.

Madrid held out against all the attacks of 1937 and 1938 but the Nationalists inched their way into Republican territory until, in January 1939, Barcelona was taken. The Spanish Civil War ended in March with the fall of Madrid but the bitterness and the emotional involvement of millions of people have not yet subsided.

Labour's attitude   In Britain, feelings ran high. The Labour Party, so long devoted to the cause of peace at almost any price (George Lansbury once said that he would disband the Army and dismiss the Air Force), came to demand direct intervention in Spain on the side of the Republicans. With a scathing attack on Lansbury's pacifism, Ernest Bevin swung Labour opinion over to a realisation of what Fascism meant to the working-class movement everywhere, though there was little understanding of the ways in which the Communists were exploiting the situation for their own ends. Lansbury resigned from the Party leadership and was succeeded by Clement Attlee,* who was an officer in the First World War and no pacifist. After Abyssinia and the outbreak of the Spanish War, it was Labour that appeared to be ready to fight (though they opposed conscription as late as April 1939), while the Conservatives were increasingly accused of weakness and of appeasing the Fascist aggressors.

Yet appeasement, until it became a term of abuse, was exactly what the country wanted and what the Labour Party in particular had always supported. Labour's Peace Crusade of the thirties condemned the use of force, the manufacture and sale of armaments and the failure to set an example by drastic disarming. To men like Lansbury and Henderson, as to Baldwin and Neville Chamberlain, the sensible way to settle disputes was to argue them out round a table. Their mistake was to imagine that dictators could be influenced by the views of decent, reasonable men like themselves.

* Clement Richard Attlee, born 1883 at Putney, educated Haileybury and Oxford. A barrister, interested in social work in London's East End. 1919, Mayor of Stepney; 1922, M.P.; 1923 Under-Sec. of State for War; 1927, member of Simon Commission to India; 1930, Chancellor of Duchy of Lancaster; 1931, Postmaster General; 1935, Leader of Opposition; 1940, Lord Privy Seal; 1942, Dominions Secretary; 1943, Deputy Prime Minister; 1945–51, Prime Minister; 1955, became Lord Attlee.

HITLER
AND
GOERING

14 The Road to Munich

THROUGH the twenties and up until 1934, Britain adopted a policy of disarmament which had the support of almost everyone except Churchill. The British people were solidly anti-war. Lacking the cynicism of the French, they genuinely believed that the 1914–18 War had been fought to end war and that the League of Nations had been created to maintain peace. Since weapons produced wars, they ought to be abolished and there were many idealists and pacifists, especially in the Labour Party, who felt that if Britain were to disarm completely, other nations would follow her example. Some people agreed with Neville Chamberlain when he said that to spend £78 million on the armed forces would well-nigh ruin the country, and there were those who thought that Russian Communism was a greater threat to peace than a strong Germany.

The watchword of ex-servicemen was " Never again ". A spate of war books informed their sons and daughters that war was a measureless horror that harvested ruin for victors and vanquished alike. So they joined the Peace Society or the Peace Pledge Union. In the Peace Ballot of 1935 an overwhelming majority of its 11½ million voters answered in favour of the League and drastic disarmament. Two years earlier, students of the Oxford Union had passed their celebrated resolution " That this House will in no circumstances fight for its King and Country ". A great deal of fuss was made about this incident which was supposed to have convinced Hitler that Britain had gone soft. But the young men at Oxford were merely expressing their countrymen's fervent hope that they would never *have* to fight. It was the peace-at-any-price attitude of persons much older than the Oxford undergraduates that gave Hitler the impression that Britain and France would put up with anything rather than war.

With splendid impartiality, Churchill laid the blame for Britain's military weakness on all three political parties. It was their " refusal to face unpleasant facts, the desire for popularity and electoral success . . ." that helped to unleash the horrors and miseries of war.

He himself was sounding the alarm as early as in 1932. Out

CHURCHILL
IN 1930

of office, he still possessed a semi-private intelligence service that kept him closely informed about what was going on in Europe, and when, in 1934, there was a modest increase of forty aeroplanes to Britain's air strength, he was on his feet complaining that, with Germany arming fast, this was not enough.

Later that year, the Government's five-year programme to expand the R.A.F. to 1,300 aeroplanes was opposed by Labour and the Liberals on the grounds that there was absolutely no need for increased armaments. When Churchill presently told Parliament that the German Air Force was already almost as strong as the R.A.F., and that by 1937 it would be twice as large, Baldwin flatly denied this alarming statement. Within six months he was eating humble pie:

" with regard to the figure I gave in November of German aeroplanes . . . I believed at the time it was right. Where I was wrong was in my estimate of the future. There I was completely wrong."

Churchill's unpopularity
By 1935 disarmament was at an end and Britain began to try to catch up, but in continuing to hope that war would never come, the public showed no liking for Churchill. His well-known pugnacity and his opposition to Indian self-government reduced the effectiveness of his warnings. The very style of his speeches with their blood-curdling prophecies of disaster made people impatient. Here was a man, they reminded themselves, who had always been wayward and self-opinionated. Now he was telling them what they did not want to hear and, worst of all, he had put honest Mr Baldwin into an embarrassing position.

Churchill's position was an extraordinary one. Blessed with more vitality, talent and experience of action and high office than anyone else in his Party, he was also cursed with a tempestuous nature that loved a fight. This often led him to act and speak rashly. There was a kind of wilful naughtiness about him. Aristocrat though he was by birth, he still looked and behaved like an impish schoolboy—bizarre hats, cigars, bow-tie, paint-brushes, membership of the bricklayers' union, all seemed to belong to a man who had never quite grown up. Labour looked on him as the Minister who had sent soldiers to fire on workers; Liberals and Conservatives regarded him as a turncoat whose undeniable abilities did not include trustworthiness. An imperialist whose mind was shut on the subject of India, he nevertheless had the power to see great issues and

JUBILEE CELEBRATIONS IN LONDON'S EAST END

the trend of history with a clarity that was irritating to lesser men. The Conservatives had no affection for him (that came later) and he only came to the Premiership in 1940 because Attlee and the Labour Party refused to serve in a Government headed by Chamberlain.

In May 1935 the country celebrated the Silver Jubilee of George V's accession. The last great procession of reigning monarchs made its way through London's decorated streets and the nation showed its affection for the monarchy with a warmth that surprised the modest conscientious man who had occupied the throne for twenty-five years.

Soon after the Jubilee, Ramsay MacDonald resigned the Premiership. He was unwell and his position at the head of a Government consisting almost entirely of Conservatives had become, in his own words, " more and more degrading ". So, with pathetic dignity, he shuffled off to change places * with Baldwin who, in any case, had long been ruling from the background. *Baldwin in office*

The change made little difference. Nor did the General Election that took place in the autumn, the last election for ten years. A so-called National Government was returned, consisting of 387 Conservatives, 33 Liberal-Nationalists and 8 National-Labour members. The Opposition was stronger,

* MacDonald took Baldwin's post as Lord President of the Council and held it until 1936. He died in 1938.

for Labour now had 154 M.P.'s compared with 46 in 1931, but there were only 17 Liberals and Lloyd George's family party of 4. Baldwin, more popular than ever, was of course Prime Minister. Neville Chamberlain, the Chancellor, was the strongest man in the Government, Sir Samuel Hoare had already taken Simon's post as Foreign Secretary and Anthony Eden entered the Cabinet. There was no place for Winston Churchill.

This was the Government that had to face a mounting series of crises during the next four years—Abyssinia, the Rhineland, the Spanish Civil War, Austria, Sudetenland, Munich and Poland. During these critical years, the dictators were never faced by a resolute partnership between Britain and France, but only by wobbling uncertainty and half-hearted measures too feeble to impede the aggressors but sufficient to cause irritation. Rearmament did nothing to stiffen Baldwin's spine; he felt that it only made war more likely: " I am prepared to devote all our efforts . . . to do what is necessary but I am conscious all the time of the folly of all of us." But when it came to a domestic crisis, Baldwin could act with a resolution that he never showed in foreign affairs.

George V died in January 1936 and was succeeded by Edward VIII who had been a very popular Prince of Wales. The new King was unmarried and had formed a close friendship with an American lady, Mrs Simpson, who had divorced one husband and was about to divorce another. When Baldwin learned that the King intended to marry Mrs Simpson, he made it clear with tactful firmness that the lady was not acceptable as Queen. There was much support for Edward VIII but Baldwin skilfully persuaded the House of Commons that no compromise was possible; the position of the monarchy demanded that if the

EDWARD VIII
THEN PRINCE
OF WALES VISITS
MINERS' HOMES
IN DURHAM

King was determined to marry this lady, he must abdicate. In *The Abdication crisis* December, a Declaration of Abdication Act was put through and the Duke of York became King George VI. It all happened so quickly that the public was taken by surprise and the decision was made before people had time to think the matter out. For once, Baldwin had acted with authority, doing what he believed to be right and in the best interests of the country. In fact, the monarchy did not suffer, for George VI and his Queen possessed all the qualities that the people had come to expect in royalty.

After the Coronation in May 1937, Baldwin retired with an earldom and the esteem of the nation. In a very short time, his reputation was in the dust. By 1940 he was reviled as the chief of the " guilty men " who had brought Britain to the verge of disaster. He did not deserve all the abuse that was poured upon him and which he scorned to answer. In many respects he had been a wise and tolerant politician, but his abiding defects were his indolence and his inability to grapple with dangers abroad. As Churchill said, " He knew little of Europe, and disliked what he knew ".

Neville Chamberlain became Prime Minister. An alert *Neville Chamberlain, peacemaker* beady-eyed administrator as efficient and unlovable as a rasp, he possessed all and more of the self-confidence that his successful career entitled him to entertain for his own talents. His mission was to bring peace to Europe and he was certain that he knew how to handle the troublemakers.

In his view, it was necessary to get on good terms with the two principal dictators while contriving to separate Mussolini from Hitler. The League of Nations was as good as finished and he said himself that no one could look in that direction for protection. As for alliances, the United States was wedded to isolation, and France, beset by civil discord, seemed no better than a broken reed. Russia, France's ally, inspired no confidence, for Stalin had recently carried out a savage purge of the Red generals and, as always, little was known of Russian intentions and military strength.

Chamberlain's policy therefore was to establish himself as the Peacemaker of Europe and this he would do by getting into personal touch with the dictators and discussing in man-to-man talks the things that would satisfy their aspirations. If necessary, they could be appeased by the return of Germany's former colonies and by recognition of the Italian conquest of Abyssinia.

This approach was contrary to all that Anthony Eden, the

Foreign Secretary, stood for. He believed in close co-operation with France, support for the League, better relations with Russia and, above all, a firm attitude towards the dictators. Hitler was fully aware of this and, in London, von Ribbentrop, the German Ambassador, made it his business to drop hints that Eden's unfriendliness was displeasing to the Führer. This impudence should have been ignored but the British Ambassador in Berlin had already been replaced by Sir Nevile Henderson, an out-and-out appeaser, and it was not long before Sir Robert Vansittart, who detested the Nazis, was removed from his post as permanent head of the Foreign Office.

Two incidents led to Eden's resignation. In January 1938, President Roosevelt sent a confidential message to Chamberlain asking for the British Government's views on his proposal to call a meeting of the leading Powers to try to reduce tension. Without informing Eden, who was on holiday, Chamberlain sent a most discouraging reply. He hoped that the President's proposal would be postponed since he was making efforts of his own which might include recognising Italy's occupation of Abyssinia. Roosevelt was perturbed by this news and Eden, when he heard of the matter, was horrified. He managed to have a more cordial message sent to America but the damage was done and the President made no further effort to influence affairs in Europe.

Almost immediately, talks took place between Grandi, the Italian Ambassador, and Eden who was accompanied by and frequently overruled by Chamberlain. Suspecting that Mussolini was unhappy about Hitler's designs on Austria, Eden wanted to take a firm line, particularly over the Italian army helping Franco in Spain. In his opinion, it should be withdrawn before an Anglo-Italian agreement was signed, but Chamberlain would not allow quibbles to stand in the way of appeasement. He insisted that discussions must be started in Rome, so Eden resigned and was replaced by Lord Halifax, who had already paid an unofficial visit to Hitler and Goering and was far more likely to support Chamberlain's policy.

The Anschluss Meanwhile, Hitler had annexed Austria. In March 1938 the Austrian Chancellor was forced to resign, German tanks crossed the frontier and Hitler entered Vienna to announce that Austria was now part of the German Reich. Mussolini did nothing at all and Hitler was able to retort, in reply to Chamberlain's protest, that Austria was no business of Britain's. But it was.

The "Anschluss", or union of Germany and Austria, was forbidden by the Treaty of Versailles, and now that Austria, a fellow-member of the League of Nations, had been taken, Czechoslovakia and south-east Europe lay exposed to the aggressor. However, Hitler knew what he was about: here is what he said to the Austrian Chancellor:

"Don't believe that anyone in the world will hinder me in my decisions! Italy? I am quite clear with Mussolini: with Italy I am on the closest possible terms. England? England will not lift a finger for Austria . . . And France? Well, two years ago when we marched into the Rhineland with a handful of battalions—at that moment I risked a great deal. If France had marched then we should have been forced to withdraw . . . But for France it is now too late!" *

His calculations were right. The dictator had grown into a monster who, by means of terror and a fearsome ability to appeal to the worst and the best aspects of the German character, was now backed by a powerful nation thirsting for fresh triumphs. But, to Chamberlain's mind, nothing should be done to cause offence. When the Russians suggested talks and

* *The Second World War*, W. S. Churchill, quoted from the memoirs of Schuschnigg, the deposed Austrian Chancellor.

the National Council of Labour called for a Franco-British-Russian alliance, Chamberlain was unmoved. He distrusted Russia and had already decided that Czechoslovakia was doomed:

"You have only to look at the map", he wrote, "to see that nothing that we or France could do could possibly save Czechoslovakia from being overrun by the Germans . . . I have therefore abandoned my idea of giving guarantees to Czechoslovakia or the French in connection with her obligations to that country."

Thus, he dismissed the obligation to support the one democratic state in central Europe. A "look at the map" was sufficient reason to abandon the country which had been created by the Treaty of Versailles, which possessed a treaty with France, a Pact with Soviet Russia, a large army and one of the most modern armament works in the world.

*The
Sudetenland*

The spotlight fell upon that part of north-west Czechoslovakia known as the Sudetenland. Its inhabitants included just over three million German-speaking persons who had earlier belonged, not to Germany, but to the Austro-Hungarian Empire. Not unnaturally, they felt more affection for their Austrian cousins than for the Czechs and, to this extent, there was a Sudeten problem before Hitler took advantage of it. Acting on his orders, the Sudeten Nazis began an outcry against Czech "persecution" but, for the moment, Dr Benes, President of Czechoslovakia, was not greatly perturbed. He believed in the support of France and the friendship of Britain. Unfortunately he also believed that his own undoubted cleverness would see him through in his dealings with Germany. The situation caused Daladier, the new French Prime Minister, to visit London where he told Chamberlain and Halifax that if Czechoslovakia was attacked, France would fight. He urged them to join him in issuing a strong warning to Hitler.

Chamberlain refused. In his opinion, the Sudeten problem should be settled by negotiation and he would go no further than to say that if France became involved in war, Britain might not stand aloof. Daladier's resolve, never very firm, was hardly strengthened by this reply. However, in May 1938, when a border incident led to German troop movements, France and Russia were prepared to act. Halifax warned the German Ambassador of the danger of a general war and Hitler backed down for the time being. He was still determined to see what could be gained by threats and bluff.

All through the summer of 1938, Czechoslovakia was kept under pressure. The Sudeten Nazis complained unceasingly, Britain urged concessions and Chamberlain sent a mission to Prague to assist negotiations. France would have nothing to do with this but her war-like resolve was weakening, for there were appeasers and defeatists * in plenty to oppose Daladier and to point to the German defence line that faced the French frontier. Although Benes offered to accept the Sudeten demands, matters were deliberately brought to boiling point in September when Hitler made a violently hostile speech and the Sudeten Nazi leader " fled " to Germany.

Chamberlain felt that he alone could avert catastrophe. He sent a telegram to Hitler asking for a personal meeting

* Their leader was M. Bonnet, the French Foreign Secretary.

CHAMBERLAIN AND HITLER TAKE TEA TOGETHER. ON THE RIGHT, VON RIBBENTROP AND SIR NEVILE HENDERSON

and on the 14th, to the dismay of the Czechs, he flew to Berchtesgaden to reason with the dictator in his mountain retreat.   In a three-hour talk he became convinced that Hitler

*Czechoslovakia
doomed*

was determined to have his way and Hitler became equally convinced that Chamberlain would not stop him.   On the following day the British Prime Minister came home to bring about the ruin of Czechoslovakia as surely as if he had been that country's mortal enemy.

To the Cabinet he put forward his proposal that all districts of Czechoslovakia with a German-speaking population of more than 50 per cent should be handed over immediately to Germany. With some demur, his colleagues accepted.   So did Daladier and Bonnet, who thereby agreed to destroy the Czech alliance which had been made for the express purpose of giving France the security she craved.   By now all sense of honour had vanished, and the Czechs were told by their allies to accept the proposals without argument or delay.   The alternative was war and the blame would be Czechoslovakia's!   Benes bravely rejected this shameful proposition and offered to submit the Sudeten problem to arbitration but when he was sternly advised to face up to reality, i.e. to the fact that his friends would no longer assist him, he gave in.

Joyfully, Chamberlain flew to Germany again, only to find that Hitler had stepped up his demands which, as set out in a paper known as the Godesberg Memorandum, amounted to an ultimatum.   By this time, public opinion in Britain was beginning to harden.   Halifax and the Cabinet informed Chamberlain that the Godesberg Memorandum must be rejected and when Daladier agreed with this view and ordered partial mobilisation of the French Army, it looked as if Hitler's bluff had been called.   The British Fleet was ordered to

DR BENES OF
CZECHOSLOVAKIA

mobilise and the Czechs had $1\frac{1}{2}$ million soldiers standing ready.

What of Russia?   On 21st September, Litvinov told the Assembly of the League that the Soviet Union was ready to give immediate aid to Czechoslovakia if France would render similar assistance.   This offer was repeated two days later, but Chamberlain took no notice and he behaved throughout the crisis as though Stalin and the Red Army did not exist.   Hitler's almost insane hatred of Russia was well known and Chamberlain doubtless assumed that his hopes of a friendly understanding with Germany would be ruined if he paid attention to Stalin's offer.   Yet it was obvious that with the Red Army in the scale alongside the French, Czech and British forces, the balance would be tilted decisively against Germany. The German generals knew this and they solemnly warned Hitler of the risks that he was running. But the Führer knew his man. He had met Chamberlain and he must have reckoned that this cold dedicated politician, utterly sincere and utterly mistaken, would play his game to perfection.

On 26th September, Hitler made another speech full of violent abuse and threats against Czechoslovakia. War appeared to be certain and, in Britain, air-raid precautions were being taken. Volunteers were digging slit-trenches when Chamberlain made a broadcast speech that showed to what shameful depths his love of peace had brought him:

"How horrible, fantastic, incredible it is that we should be digging trenches and trying on gas-masks here because of a quarrel in a far-away country between people of whom we know nothing."

The "far-away country" could still be sacrificed and, in reply to a message from Hitler, he told him that he felt certain that Germany could get "all essentials without war and without delay". Mussolini and Daladier were invited to attend a Four Power meeting (no need to bother about Benes or Stalin) and a dramatic moment occurred, by accident or design, in the House of Commons when Chamberlain's speech was interrupted by the arrival of a telegram. Herr Hitler had invited him to go to Munich on the following day. The peace of the world would be saved.

At Munich, on 30th September, Hitler, Chamberlain, Daladier and Mussolini reached agreement and the Czechs, who had not been invited to be present, were curtly informed that the areas which Germany demanded were to be handed over at once with all fortifications and weapons. Czech defences were gone, the treaties with France and Russia were cancelled and in their place a "guarantee" of new frontiers would be arranged under a German chairman. *Munich 1938*

On the following day, Chamberlain came home to a hero's welcome. In the hand that waved to the cheering crowds, he held a piece of paper. It was a document signed by Hitler, promising that the peoples of Britain and Germany would never go to war with one another again.

"I believe it is peace in our time," cried the exultant Prime Minister.

" PEACE IN OUR TIME." CHAMBERLAIN AT HESTON AIRPORT, SEPTEMBER 1938

At the time, most people agreed with him. They felt that he deserved every word of the praise that was showered upon him, for he had saved them from war and thêy regarded war with the uttermost dread. In 1938, Hitler's villainy had not been fully revealed and it was not unreasonable to believe him when he said, " This is the last territorial claim I have to make in Europe ". After all, Germany seemed to have a moral right to the Sudeten territory and Munich might well provide a much more stable peace in Europe. As Mr Chamberlain wrote to the Archbishop of Canterbury, " Some day, the Czechs will see that what we did was to save them for a happier future ".

Parliament approved the Munich Agreement by 366 votes to 114 but, as the waves of hysterical relief subsided, the voices of the critics were heard and feelings of shame came creeping in. Attlee condemned the triumph of brute force; Duff Cooper resigned his post as First Lord of the Admiralty and Churchill spoke of " a total and unmitigated defeat ". They pointed to what had been lost: Britain's good name, the trust of small countries, the respect, if any, of Russia, the Czech alliance and the great Skoda arsenal which was now turning out weapons for Germany.

" *A total defeat* "

Supporters of appeasement were to claim later on that

Chamberlain gained a breathing-space, that he made it possible
for Britain to enter the fight with more aeroplanes, guns and
tanks. But Chamberlain did not go to Munich with the idea of
playing for time. He went to secure peace and he honestly
believed that he had won it, not for twelve months, but for many   *A breathing-*
years to come. As for the gains in armed strength, Britain was   *space?*
certainly weak in 1938, for her army amounted to only two
fully-equipped divisions and her air force to 1,854 planes.
The Spitfires which played a decisive part in the Battle of
Britain were only just coming into production. On the other
hand, France could put 60–70 divisions into the field and the
British Navy was supreme at sea. In the year that followed
Munich, Germany's lead was bound to increase because her
industry was already geared to producing planes, tanks and
army equipment, whereas Britain was still in process of organising the labour, machinery and materials for producing arms.
Thus, by 1939, Britain's strength had risen to 5 divisions and
1,978 planes but Germany's had grown to 106 divisions and
3,609 planes. Churchill believed that France was stronger than
Germany in 1938 but not in 1939.

There are those who hold that the Second World War was
caused more by the blunders of French and British politicians
than by Germany's aggressive intentions, but it is worth noting
that in 1934, Germany spent £280 million on armaments to
Britain's £99 million and in 1938, £1,710 million to £358
million. It is hard to believe A. J. P. Taylor when he writes:

" The state of German armament in 1939 gives the decisive
proof that Hitler was not contemplating general war, and
probably not intending war at all." *

For Hitler, threatened by no one, had caused his country to
spend a quarter of its national income upon armaments. The
German nation was keyed up, exultant in its recovered might.
What then was Hitler contemplating? What, other than war,
were the aims of the dictator who had caused his country's
industry to turn out, not the manufactures of peaceful trade, but
the materials of war? It seems clear that Hitler built up
Germany's armed strength in order to recover all and more than
all of the 1918 losses. If he could achieve this without a war
against France and Britain, so much the better for he intended,
sooner or later, to attack Soviet Russia.

* *The Origins of the Second World War*, (1961)

15 Last Months of Peace

DURING the winter that followed Munich, Chamberlain remained full of optimism. He saw no need to listen to Halifax's doubts or to bring men like Churchill and Eden into the Cabinet. A certain amount of rearmament was a wise precaution but, on 15th March 1939, he had just declared that " Europe is settling down to a period of tranquillity ", when Hitler struck again.

The new President * of Czechoslovakia was summoned to Berlin and compelled to sign a treaty putting the remnant of his country under Germany's " protection ". German troops moved in, Prague was occupied and, to mark the occasion with the presence of the new master, Hitler spent one night in the Czech capital.

Chamberlain was hurt. He complained that Hitler might at least have consulted him, even though the end of Czechoslovakia " may or may not have been inevitable ". But he was taken aback by the indignation of the British public who, remembering their own joy at the time of Munich, were all the angrier to see how easily they had been duped.

This outburst of feeling had its effect on Chamberlain who publicly, instead of privately, warned Hitler that Britain would resist any attempt to dominate the world by force. For all that, Chamberlain refused a Russian suggestion for a conference and proposed instead a declaration by Britain, France, Russia and Poland that they would act together against any further aggression.

Poland Why had Poland moved into the limelight? Resurrected by the Treaty of Versailles, Poland had been trying for twenty years to play the part of a Great Power independent of her powerful neighbours. The Polish Corridor separated Germany from East Prussia, and the Free City of Danzig was populated largely by Germans, who were clamouring to be taken into the Fatherland.

The Poles were too nervous of Russia to agree to Chamberlain's plan. Instead, with an army of two million soldiers and a courageous Foreign Secretary in Colonel Beck, they were

---

* Emil Hacha. Benes had gone into exile.

disposed to stand up to Hitler or at least to negotiate on equal terms. On 21st March, however, they were told that Danzig must be handed over to Germany and a right of way through the Polish Corridor must be granted. Two days later, Lithuania ceded the port of Memel to Germany.

In view of his previous record, Chamberlain's reaction was astounding. On 31st March, the man who dismissed Czechoslovakia as a "far away country", gave Poland a guarantee of support against aggression. Never mind that it was even farther away, with poorer defences and a less up-to-date army. Never mind the fact that, as Lloyd George pointed out, it was impossible to help Poland without having a close understanding with Russia. Hitler must be checked and surely this form of declaration, backed by France, would bring him to his senses? Similar guarantees were given to Rumania and Greece in April when Mussolini suddenly attacked Albania.

In May a languid effort was begun to form an understanding with Russia but, after years of cold-shouldering, progress was slow, especially as Poland and Rumania recoiled with horror from the thought of allowing Russian troops to cross their territory. On both sides there was suspicion and neither Chamberlain nor Halifax thought it worth paying a personal visit to Stalin. It should have been noted with alarm that Russia's Foreign Commissar, Litvinov, who favoured co-operation with the Western Powers, was suddenly replaced by Molotov, a close associate of Stalin and a dedicated Party man who, if it suited Russia's purpose, would be pro-Hitler or pro-Satan.

On 24th August a bombshell exploded. With horrified disbelief, the world learnt that Germany and Russia had signed a Non-Aggression Pact. The one certainty in international affairs had seemed to be the undying hostility between these countries. Hitler's violent hatred of Communism and his evident intention to dominate Eastern Europe made him the natural enemy of Stalin. The fact that the two had joined hands was a disaster which must have terrible consequences.

The Russo-German Pact

Yet it had been naïve to suppose that rival dictators could never come to terms. For Stalin, the Pact meant safety, at least for a time. It gave him the chance to grab the Baltic States and to push Russia's frontiers some distance to the west. For Hitler, it meant that he could deal with Poland without the spectre of a war on two fronts, for he was confident that France and Britain must now abandon their guarantee to Poland as they had abandoned Czechoslovakia. Ribbentrop had assured him that Britain would not fight; the despised democracies would bow to the inevitable.

To his annoyance, they did no such thing. Chamberlain sent him a letter of warning and reaffirmed the Anglo-Polish treaty. Daladier took the same line. Appeals for peace were made by Roosevelt, the Pope and the King of the Belgians. Hitler's friend Mussolini admitted that he was not ready for war on Germany's side. For a moment, Hitler wavered. Orders to invade Poland on 26th August were cancelled and, in Berlin, Henderson was told that the Führer would come to the defence of the British Empire anywhere in the world!

Meanwhile, although agreeing to negotiate, the Polish Government ordered mobilisation. The German Press reacted with hysterical accounts of Polish " atrocities ". Hitler lost his temper and demanded that Poland send a representative to Berlin to accept whatever Germany proposed. The Poles replied that they would negotiate but not on the terms for a defeated nation. This was enough for Hitler.

In the small hours of 1st September German forces invaded Poland. For two agonising days Britain and France appeared to hesitate but on 3rd September, to the " stunned surprise ", it is said, of Hitler, Goering and Goebbels, both countries *September* declared themselves at war with Germany. The Dominions, *1939* which had not on the whole approved Britain's foreign policy prior to 1939, rallied to Britain's side. Australia and New Zealand regarded themselves at war immediately. Canada and South Africa declared war with the approval of their parliaments. Only the Irish Free State, renamed Eire since 1937, decided to remain neutral.

EVACUEES.
SCHOOLCHILDREN
LEAVING LONDON
WITH NAME-
TAGS TIED TO
THEM AND GAS-
MASKS IN
RECTANGULAR
BOXES

16 The Nature of World War

THE Second World War was fought by pretty well the same contestants and for much the same reasons as the First. It began in the same way with an attack on a small country and it ended in the same way with the defeat of Germany. In both cases, there was a scapegoat whose wanton aggression seemed to have caused the war, though the Kaiser was never regarded with such detestation as Hitler nor did he ever possess the power and strength of character of the Austrian-born dictator.

Hitler was undoubtedly a monster of wickedness, not because of his cunning and duplicity in the conduct of foreign affairs (plenty of statesmen have shown similar qualities in the service of their countries) but because, as the author of the foul doctrines of Nazism, he was responsible for the enslavement, torture and murder of millions of human beings, many of them German citizens. Nazism, with its half-baked theories of racial superiority, its secret police, corrupt Youth movements, concentration camps and gas chambers, was a loathsome creed.

But it was not the sole cause of the war. There were deeper causes than Nazism, and the war might still have come about if Hitler had died of his war injuries in 1918.

Germany would have found another leader, possibly one less unpleasant, for there were others working to overthrow the Weimar Republic and to rebuild Germany before Hitler came on the scene. The cause of both wars was the position, indeed the very existence, of Germany. Because of her size, population, industrial skill and ambition, she was bound to become the strongest power in Europe and was bound to come into collision with Britain and France who, while keeping up their uneasy alliance, never agreed on methods of dealing with the German problem.

France would have preferred to keep Germany weak and impoverished but, finding that this was not possible, she sought security in alliances with Eastern Europe and in building the Maginot Line to protect herself from invasion. Britain's aim was to bring Germany back into the family of nations and to win her co-operation through appeasement. After Versailles, Germany could be neither kept down nor appeased and, although twice defeated and brought to the depths of exhaustion and apparent ruin, she has twice bounded up again in less than twenty years.

The Second World War differed from the First in a number of ways. In extent, it was very much wider; instead of being confined to the Western Front and a few minor theatres of war, it was fought right across Europe and, significantly, into Germany itself. Major campaigns took place in North Africa and the Atlantic Ocean and, with Japan's entry, all South-East Asia and the Pacific became a battle zone. In nature, it was " total war " to a much greater extent than in 1914–18.

Modern war had become a contest in production so that, in the end, victory went to the side that could turn out the greater volume of weapons and supplies. Factory-workers were as important as fighting-men and therefore the homes, factories, food and the will of civilians were targets for attack. Millions of civilians died from disease, starvation and bombing, besides those, such as the Jews, who were deliberately murdered. Terror became a weapon as potent as artillery. Civilian morale was ceaselessly attacked by propaganda, rumour, bombing, mass-executions and fearsome reprisals against any who resisted the conquerors. But, in some ways, brutality defeated its own ends. It strengthened the will to resist, and hatred became so intense that neither side could contemplate coming to terms with the other. Nothing less than " unconditional surrender " would do and the struggle had to be prolonged until the victors had pounded their opponents into the dust.

There were differences, too, in the actual fighting. The stalemate of trench warfare did not occur, for the technicians had solved the generals' problems of attack. Unlike the French and the British, the Germans had learnt from the mistakes of the First World War and had arrived at a technique founded upon speed, surprise and air power. Known as the " blitzkrieg " or *Blitzkrieg* " lightning war ", this consisted of violent bombing attacks on communications and key-positions behind the enemy lines; then, at the height of confusion which was added to by dive-bombers, parachutists and traitors, powerful columns of tanks would strike at chosen points, crash through the defences and penetrate deep into enemy territory. Motorised infantry accompanied this armoured spearhead and the rest of the army

AIR-RAID CASUALTY: THE INJURED WOMAN HOLDS THE HAND OF THE
MAN WHO HAD BURROWED THROUGH THE WRECKAGE FOR 13 HOURS TO
RESCUE HER

poured through the gaps and fanned outwards to mop up the
broken forces of the enemy and to seize control of the country.

In the early part of the war, these tactics enabled the Germans
to defeat countries like Poland, Holland and France with
astounding speed. Tanks and aeroplanes were the key weapons
in which, for a time, they had overwhelming superiority. There
was, however, a defect in this form of attack. It succeeded
against a small country in which rapid advances of seventy or
eighty miles a day speedily took the invaders clean across the
entire state. It also succeeded against a large country, such as
France, where defeatism and military incompetence failed to
stand up to the shock of novel tactics.

But tank columns could not advance indefinitely. Eventually,
human weariness and the need for fuel must bring them to a
halt and then might come the opportunity to cut them off, to
form a defensive front and, one day, to counter-attack. This is
what happened in Russia when Hitler turned upon his ally.
The Russians possessed the space, the fighting-spirit and the
numbers that were needed to cope with blitzkrieg tactics. They
suffered defeats and losses of territory but, with every mile of
retreat, they lengthened the German communications and drew
their enemy farther from the supplies that nourished his armies.
Hence, there eventually occurred slogging matches like those of

the First War and the casualties were correspondingly high. At least 4 million Russian soldiers were killed and 2 million Germans; but Britain, whose troops did not have to endure much of this kind of fighting, suffered but one-third of her 1914–18 losses in men killed.

At sea, the British Fleet of 1939 was overwhelmingly superior on the surface, for the Germans had not been able to rebuild the great navy of 1914 and there was no prospect of another Jutland. They possessed, however, a number of formidable vessels, specially designed for their nuisance value, including three " pocket battleships " and some fast cruisers, as well as two battleships nearing completion in the shipyards. As before, the main threat was to come from German submarines *War at sea* whose numbers and range increased to an alarming degree as the war progressed. Early on, there was also the menace of magnetic mines which were laid on the sea-bed of our coastal waters. The outstanding development in naval warfare was the use of aircraft and of aircraft carriers in which the Japanese were so far ahead of their contemporaries that they gained a series of whirlwind triumphs in 1941.

Aircraft, which had played a minor role in the First World War, dominated the Second. Paradoxically, there was a tendency both to exaggerate and to underestimate the usefulness of air-power. Bomber-raids, which in 1938 and 1939 were dreaded with an intensity of fear that amounted almost to panic, were *Air-power* considered to be so effective that they would wipe out cities overnight and would so disrupt civilian life and war-production that collapse would surely follow. In fact, until 1945, this was not so. Germany and Britain delivered innumerable bombing attacks upon each other without decisively affecting the course of the war.

Both sides inflicted fearful damage but the dispersal of war-factories, the strengthening of defences and the speed with which airfields and railways, for instance, could be repaired caused the raids to be more costly than they were worth. They certainly produced delays in production and transport but, as was proved when the war was over, each side exaggerated the effectiveness of its own bombing raids.

This does not detract from the heroism of the airmen and it is unfair to dismiss the Allied policy of bombing Germany into submission as a piece of senseless barbarity. For three years, Britain had scarcely any other means of striking at the enemy

A HALIFAX BOMBER

or of relieving the pressure upon Russia. In total war, the state of civilian morale was of absolute importance. Bombing actually strengthened the will of brave, determined people like the Germans and the British, but it might have been unbearable without the thought that the enemy was being paid back with interest. In the end, however, the war had to be won by armies on the ground and it was here that aircraft were essential weapons of attack; but Britain's policy of concentrating upon long-range bombers meant that her Army was kept short of support-aircraft.

The obvious exception to this was Japan which surrendered when its armies were undefeated. However, by that time, the atom bomb had reached a destructive power which previously existed only in the imagination. The early dramatic successes of the Germans and Japanese were due not only to their temporary superiority in air-power but to the fact that their senior commanders had studied how to use aircraft in close co-operation with land and sea forces. The Allies, particularly the British with their three separate Services, had to suffer some painful reverses before they, too, learned that it was suicidal to attempt landings or to move warships without powerful air support.

The war was more scientific and ruthless than any previous conflict. German scientists produced the magnetic mine, the " V.1 " Flying Bombs and the " V.2 " supersonic rockets which caused a great deal of damage in southern England. British scientists found an answer to the magnetic mine and, by producing radar they provided a means of tracking hostile aircraft, guiding bombers to their targets and enabling ships to locate the enemy. In addition, they helped the Americans to produce the atom bombs which, first tested in the desert of New Mexico, caused Japan's sudden surrender in August 1945.

More humanely, science reduced the number of deaths, for improved medical knowledge, surgery and, above all, the use of penicillin saved countless lives which otherwise would have been lost.

The key commodity of the war was oil, since, without it and its product petrol, the armies, navies and air forces were *Oil* unable to move. Much of the strategy of Britain and Germany was directed towards defending or obtaining the oil-wells which they lacked in their own countries. The failure of the Germans to seize the oil fields of the Caucasus and the Middle East was a major factor in their defeat.

The most distressing feature of the war was the inhumanity towards those for whom civilised persons would normally feel compassion or at least decency. Mass bombing of cities of no considerable military significance, such as Rotterdam and Munich; ill-treatment and murder of prisoners-of-war, as in *Inhumanity* Burma, Russia and Germany; reprisals against entire populations of villages, as in Lidice; and the brutal enslavement of workers forced to labour for their conquerors—all these pale into insignificance compared with the treatment meted out by Hitler's criminals to Jews and others who were sent to concentration camps.

There, with deliberate bestiality, mankind reached depths of cruelty almost beyond belief, but which can perhaps be faintly realised by the words of the German judge who presided over the trial of a few of those who carried out the work for Hitler:

" Auschwitz. . . . That hell inconceivable to any normal mind.   The poor human beings arrived, their possessions were taken from them, their clothes, their hair was shorn; they were given a few rags, or even left stark naked, here they were at the mercy of their cynical prefects and S.S. guards, plagued by vermin, covered in sores, hungry day and night . . . driven along roads like cattle and to do hard unaccustomed work; they were beaten, they were kicked, they were mocked and in the evening their guards rejoiced in making the exhausted creatures do exercises, " doing sport ", as it was called, until the poor martyred bodies fainted and this became an excuse to shoot them.

" This was their daily existence, until life itself was taken from them in the gas chambers. There they died, naked, packed one against another, with their prisoner's number scrawled on their skin, men separated from their wives and children. It was death by suffocation, after a last struggle for air, the still living standing on the bodies of the dead."

BELSEN: VICTIMS
OF NAZI
BRUTALITY

17 The Second World War

In September 1939, the blitzkrieg went into action. Poland was invaded from a number of points by armoured divisions which pressed swiftly across the flat countryside, by-passing strong points of resistance which were dealt with by the follow-up armies. Complete air supremacy was gained from the outset when the Polish air force was mostly destroyed on the ground, and thereafter the Germans were able to give undivided air support to their own forces.

The Poles, who had not had time to mobilise fully, made the mistake of spreading their forces along the frontier so that, when the enemy broke through, there were insufficient central reserves to check his progress. In a matter of days, the Polish High Command had lost control of the situation and, on 17th September, when resistance had practically collapsed, the Russians crossed the almost undefended eastern frontier. Stalin was anxious to grab his half of Poland before Hitler had taken the entire country. Warsaw held out bravely for another ten days but, within a month, Poland had been conquered.

Britain and France watched the destruction of their ally with stupefied amazement. But they did nothing to help her. While the bulk of Germany's armed strength was engaged in the East, the French Army commanded by General Gamelin sat tight behind the Maginot Line and did not disturb the smaller German Army opposite by so much as firing their guns. As in 1914, the British transported their small army across the Channel but, apart from one air-raid on German warships, they confined their activities to dropping leaflets, because the French felt that bombing raids would lead to attacks on their own factories.

In some ways, this inactivity on the part of the French High Command was justifiable. By the time they could have been ready to launch an offensive, Poland had fallen and the German divisions were returning to the West. The memory of French losses in the previous war and the influence of that aged pessimist, Marshal Pétain, were enough to make them hesitate to hurl their young men against Germany's fortifications. Almost all the generals believed that attack was a suicidal policy. However, what should have been more alarming than the French caution was the shortage of armour in the Allied forces (the British Expeditionary Force did not have *one* armoured division) and the obvious decay of the Frenchman's traditional fighting spirit.

2. " THE PHONEY WAR "

Through the winter of 1939, so little happened on the Western Front that the Americans dubbed this the " Phoney War ". The British Army, under General Gort, busied itself with defence works opposite the Belgian frontier; the French made a cautious advance towards the enemy and drew back to the Maginot Line before anything happened; the Belgians, anxious to avoid provoking Hitler, refused to form a common front with the Allies.

At home, in Britain, the non-arrival of the dreaded air-raids brought the evacuees back to the towns, air-raid shelters appeared in back-gardens, and food rationing came into force. This time, there were no enthusiastic queues at the recruiting offices, for a measure of conscription had been introduced in April 1939 and the country's manhood waited its turn to be called up for service according to age and occupation.

There was nothing phoney about the war at sea. The Navy had been busy from the first day, when the Germans announced their intentions by torpedoing the liner *Athenia*. In October, to the consternation of the Admiralty, a U-boat penetrated the great naval base at Scapa Flow and sank the battleship *Royal Oak* as she lay at anchor. Further alarms were provided by the magnetic mines and by the brief appearance in the Atlantic of two German battle-cruisers which were heroically tackled by the converted passenger-ship, the *Rawalpindi*. In December, the pocket battleship *Admiral Graf von Spee*, on a voyage of destruction, was attacked off South America by three British cruisers and driven into the estuary of the River Plate where she was scuttled on Hitler's own order.

For the most part, the Royal Navy's tasks were less dramatic but equally vital to the nation's survival. In addition to keeping a ceaseless watch against U-boats and surface raiders, to guarding our coasts and the transport of troops, ocean convoys (intro-

duced, this time, from the beginning) had to be brought safely into port since upon them depended Britain's food and the supplies of war.

3. FINLAND, DENMARK AND NORWAY

Half of Poland had fallen into Stalin's grasp and, to push forward Russia's Baltic defences, he decided to seize the states of Estonia, Latvia and Lithuania. These were taken without difficulty and demands were then made upon Finland, whose borders ran uncomfortably close to Leningrad. Russia required certain islands, ports and frontier changes which the Finns refused and, in November 1939, Russian forces invaded Finland, a country with 4 million inhabitants and an army of some 200,000 men. To everyone's astonishment the Finns held the Mannerheim Line (a defence-system named after their veteran leader General Mannerheim) and inflicted some humiliating set-backs upon the Russians. However, weight of numbers told and, by March 1940, the Finns had to admit defeat and yield the territory that Stalin required.

The Russo-Finnish campaign

The Finnish campaign convinced Hitler, among others, that the Russians would be easy to defeat; in fact, they had learned from their mistakes much more thoroughly than anyone gave them credit for. The French and British, who had done virtually nothing in the war so far, were actually on the point of sending an army to help the Finns. This would have meant taking on Russia as well as Germany, not to mention Norway and Sweden who would have refused the passage of troops!

A more realistic reason for the Allies' interest in Scandinavia was Germany's dependence upon Swedish iron-ore which was carried in German ships along the coast of Norway. It was therefore sensible to try to cut off these vital supplies, as well as to do something active in the war, because defeatism was seeping into France's huge army of bored soldiers.

As a first move, mines were laid in Norwegian waters and,

on 4th April, buoyed up perhaps by an apparently successful meeting with the new French Premier, M. Reynaud, Chamberlain announced that Hitler had " missed the bus ". The Allies, he felt, had overcome their former weakness and the enemy's chance of victory had slipped away. Chamberlain's knack of making utterances which bounced back disastrously had not deserted him. Five days later, the storm broke.

On 9th April German troops overwhelmed Denmark and seized every town and airfield in Norway, except Narvik. Here, the British Navy sank some German destroyers and *Norway* covered the landing of a small Allied force. Further south, *conquered* French and British troops were put ashore near Trondheim but, lacking air-support, their position was so hopeless that the survivors soon had to be evacuated. Norway, with its long coastline facing the Atlantic, fell into the hands of the Germans whose swift assault was aided by a home-bred traitor named Quisling.

The proximity of Germany and the difficulties of rendering military aid at short notice made Norway's downfall certain and the Allied intervention was no more than a token gesture of friendship. But the British public did not see it that way. The miserable showing of their own troops and the insolence of Hitler's easy triumph after Chamberlain's talk of " missing the bus ", filled them with angry indignation. Their demand for a new leader, one who had never taken Hitler's hand or tried to appease him, led to Chamberlain's resignation and to Churchill's acceptance of the office of Prime Minister.

NARVIK BAY
10 APRIL 1940,
AFTER ATTACK
BY BRITISH
WARSHIPS

It was 10th May 1940 and Churchill, deep in thought about his new responsibilities, had walked from Downing Street to his old office at the Admiralty when he became aware of visitors:

"The Dutch Ministers were in my room. Haggard and worn, with horror in their eyes, they had just flown over from Amsterdam. Their country had been attacked without the slightest pretext or warning. The avalanche of fire and steel had rolled across the frontiers, and when resistance broke out and the Dutch frontier guards fired, an overwhelming onslaught was made from the air. The whole country was in a state of wild confusion."

Attack on Holland

Hitler had launched his attack on the West and the phoney war was over.

4. THE FALL OF FRANCE

Holland was overwhelmed in four days. The speed and power of the assault paralysed her defences and her civilian population was terrorised by the bombing of undefended Rotterdam. On 14th May the Dutch Army surrendered and Queen Wilhelmina escaped to England.

Meanwhile, a simultaneous attack on Belgium had caused the British and French to move up to the assistance of the Belgian Army which had already lost the Albert Canal line. However, there was a second defence line along the River Dyle which was held by the Belgians in the north, by the British in the centre and by the French 1st and 9th Armies from Wavre to the French frontier.

The 9th Army, the worst equipped of the French forces, covered the Ardennes, a stretch of forested country thought to be so unsuitable for attack that its prepared defences had been neglected.* But in this very area, between Sedan and Namur, the Germans concentrated powerful armoured forces under General von Rundstedt which broke clean through, crossed the Meuse and came out into open country. Rundstedt swept on due west towards the Channel coast. This colossal blow, perfectly aimed at the weakest point, threatened to cut off the Allies in Belgium from the rest of the armies in France.

* It was said that tree-felling would have halted the German tanks, but this was not carried out because it would have hampered the French cavalry!

In actual numbers, there was little difference between the
contestants, but, in all other respects, the Germans were immensely superior, with eight armoured divisions plus six more
of light tanks, against four French armoured divisions. In the
air, the German superiority was three to one and this was
increased when the small Belgian air force was wiped out and
the French aeroplanes were driven from the skies. The R.A.F.
squadrons fought well but were soon reduced to about fifty
machines and although four fresh squadrons were sent from
Britain, the R.A.F. found itself operating from airfields so far
in the rear that its effectiveness was much reduced.

German morale was high. Their troops moved forward
with the confidence and experience of earlier successes, reinforced by good radio communications which enabled fighters
and dive-bombers to operate in close support of the advancing
columns. The Allies, on the other hand, were confused by the
speed of events. Their communications were imperfect and the
French tanks were scattered along the front, instead of being
held in concentration to make counter-attacks against the enemy
flanks.

The German thrust through the Ardennes made it essential
for the British and French forces in the north to rejoin the main
French Army without delay. Precious time was lost, however,

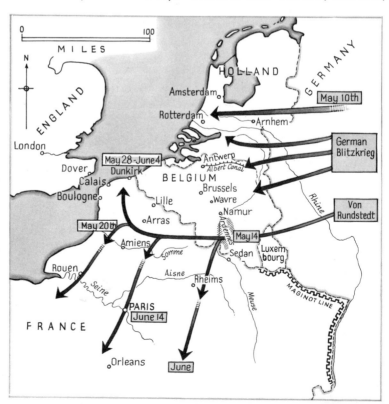

THE BATTLE OF
FRANCE, 1940

while the French general waited for orders and it was not until 16th May that the withdrawal began. By this time the roads were choked with refugees and the Germans were pouring troops into the gap made by Rundstedt.

Although M. Reynaud replaced General Gamelin by General Weygand, the French were showing a marked lack of determination and the Belgians, under severe pressure, were beginning to crumble. By 19th May, when the Germans took Amiens, the B.E.F., the Belgians and the French 1st Army were well nigh trapped. Gort, who had already thrown garrisons into Calais and Boulogne (the latter had to be abandoned), made a determined effort to break out on 21st May but the enemy was too strong and Weygand's attack from the south on the German wedge did not succeed. Still fighting, the B.E.F. and the French 1st Army had reached the River Lys when, on 24th May, the Belgian Army's surrender made their position desperate. Gort's left was undefended and German armour pressing down the coast would complete the encirclement.

In order to save his army from annihilation, Gort therefore decided to make for the coast in the hope that as many troops as possible would be taken off by sea. Although he would assist the French to escape, he felt that his first duty was towards his own men. On 28th May he had formed a defensive perimeter round Dunkirk which steadily shrank to a small area west of the town where, on the open beach, thousands of British and French troops, bereft now of their stores, equipment and even their weapons, waited for rescue.

DUNKIRK: THE LAST OF THE BRITISH TROOPS

Belgian surrender

Dunkirk

A spirited defence of Calais held up the Germans for several precious days during which 337,000 troops were taken off by a fleet of " little ships " ranging from destroyers to fishing-boats. Overhead, the R.A.F., operating from home bases, did its utmost to lessen the severity of the German air attacks and, by 4th June, the mass of the B.E.F. had been saved and about 110,000 Frenchmen.

In some ways, Dunkirk was a triumph, especially for the Royal Navy whose admiral organised the rescue. The British elevated Dunkirk to the level of a victory. In fact, it was a most disastrous defeat. The Army's entire equipment was lost so that, even if the men could be returned to help France in her agony, they had nothing to fight with. Worse, the French, who could scarcely be expected to think highly of an ally whose 40-odd million inhabitants had contributed an army of only 230,000 men, felt that they had been left in the lurch and this did nothing to stiffen their resistance to the blows that now fell upon them.

On 5th June the Germans attacked south of the Somme and swept towards Rouen. By the 10th they were over the Seine; on the 12th the French Government left the capital, and on the 14th Paris was taken without resistance. Frantic appeals were made for help and although the R.A.F. continued to assist France until the end, the British Government refused to release its last reserves of air strength.

In a final attempt to encourage the French to keep up the struggle, Churchill offered a complete union of the two countries and a promise to assist the fight even into North Africa. Reynaud accepted but the rest of his colleagues rejected the offer with angry disdain. " Better be a Nazi province! " cried one minister and Pétain declared it would mean " union with a corpse ".

Collapse of France

The French armies collapsed, some without even going into action; Reynaud resigned and old Pétain, who embraced defeat almost lovingly, came to the head of affairs. On 16th June he asked for an armistice. The Germans, bent on total humiliation of their enemy, did not reply at once and this gave Mussolini time to join in the kill, though his attack in the south was easily repulsed and his gain amounted to one French town. On 22nd June France surrendered.

Germany's terms were hard. The whole of northern France and all the Atlantic coast were to be occupied by German troops. The French would pay for the occupation, would hand over all war equipment, prisoners and refugees and would allow their country to be used as a springboard for attack on their ally. The southern remnant of the country was given a pro-German French Government at Vichy where the leading ministers were Pétain and Pierre Laval.

Only one Frenchman of note was prepared to fight on. He was General de Gaulle who had commanded an armoured division with some success. This proud uncompromising officer escaped to London where he placed himself at the head of the " Free French " forces who joined him in exile, though, considering the proximity of France, these were but a handful of his countrymen.

Britain was deeply concerned about the future of the French Fleet, since, with Italy in the war and certain to try to dominate the Mediterranean, it was essential to prevent a large number of warships from falling into enemy hands. Unfortunately the French Navy, apart from a few small vessels, showed no sign of wishing to join Britain. French ships at Portsmouth and Plymouth were therefore taken over and, at Alexandria, a French squadron had to be disarmed under threat of sinking. At Oran, in French Morocco, the admiral was given the choice of joining the British fleet or sailing to a British port or to a French port in the West Indies. All were refused, whereupon the British opened fire and inflicted crippling losses upon his force. This attack and another upon a battleship at Dakar provoked bitter feelings in France and in the French colonies. Indeed, in some quarters, Britain was regarded as an enemy only slightly less hateful than the German conqueror.

5. THE BATTLE OF BRITAIN

The British Commonwealth now stood alone. " In three weeks England will have her neck wrung like a chicken ", remarked General Weygand; and Hitler, like almost everyone else, expected that Churchill would ask for terms. The position seemed hopeless and there were many responsible persons who felt that the only prudent course was to end the war before complete disaster enveloped the nation. At this sombre moment, Churchill spoke out:

" What has happened in France makes no difference to our actions and purpose ", he said on 17th June. " We

CHURCHILL
LEAVES 10
DOWNING ST.
TO MAKE HIS
SPEECH ON 17
JUNE 1940

have become the sole champions now in arms to defend the world cause . . . We shall defend our Island home and with the British Empire we shall fight on unconquerable until the curse of Hitler is lifted from the brows of mankind."

On the next day, he ended another speech with these memorable words,

"Let us therefore address ourselves to our duty and so bear ourselves that if the British Commonwealth of Nations and Empire last for a thousand years men will still say 'This was their finest hour'."

The effect of these defiant words upon the British people was incalculable. As always in their history, they responded to real leadership and, having been told the worst, they decided to get on with the job of beating Hitler. How it would be done, neither they nor anyone else knew, but at least there was plenty to do for the time being.

Strenuous efforts were made to prepare for the expected invasion by fortifying the south and east coasts, by reorganising the Dunkirk troops and replacing their lost equipment as speedily as possible. Additional age-groups registered for military service and older men enrolled in the local Home Guard, in order to attack parachutists with shotguns, pikes and any improvised weapons that came to hand.

Realists might consider that such fortitude amounted to folly but the nation found courage and unity that it had never known when facing Napoleon or in the darkest days of 1918. Even so, this brave determination might have been of no more avail than it was in, say, Norway or Belgium, had it not been for the narrow stretch of water that divided England from the continent.

The Battle of Britain The Channel stood between Hitler and complete victory. His tanks, shock-troops and the victorious divisions that had sliced through so many defences could reach their last opponent only in ships. While the ships and troop-barges were being assembled, the R.A.F. must be destroyed for, with air support, the Royal Navy could deal with any invasion fleet. Thus, the key to the situation was control of the air.

On 8th August, the Battle of Britain began with heavy bomber attacks on shipping along the south coast. Next, the enemy switched to fighter airfields in the south and south-east. Goering, Commander-in-Chief of the German *Luftwaffe*, had planned to drive the R.A.F. from its advanced bases and then,

"SCRAMBLE!" FIGHTER PILOTS DURING THE BATTLE OF BRITAIN

by attacking targets which Fighter Command must defend, to destroy the British fighters in the air. Against him were barely 1,500 pilots in fifty-five fighter squadrons which included six night-fighter squadrons of Blenheims, too slow to take much part in day operations. The rest were Hurricanes and Spitfires (the former outnumbering the latter by four to one) with two squadrons of Defiants.

The Luftwaffe possessed fully twice as many aircraft but many were necessarily bombers and, for the first time, the Germans were opposed by an extremely efficient air force. In the first phase of the battle, their losses numbered several times those of the R.A.F. and so, after a period of rest for the air crews, a fresh series of attacks was launched with more fighters accompanying the bombers.

Between 1st and 5th September there were eleven major attacks against inland targets in which the R.A.F. claimed 562 enemy aircraft destroyed to their own loss of 219 with 132 pilots saved. On the 7th, a mass daylight attack was made on London, followed by a night assault when the bombers were guided in by the fires still burning below. Day and night attacks were kept up until 15th September, the day of the greatest onslaught, when the engagement was fought all day high above the fields of Kent and Sussex. The German losses were very heavy, though perhaps not more than a third of the number that the R.A.F. claimed. At all events, they were too costly to be endured, especially as the destruction of every bomber meant the permanent loss of about five trained airmen who were far more difficult to replace than machines. In all, the Luftwaffe lost 1,733 aircraft to the R.A.F.'s 900-odd.

After the peak of the battle on 15th September, the attacks tailed off and by about 5th October the day-bombers came no more, apart from a few heavily escorted fighter-bombers. By the end of the month, the Battle of Britain may be said to have ended. Goering broke it off because the Luftwaffe was beaten, though, as the country was soon to learn, it was far from broken. The invasion, which was probably cancelled before the air-battle ended, had to be abandoned.

The Battle of Britain, fought by a few thousand pilots, mechanics and operations-room personnel, was one of the decisive victories of the war.

A decisive victory   A number of factors saved Britain from becoming a German colony. First, whilst the opposing air forces were closely matched, the Spitfire was slightly superior to the Messerschmidt 109 and the Me. 110, and the Hurricane, slower than these three, was nevertheless a first-class aeroplane and highly effective against the bombers. Second, the R.A.F. fighter-pilots, who knew themselves to be every bit as good if not better than the enemy, had the advantage of fighting above their own country for the most part, so that if a pilot was forced to " bale out ", he usually came safely to ground and was quickly back in his own squadron. Moreover, they were attacking an enemy who was usually flying in formation, with the fighters guarding the bombers on their way to an ascertainable target. Third, Fighter Command was well organised for its task. A chain of radar stations tracked incoming aircraft and passed the information (supplemented overland by Observer Corps reports) to Group and Sector operations rooms whose controllers dealt with the situation and organised defences where they were most needed.

By the end, every day-fighter squadron but one had taken part in the battle and many were near to exhaustion. Bomber Command played a vital role in the struggle by attacking enemy airfields and barge-concentrations along the French coast with such resolution that their own losses were actually greater than those of Fighter Command.

From the autumn of 1940 the Germans concentrated on night-bombing of London and the larger ports and cities. The chief

DURING THE
" BLITZ " THE
LONDON
UNDERGROUND
BECAME AN
AIR-RAID
SHELTER

sufferers were Southampton, Bristol, Liverpool, Glasgow, Coventry and Birmingham in which, as in many smaller towns, widespread damage was caused and nearly 18,000 civilians were killed in three months. Defences against the night-bomber were still in their infancy. Anti-aircraft guns and searchlights, few in numbers and as yet relatively inaccurate, accounted for only a tiny percentage of the raiders, and night-fighters had to rely on luck and keen eyesight. However, the use of radar began to bring better results.

The R.A.F. retaliated with raids on Western Germany and, during the winter, Berlin itself was reached. Attacks were also made across the Alps on Milan and Turin but whereas the Germans could operate from airfields close to Britain, the R.A.F. had to cover immense distances to reach its targets.

6. THE BALKANS AND NORTH AFRICA

While the air war was being fought in Europe, Mussolini attacked the British-held Middle East. Here General Wavell had but 90,000 troops and miserably inadequate supplies of tanks and aircraft to oppose the Italian armies of over 400,000 men poised in Libya and Abyssinia. However, Italian morale was even feebler than that of the French, and after Wavell had repulsed a hesitant advance upon Egypt, the arrival of fifty tanks enabled him to carry out a bold counter-attack.

Wavell's victory

In January 1941 the Italians fled in disorder towards Benghazi, abandoning the coastal towns and masses of equipment. In a simultaneous campaign, British and Commonwealth forces liberated Abyssinia and restored Haile Selassie to his throne. In both theatres, thousands of prisoners were taken and Wavell would have driven the Italians clean out of Libya but for events in the Balkans.

Here Mussolini had attacked Greece from Albania, but his gimcrack legions which were meant to revive the glories of the Roman Empire received a beating from the fiery Greeks. Hitler meanwhile had compelled Rumania, Hungary and Bulgaria to join the Axis alliance and was therefore in a position to finish the work that Mussolini had started so badly. In April 1941 a blitzkrieg was launched against Yugoslavia and Greece.

Having promised to help Greece, Churchill ordered Wavell to send part of his slender forces to that country. The result was disastrous. Yugoslavia was beaten in ten days and the full force of the German invasion fell upon Greece which put up a stout but hopeless resistance.

The British troops under General Wilson had to be evacuated by the Royal Navy and the decision was taken to put 27,000 men, nearly half of them Australians and New Zealanders, ashore in Crete in the hope of holding the island. But Crete was within easy reach of the airfields on the Greek mainland and the Germans mounted an air-offensive which speedily ousted the

Crete

R.A.F. and silenced the anti-aircraft guns. Although the Navy smashed an attempt to invade by sea, the Germans brought in sufficient troops by gliders and parachutes to make the island untenable and, at the end of May, under heavy bombing, about half the British force was evacuated.

In retrospect, it is possible to see that the defeats in Greece and Crete may have prevented worse defeats elsewhere. If Hitler had not invaded Greece, he would have been able to attack Russia at least a month earlier, a month which might have brought him the total victory that he so narrowly missed. Furthermore, if he had sent German troops earlier to North Africa, they might have prevented Wavell from winning his brilliant campaign.

One happier result of Britain's decision to send help to Greece had been the defeat of the Italian Navy. It had suffered losses in November 1940 when the Fleet Air Arm made an audacious attack on the battleships in Taranto harbour and, in March

1941, when attempting to prevent convoys reaching Greece, an Italian fleet was severely trounced off Cape Matapan by Admiral Cunningham.

However, at the time, the picture was exceedingly gloomy. With Yugoslavia and Greece gone, Hitler was master of almost every country in Europe, so much so that he could afford to send to North Africa one of his finest generals, Rommel, and the superbly equipped Afrika Korps. With open contempt for their allies, the Germans took over control from the Italians and forced the British to fall back to the Egyptian frontier. Wavell daringly left a strong force, mainly of Australians, behind the enemy front at Tobruk, a fortified port which proved to be a most irritating thorn in Rommel's side.

ROMMEL

7. THE ATTACK ON RUSSIA

In after years, Hitler's decision to invade Russia appeared to be an act of incredible folly, a blunder that destroyed him, his armies and all the fruits of the German victories. What then induced him to take such a course?

Churchill records a conversation with von Ribbentrop in 1937, when the then German Ambassador suggested that Britain should allow Germany to have a free hand in Eastern Europe. Besides Poland, she needed White Russia and the Ukraine to provide *Lebensraum*, living-space, for her growing population.

This ambition was never far from Hitler's mind. His conquest of the West was only a preliminary to the essential task of expunging Communism from the face of Europe and giving Germany the rich farm land, the minerals and the oil that the " master race " required. To gain these, he must destroy Russia's armies and, after their showing against the Finns, he had no doubts on that score. His panzer divisions would advance even more swiftly against a foe who was still using horse-drawn transport than they had done in Poland, and to those of his generals who dared to murmur their doubts, he could retort that he had no intention of losing his magnificent armies in the wastes of Siberia.

European Russia would suffice; a line from Leningrad to the mouth of the Volga would mark the limit of his conquest. It would enclose all the worthwhile wealth of Russia and he would have it all by the autumn of 1941 or, at worst, by the following summer.

Stalin appears to have been curiously unaware of the German preparations. He made no effort to check Hitler's advance into the Balkans nor did he pay attention to a warning sent by Churchill.

On 22nd June 1941, the Germans attacked along an immense front, with some 150 divisions to which could be added more than twenty others from Rumania, Hungary, Finland and Italy. The Russians mustered a similar number of divisions and, if the war lasted, they could call upon far more numerous reserves. In armour, equipment and aircraft, they were inferior, but by no means to the degree that Hitler had expected, and it was soon apparent that the Russian soldier had lost none of his stubborn fighting qualities.

German victories

Progress across eastern Poland was rapid and by 1st July the Germans were in Minsk. They advanced in three main thrusts, north-west through the Baltic States towards Leningrad, eastwards in the centre towards Smolensk and Moscow and south-east through Kiev to the Ukraine. There was also a drive from Rumania towards Odessa on the Black Sea.

THE RUSSIAN
FRONT

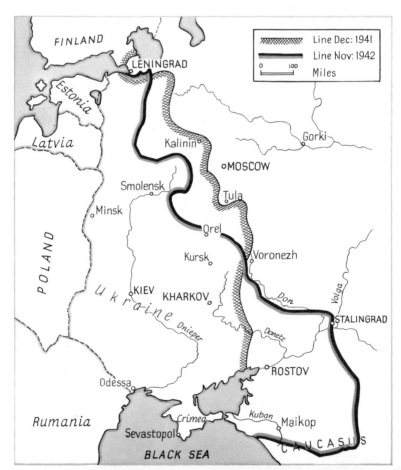

Smolensk was reached on 16th July but three weeks of hard tank fighting took place before it fell. This was an unexpected delay, and the Germans were beginning to feel the effects of bad roads and of large bodies of partisans attacking their communications. Colossal efforts were made by the Todt labour organisation to rebuild roads and railways and to establish supply depots behind the advance but time was passing and although the Russians were suffering one defeat after another, they showed no sign of cracking.

By mid-August the offensive was slowing down, except in the Southern Ukraine where a Russian collapse carried Rundstedt's army to the Dnieper. This enabled the Germans to envelop a huge pocket of Russians around Kiev where over half a million men were captured. On 1st October Hitler renewed the offensive against Moscow which he had slackened in order to make territorial gains to the north and the south. In a fearsome onslaught that lasted right through November, the Germans came to within 30 miles of the capital. But the Russians, now under General Zhukov, their finest commander, resisted every yard of ground and, on 5th December, the Germans decided to cease offensive operations for the winter. Since June they had advanced 700 miles. Although they had not captured Leningrad or Moscow, their line ran from the Baltic to Rostov and they had inflicted such tremendous damage upon Stalin's

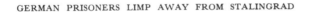

GERMAN PRISONERS LIMP AWAY FROM STALINGRAD

armies and industry that it seemed unlikely that Russia could survive another campaign.

Churchill's response to the German attack had been an immediate offer to Russia of such help as Britain could give. He still hated Communism and could barely conceal his distrust of Stalin but he made it clear that any country attacked by Hitler could count on Britain's friendship. At the same time, he once again reminded the United States of America of the danger of standing by while Hitler triumphed.

8. AMERICA ENTERS THE WAR

In 1939, despite President Roosevelt's sympathy for the Allies, the United States Congress and the American people were resolved to keep out of a European war. Thus, to obtain war supplies, Britain had to pay for them in dollars and carry them in her own ships.

By December 1940 there were practically no dollars left, but Churchill's personal letter to Roosevelt convinced the President that some way must be found to aid Britain. It was Lease-Lend, " the most unsordid act in the history of any nation ". From March 1941 the President was permitted to manufacture, lease or lend supplies to a government whose defence he deemed " vital to the defence of the United States ".

Thus the U.S.A. came actively to Britain's aid and, in August 1941, Churchill and Roosevelt met at sea off Newfoundland to draw up the Atlantic Charter. Together, they announced to the world their reasons for resisting tyranny and their desire *Atlantic* to establish peace, freedom and liberty everywhere. In spite *Charter* of the close understanding between these two leaders, it would have been more than difficult for the President to induce his countrymen to enter the European war had not Japan's attack been followed by Hitler's declaration of war on the United States.

Japan had been at war since 1937 with China whose vast size and population enabled her to put up an enduring resistance. Supplies of arms reached China through French Indo-China and over the Burma Road, and when Japan decided to close this door, Pétain, in France, was in no position to resist. By July 1941 the Japanese had occupied Indo-China. At this, the United States, followed by Britain and the Dutch East Indies, put a complete stop to all trade with Japan.

Japan's leaders, notably General Tojo, realising that their country's overstrained economy had suffered a critical blow, decided to take a gamble that offered the most dazzling prospects of success.

In South-East Asia there were vast riches, most of them belonging to Britain and Holland who, owing to the situation in Europe, could do little to defend their possessions. Above all, there was oil in the Dutch East Indies and, provided the U.S.A. did not interfere, it would be easy to conquer Malaya and the East Indies. The key to war in this area was naval strength and if America's fleet could be drastically reduced, Japan's superiority must surely lead to limitless triumphs.

Thus, on 7th December 1941, a force of 105 Japanese carrier-borne aircraft attacked the American fleet anchored in Pearl Harbour in the Hawaiian islands. Despite warnings, the American commanders had taken no serious precautions and in a very short time five battleships were sunk, three put out of action, with three cruisers and many smaller craft destroyed, besides well over 100 aircraft. At one stroke, Japan achieved sea and air supremacy in the Pacific.

Pearl Harbour

Pearl Harbour was followed by a series of lightning blows. The American naval bases at Guam and Wake Island were taken; two of Britain's largest ships, the *Prince of Wales* and the *Repulse*, sailing without adequate air-cover, were sunk by bombers in December; Hong Kong fell on Christmas Day, Manila in the Philippine Islands on 2nd January and Singapore on 15th February.

This " impregnable " British naval base surrendered to a

PEARL HARBOUR IMMEDIATELY AFTER THE JAPANESE ATTACK

Singapore comparatively small Japanese assault force that came down the Malayan peninsula and easily entered the mighty fortress by the back door. All its guns and defences faced seawards. 70,000 British troops, many of whom had just landed, went into captivity where they had to endure the torture, starvation and forced labour which the Japanese gleefully inflicted upon their prisoners.

By March 1942 the Dutch East Indies had fallen; by May the Americans, fighting strongly now, suffered further defeat in the Philippines, and the British were driven out of Burma to the Indian frontier. Everywhere the Japs proved themselves to be ruthless and efficient fighters, especially in the jungles where, almost naked and carrying only a rifle and bag of rice, they could outwit opponents encumbered by heavy stores and equipment.

When most of New Guinea fell, Australia's position was critical but the American victory in the Battle of the Coral Sea (7th–8th May) checked the Japanese advance. This was *Midway* followed by a greater victory on 3rd–5th June, off Midway *Island* Island where the destruction of Japanese aircraft-carriers tipped the balance of strength back in America's favour. After this, under General MacArthur's leadership, the Americans and the Australians began to fight back, "island hopping" towards Japan. In August 1942 there began the struggle for Guadalcanal in the Solomon Islands which lasted for six months. In the end the Japanese were driven out and MacArthur was ready for his next leap forward.

9. STALINGRAD

During the winter of 1941 the Russians showed enormous perseverance in pushing back the front opposite Moscow and in transferring entire factories far to the east out of range of the enemy. In addition, Lease-Lend was extended to Russia so that Britain gave up huge quantities of war-supplies which otherwise would have come to her own use. The Russians clamoured for more help and constantly reproached their ally for not opening a Second Front in the West although, as Churchill pointed out, Britain was already stretched to the limit.

The Germans, who had stoically endured the Russian winter, were ready to renew the offensive in early summer of 1942. Hitler, having taken supreme command of his armies, did not intend to resume the attack on Moscow. His plan now was to break Russia by a colossal drive to the south-east. This would give him the industrial region of the Donetz basin, the grainlands of the Kuban area and the oilfields of the Caucasus.

Sevastopol in the Crimea was captured in July and the oil-fields had been reached by August. With the Germans driving on towards the Caspian Sea, the whole of south-east Russia seemed to be lost. However, the Russians were holding out obstinately in two towns, Voronezh on the Don and Stalingrad on the Volga. It was risky to continue with the advance until at least one of these strong points had been taken. Hitler therefore halted the Caucasus offensive in order to concentrate upon capturing Stalingrad.

A grim yard-by-yard struggle took place amid the ruins of the city where tanks were largely useless and even aircraft could do nothing to dislodge the defenders. In November the Russians counter-attacked from north and south, broke through the Rumanian and Italian divisions holding the flanks and succeeded in surrounding the city and isolating the German Sixth Army. Hitler ordered its commander, General Paulus, to fight to the end, and the Germans did so until 2nd February 1943 when 22,000 half-frozen survivors out of an army of 200,000 surrendered.

This disaster, the turning-point in the East, forced the Germans to abandon their conquests farther south and to withdraw from the Caucasus altogether. Thus, by March 1943, their reduced line ran from near Leningrad (still uncaptured) to 275 miles west of Moscow to Orel, Kharkov and Rostov in the south. *The turning-point of the war*

The Russians had pushed the invader back some 200 miles and had wiped out hundreds of thousands of his best troops. Furthermore, the R.A.F.'s heavy raids on Germany were reducing aircraft production and holding down large numbers of fighters to defend the West so that the Soviet Air Force was able to operate on equal terms, and by the middle of 1943 it had gained air superiority. After Stalingrad, the German armies were always on the defensive. They won no more victories.

10. ALAMEIN

In North Africa, Wavell was replaced by General Auchinleck who, in November 1941, launched an offensive from Egypt that drove Rommel back and brought relief to Tobruk. In order to

Malta besieged

assist Rommel, the Axis air forces opened a heavy assault upon Malta, the base from which British submarines and aircraft had been attacking convoys of German troops and supplies. Operating from nearby Sicily, enemy bombers pounded the island for weeks on end and did such damage to the Navy and to incoming British convoys that, although Malta survived, Rommel received the supplies that he needed.

In May 1942 he attacked the British Eighth Army and in a series of tank battles drove it back with heavy losses, captured Tobruk with more than 20,000 prisoners and, pushing on at thirty miles a day, forced his way across the Egyptian frontier. Auchinleck, unable even to hold the position from which Wavell had begun his offensive eighteen months earlier, fell back to El Alamein where, in the thirty-five mile gap between the sea and the impassable Qattora Depression, he formed a defence line. If it broke, Egypt, the Suez Canal, the Middle East oil, India and perhaps the war itself were lost. On 1st July, Rommel attacked and was sharply repulsed. He therefore decided to pause until adequate supplies, particularly of petrol, could reach him along his immensely long communication lines.

Meanwhile Britain, powerfully aided by America, was pouring men and materials into Egypt at such a rate that, for the first time, there was superiority in numbers of troops, with guns, tanks and aircraft as good as the enemy's. They also possessed a new spirit of confidence. Auchinleck, a fine courageous soldier, had to make way for another commander and General Alexander, who had distinguished himself in

MEN OF AN ADVANCED MOTOR COLUMN HARASS ROMMEL'S SUPPLY LINE

NORTH AFRICA

Burma, became C.-in-C. Middle East with General Montgomery in command of the Eighth Army.

Montgomery, a razor-sharp personality with an eye for his soldiers' welfare and a nose for victory, made the most of his good fortune in reaching the top when his country's war-effort was in full swing. He had complete faith in himself, and his army came to share that faith. At a time when the public badly needed a soldier-hero, Montgomery proved himself to be their man. *Montgomery*

Realising that Rommel was bound to attack, Montgomery prepared a trap for his redoubtable enemy. Leaving the southern part of his line comparatively weak, he concentrated his strongest forces in an east-west ridge (Alam Halfa). So, when on 31st August 1942 Rommel made a deep penetration in the south and turned north to roll up the British front, he ran into a powerful concentration of British armour and artillery. After a week's severe fighting, he was forced to retire and to await Montgomery's counter-attack.

It did not come until 23rd October because a full moon was necessary for negotiating enemy minefields and Montgomery, never a general to take unnecessary risks, needed time to complete his plans. Preceded by a colossal bombardment by 800 guns, the attack was a success. In a hard, drawn-out battle, both sides suffered heavy losses but Montgomery, confident that in men and materials he had the measure of the enemy, coolly kept up the pressure until Rommel had lost the greater part of his tanks and fully half of his men. Abandoning the Italians, Rommel retreated to his old position at Agheila where he at least had the advantage of shorter supply lines whereas the British had now to move materials over ever-increasing distances.

Alamein was a great victory even if it did not annihilate the enemy as Montgomery had hoped. However, he forced Rommel to fall back another 250 miles, prised him out of his next position and, by January 1943, had chased him as far west as Tripoli. In tremendous heart, the Eighth Army pressed on into Tunisia where Rommel took up position in the fortified line at Mareth. Meanwhile an Allied force had landed in the rear of the Germans.

On 8th November American and British armies went ashore at Casablanca, Oran and Algiers in French North Africa. The French, showing little sympathy for de Gaulle's Free French movement, put up a brief but truculent resistance. However, some French troops, led by General Giraud, came over to the Allied side.

Eisenhower

In command of the operation was the American general, Dwight Eisenhower, a gifted organiser rather than a great soldier, but a man of such charm and firm resolve that he was the ideal choice for the difficult task of welding the allies into a harmonious team.

Hitler responded to this move by pouring fresh troops into Tunisia and by occupying the whole of southern France where, at Toulon, the French scuttled the remainder of their Fleet.

On 20th March Montgomery smashed his way into the Mareth Line with such power that on 7th April the Eighth Army joined hands with Eisenhower's troops. From now on, these combined forces were commanded in the field by General Alexander who finished off the Tunisian campaign with sledge-hammer blows. Hitler had Rommel flown out to safety, but for the rest of the Axis forces there was no escape. Hemmed in by land, blockaded from the sea and hammered mercilessly from the air, they fought on until 12th May when a quarter of a million Germans and Italians surrendered. North Africa was cleared, the Middle East was safe and the Mediterranean belonged to the Allied navies.

ALEXANDER

A momentous year

1942 had been a momentous year. It began with enemy triumphs on all fronts—in Russia, in the Pacific, in North Africa and in the Atlantic where the U-boats sank several million tons of shipping. Yet, by the end of the year, an astonishing series of changes had taken place. The Japanese had been defeated at Midway Island, the Germans at Stalingrad, the Germans and the Italians at Alamein. With these three victories, the tide had turned and, as Churchill said, " Up to Alamein, we survived. After Alamein, we conquered."

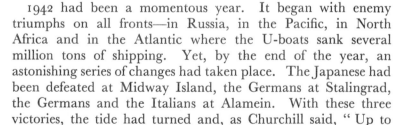

EISENHOWER

II. THE WAR AT SEA

From the middle of 1940, Hitler's conquests gave Germany control of Europe's coastline from northern Norway to the border of Spain. The U-boats could also operate freely in the Mediterranean and along the West African coast. As a result, Allied shipping losses rose alarmingly and actually became worse for a time after the U.S.A. entered the war, owing to Japanese activity, especially in the Indian Ocean, and to German raids into American coastal waters. In addition, there were serious sinkings in the convoys to Malta and to Russia.

The worst period of destruction was from the beginning of 1942 to the middle of 1943 when seven million tons of merchant-shipping were sunk in the Atlantic and, in one month alone (November 1942) 117 ships were lost. By this time, the U-boat captains were operating, not singly, but in " wolf-packs " which were frequently guided to their targets by spotter-aircraft. Handicapped by being unable to use the ports of southern Ireland and by the fact that aircraft did not yet possess the range to patrol the entire expanse of the Atlantic, the Allies hit back at the U-boats with every means in their power. Coastal Command aircraft equipped with radar and searchlights had many successes, especially against submarines which had to come to the surface at night to recharge their batteries and air-supply. The German invention of the Schnorkel tube removed this need to surface but the American shipyards were launching vessels quicker than the Germans could sink them and these included ships specially designed to combat the U-boats and others to form Support Groups which worked independently of the convoy escorts.

The U-boats

The end of 1942 saw the introduction of six escort-carriers able to provide continuous air-cover for the convoys and it was by such methods, together with Bomber Command's persistent attacks on the submarine bases, that the U-boat menace was checked. It was never mastered. At its peak, the Germans had 235 U-boats in action and, when the war ended, there were 49 still at sea, while over 100 surrendered in harbour and 220 others were destroyed by their crews. Throughout, German production was able to stand the losses inflicted by the Allies (781 U-boats altogether, 40 in May 1943) but it became increasingly difficult to replace the highly-trained crews who failed to return to base.

Besides U-boats, the Royal Navy was forever on guard against German surface raiders getting loose into the Atlantic, since one enemy battleship would be able to destroy entire convoys and all their escorts without sustaining a scratch. In 1941 the *Scharnhorst* and the *Gneisenau* sank twenty-two ships before taking refuge in Brest where the R.A.F. made numerous but unavailing attempts to destroy them. Then, in May of that year, the superb new battleship *Bismarck* left Norway with the cruiser *Prince Eugen*. Fortunately they were sighted and a tremendous chase took place during which the British battle-cruiser *Hood* was sunk, though not before it had damaged the *Bismarck*. Limping towards the French coast, she was hunted down by the Home Fleet and finally sunk 400 miles from Brest. She was only one ship but her destruction was a naval victory of the first order. It left just one other ship of her class in the world, the *Tirpitz*, which Hitler insisted on keeping in Trondheim fiord.

Surface raiders

To the angry dismay of the British public, the *Scharnhorst*, *Gneisenau* and *Prince Eugen* succeeded in leaving Brest harbour on 11th February 1942 and sailing through the English Channel under the very noses of the Royal Navy and the country's air defences. They were late in being picked up by aircraft and the radar " look out " had been cleverly jammed so that, despite the heroism of the Fleet Air Arm, the escape was successful and all three warships came safely, if not unscathed, into a German port. This humiliating episode had certain compensations, for it revealed to everyone the Navy's need of modern aircraft and it also showed that the German warships could venture to sea only when covered by a most powerful umbrella of land-based fighters.

12. COLLAPSE OF ITALY

By 1943 the Allies had cleared the enemy out of North Africa. What then was the next task for their victorious armies? The Americans, rightly convinced that the only way to win the war was to invade Germany, wanted to press on with a landing in France. Like Stalin, they vigorously advocated the opening of a Second Front and it was embarrassing for Churchill to have to point out the dangers and difficulties of the operation. Any attempt to invade France without complete air-mastery and a vast accumulation of landing-craft and

supplies was to invite disaster. An invasion was not possible
in 1943 for the simple reason that the necessary equipment did
not exist. Nevertheless, Churchill and his Chiefs of Staff were
unwilling to keep a million splendid troops standing idle in North
Africa. They therefore suggested an all-out attack upon Italy.

There was ample reason to believe that Italy would be
speedily knocked out. In that case, Hitler might find himself
in serious difficulty. Besides defending the peninsula at some
point, he would have to replace the twenty-six Italian divisions
that were occupying the Balkans. Yugoslavia,* which already
had a strong resistance movement led by the communist Tito,
might be encouraged to break into open revolt. There was
also the chance that Turkey would join the Allies and this
could lead to a powerful penetration of south-east Europe.

Roosevelt and his advisers were extremely dubious of the
British plan. They thought that Churchill, the old imperialist,
had worked out a deep-laid scheme to thwart Russian influence
in this area. Great man as he was, Roosevelt never shared his

* Until June 1943, Allied help was given to General Mihailovic
and his resistance fighters. However, as the Yugoslav Partisans
under Tito became more active, Mihailovic did less and may even
have co-operated with the Germans. Churchill therefore switched
support to Tito.

friend Churchill's distrust of Russia and he mistakenly believed that the danger to the post-war world would be, not the advance of Communism, but a revival of British Imperialism.

However, since there was no other course to take, the blow against Italy was decided upon and Sicily was invaded on 10th July 1943. Italian resistance was half-hearted but it took five weeks to drive out the German troops. By this time Mussolini had been deposed and arrested. As the new head of government, Marshal Badoglio conducted secret negotiations for Italy's surrender but, long before the armistice was signed (2nd September), Hitler had poured troops into Italy in order to take control of the country and to disarm the Italian soldiers. Thus, instead of an easy conquest, the Allies had to fight all the way up the peninsula. Its mountain backbone and numerous rivers running in deep channels at right angles to the line of advance gave tremendous advantages to the defenders who fell back slowly, destroying every bridge as they went.

Anzio

Naples was captured in October but the Germans stood fast on Garigliano river and there was nothing for it but a head-on slogging-match unless the enemy could be taken in the rear. Landing-craft were scarce but, in January 1944, a strong force was landed at Anzio with the object of cutting German communications and capturing Rome. Complete surprise was achieved but, instead of dashing on, the American commander (General Lucas) acted so cautiously that Kesselring, the German general, had time to seal off the bridgehead. Nothing was gained and Alexander had to renew his frontal assault on the enemy at Monte Cassino. In May, a massive blow succeeded, the Anzio force broke out and Kesselring retreated to fresh defensive positions in northern Italy.

On 4th June, two days before the Normandy landings, the Allies captured Rome, but from then on their forces were seriously reduced to feed the armies in France and the Italian front became a secondary theatre of war. Even so, the British Eighth Army and the American Fifth battled on towards the River Po which they crossed only a week before the German Army surrendered on 2nd May 1945.

Mussolini's death

By that time Mussolini was dead. Some months earlier German parachutists had rescued him from captivity and, by permission of his master, Hitler, he set up a puppet Fascist-state behind the German lines. But in April, when attempting to escape towards the Swiss frontier, he was recognised by Italian

partisans and shot without mercy. His body was hung upside
down on a meat-hook in Milan, the city in which he had started
his dictator's career.

Meanwhile, Marshal Tito, having disarmed the Italian
divisions in Yugoslavia, was conducting full-scale war against
the German occupation army.

13. THE INVASION OF FRANCE

After Alamein, the Allies' chief concern was to build up their
strength for the direct assault upon the main enemy. While
Bomber Command and the U.S.A. Air Force kept up a night
and day bombardment of Germany, large forces and enormous
quantities of equipment were assembled in southern England.

Most remarkable of all the preparations was the building of
huge hollow blocks of concrete which were to be towed across
the Channel, placed end to end and flooded so they would
sink to the sea-bed and form an artifical harbour where tanks
and heavy stores might be landed. Known as " Mulberry ",
this invention would allow the Allies to land on an open beach
instead of having to undertake the costly and time-wasting
operation of capturing an existing port. In addition, the
problem of fuel supply was solved by constructing an immense
pipeline, known as " Pluto ", which would carry petrol direct
to the armies on the continent. Nearly 2,000 vessels, many of
them specially designed for putting tanks and vehicles ashore,
were assembled along the south coast. By May 1944, the Allies
were ready. Operation " Overlord " would begin on " D-day "
but the exact date and location of the attack would be decided
by the Supreme Commander, General Eisenhower.

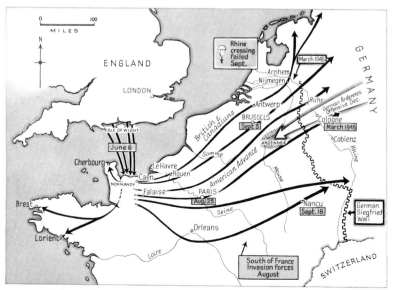

THE INVASION
OF FRANCE

A colossal air-offensive was mounted against the communications of northern France and everything was done to persuade the Germans that the landing-area would be near Calais. On 6th June, in weather that was far from ideal, the greatest sea-borne invasion in history was launched.

Before daylight, airborne forces were landed to secure vital bridges and at 6.30 a.m. the first assault parties went ashore on the coast of Normandy in the Bay of the Seine. A rapid build-up of American and British troops followed, for the Germans had been caught off guard and by the time they recovered, a firm beachhead had been established. " Mulberry " harbours were getting into position and, overhead, layer upon layer of fighter aircraft kept a protective cover above the beaches.

The Allied plan was for the Americans to dash up the Cherbourg peninsula to secure the port from the land side and also to wheel right towards the Seine. The British, under Montgomery, were to pin down the enemy's main armoured forces. In general, this plan succeeded, though the severe fighting round Caen, where the British and Canadians took on two-thirds of all the German armour, caused delay and made it appear that Montgomery's caution was holding up the advance. Meanwhile, the Americans under Bradley and Patton were making rapid progress. By July the Allies had burst into France, and in August, having destroyed enormous enemy forces in a " pocket " at Falaise, they streamed across the Seine, took Paris on the 25th, Brussels on 3rd September and

Antwerp on 4th September.   French Resistance troops aided
the Allies and de Gaulle made his entry into Paris with the
majestic air of a returning saviour.

Meanwhile, a plot by German officers to assassinate Hitler
had narrowly failed and an Allied landing had taken place in
the south of France (15th August).   This enabled American
troops to advance up the Rhone valley but, in view of the fact
that the Germans made no attempt to hold a line there, it was
doubtful if it had been worth starving the Italian front.

With the Germans in retreat everywhere, it began to look
as if the war would be over before the end of the year but the
Allies' difficulties tended to increase as they advanced ever
further from their Normandy base (Antwerp was unusable
until November).   Despite his severe losses, the enemy was
fighting as stubbornly as ever.   Progress became slower and
slower, since Eisenhower insisted upon advancing on a broad
front whereas Montgomery and Bradley would have preferred a
single powerful thrust into Germany.   An attempt by British and
American airborne divisions to outflank the Germans by a sudden
descent upon West Holland failed narrowly at Arnhem and the
ponderous advance on the Rhine continued into the winter.

DE GAULLE 1944

By this time southern England was being attacked by a
novel and most unpleasant weapon.   The V1 or " Flying
Bomb ", a jet-propelled pilotless plane carrying about a ton of
explosive did not prove too difficult to combat; but its successor
the V2, which began to arrive in September 1944, was a much
more formidable threat.   Fired from launching-sites as far
distant as 200 miles, its speed and height were such that there
was no warning and virtually no defence except the capture
of the territory from which the rockets were fired.   Had Hitler's
scientists perfected the V2 a year earlier, Britain's chances of
mounting the invasion, or even of surviving, must have been in
doubt.

V bombs

14. THE RUSSIAN ADVANCE

During the summer of 1943 the Russians, growing ever
stronger as German strength declined, pushed back the enemy's
northern front and recaptured Kharkov, Smolensk and Kiev.
The German armies in the Ukraine were therefore exposed
unless they drew back to straighten the line but, as at Stalingrad
and in Tunisia, Hitler, who by now was scarcely sane, forbade

withdrawal. As a result, the bulge was cut off and eight German divisions perished. By the spring of 1944, Russia had recovered the Ukraine and the Crimea and Stalin's armies were poised to strike where he pleased. Ahead lay the inviting prospect not merely of Germany's defeat but of Communist domination of eastern Europe.

Russian troops advanced into Rumania, Bulgaria, Yugoslavia and Hungary where local Communists embraced the victors. As each country was liberated from the Germans, it found itself in the grip of a puppet government subservient to Moscow. Greece would have gone the same way but for the landing of a British force near Athens in October 1944.

Warsaw

The worst crime was committed against unhappy Poland. In Warsaw a strong (anti-Communist) movement waited for the signal to rise against the German oppressor and this was given in July 1944. The Russians then held back and allowed the Polish patriots to be crushed in the ruins of their city. When, in their own time, the Russians eventually liberated Warsaw, there was no one left to oppose the Communists.

15. VICTORY IN EUROPE

After the attempt to kill him, Hitler liquidated everyone who might have tried to overthrow his régime and ask for an armistice. The Allied policy of " unconditional surrender " meant that there could not be an end to the fighting until Germany was beaten to a pulp. Rather than surrender, Hitler was ready to drag his country into the depths of ruin and suffering.

The Ardennes offensive

Desperately hoping for a miracle, he decided to throw his reserves into a counter-attack that might separate the British and Americans as he had separated the French and the British in 1940. He chose the same area, the Ardennes. Here, in December, Rundstedt attacked the thinnest sector of the American front with eight armoured divisions and the strongest air support that the Germans had been able to assemble for months. Driving deep into the Ardennes, he was held by the now-experienced Americans just long enough to enable the Allied air forces to make a massive reply and for Eisenhower to bring up strong reinforcements. Rundstedt withdrew with heavy losses. His Ardennes offensive had delayed the Allied entry into Germany by several weeks but it had made the Russian advance easier.

In March 1945 Montgomery and Patton were across the Rhine racing on in the hope of reaching Berlin and even Vienna and Prague before the Russians. Roosevelt, however, was dying and American policy was still to avoid offending the Russians. Political decisions were put off while the new President, Harry Truman, took over the reins. The Anglo-American armies were halted on the Elbe and the Russians were able to enter Vienna on 12th April, Berlin on about the 25th and Prague soon afterwards.

THE GERMAN SUPREME COMMANDER SIGNS THE SURRENDER, MONTGOMERY LOOKS ON.
4 MAY 1945

On 30th April Hitler committed suicide in his headquarters beneath the ruins of Berlin, and during the next few days the German armies surrendered to the Allied commanders. On the 7th May 1945, the war in Europe was over.

16. DEFEAT OF JAPAN

The Americans never wavered from their intention to avenge Pearl Harbour. The struggle in the Pacific was very much their own war but they received help from the small but first-class Australian and New Zealand forces, from the Commonwealth navies and from the British and Indian Army fighting in Burma.

In the Pacific war, the Americans displayed great resource in carrying out their " island hopping " strategy. Often they ignored some Japanese-held islands in order to concentrate upon others that were vital to communications. A series of attacks along the northern coast of New Guinea brought the Allies within striking distance of the Philippines and neutralised the great Japanese base at Rabaul. In the South Pacific the American Admiral Nimitz took one group of islands after another (Gilberts, Marshalls and Marianas) often by means of the most bloody fighting but always with marvellous co-operation between land, air and naval forces.

Guam was retaken in August 1944 and this meant that the heart of Japan could be reached by the long-range Super Fortress bombers. Now the Americans could launch their attack upon the Philippines, the control centre for the whole area. Japan accepted the challenge and sent two fleets, one from home and the other from Singapore, to attack the American Fleet. On 21st–22nd October 1944 at Leyte Gulf, Admiral Halsey won the greatest naval victory of the war and, in destroying forty enemy warships, including three battleships and four carriers, he made it impossible for the Japanese ever again to face the Pacific Fleet. MacArthur then reconquered the Philippines and Manila fell in February 1945. When Okinawa was attacked in April, the way was open for an invasion of Japan itself.

Meanwhile, Chiang Kai-Shek, with considerable aid from America, was still fighting the Japanese in China and this led to the decision to recapture Burma. Direct land communications with China could be re-established if Burma was liberated but, unfortunately, a shortage of landing-craft ruled out a sea-borne invasion of Rangoon, and the British and Indian troops had to endure the difficulties of prolonged jungle warfare.

The advance overland from India began early in 1943 when Brigadier Wingate made a remarkable penetration of Japanese-held territory. But the Japanese counter-attacked strongly and *Burma* there was a bitter struggle in 1944 to repel them at Imphal, near the Indian frontier. However General Slim's Fourteenth Army stood up to the enemy and, by the end of the year, the Allied troops were pushing towards central Burma. Meanwhile, the American General Stilwell was progressing south with

THE WAR IN THE FAR EAST

mainly Chinese forces. Air superiority enabled the Allies to supply their armies and to transport large numbers of troops from one position to another. The Burma Road was reopened in January, Mandalay was captured in March and Rangoon in May 1945. The campaign had been carried out brilliantly, in atrocious conditions.

By now Japan's position was hopeless. Nine-tenths of her merchant navy had been sunk, supplies of steel and oil were unobtainable, her homeland was within easy reach of the American bombers and Russia was preparing to invade Manchuria. Yet, once again, the demand for " unconditional surrender " prevented an armistice.

Had there been an offer from the Allies to safeguard the Emperor, the Japanese would probably have surrendered. As it was, they were compelled to do so by the horrific effects of *Hiroshima* two atomic bombs which were dropped on 6th and 9th August on Hiroshima and Nagasaki. In the face of such gigantic destruction (and not knowing that as yet no other atomic bombs existed), the Emperor overruled his Cabinet and ordered his armies everywhere to lay down arms. The Second World War ended officially on 2nd September 1945, just six years after Hitler marched into Poland.

It is now widely held that the use of the atomic bombs was a mistake. To some, it was an appalling crime. The decision was taken by Truman with Churchill's full assent; Stalin was informed and a small number of persons at the head of affairs knew that an exceptionally powerful weapon had been developed. It was, in fact, the most frightful weapon of destruction ever devised. But, at the time, no one apart from a handful of scientists had any idea of the total effects of such explosives. If the enemy had been warned, it was not likely that he would have believed the information even if it had been given in full. There had been too many threats of " secret weapons " for that. Moreover, the possessors of the bomb were not even sure it would go off. If a solemn warning had been followed by failure, the enemy would have been encouraged and the Allied forces depressed. It was certain that in defending their homeland, the Japanese would inflict enormous losses upon an invasion force and the decision to drop the bombs was taken in the belief that they might save the lives of a million Allied soldiers. In the event, they did so, and it may well be that the known effect of this terrible weapon has deterred anyone from using it again.

HOME! A
SOLDIER COMES
HOME AFTER
4 YEARS, 3 OF
THEM AS A
PRISONER OF
WAR

18 A Kind of Settlement

AT Teheran, Yalta and Potsdam there took place the three
historic meetings between the " Big Three "—the United States,
the U.S.S.R. and Britain. On each occasion, it became increasingly clear that behind the cordial phrases there were deep
differences.

At Teheran in Persia in November 1943, Roosevelt, Stalin
and Churchill talked about war aims and the Second Front but
Roosevelt declined a private conversation with Churchill lest it
should arouse Stalin's suspicion. At Yalta (February 1945),
they discussed the occupation of Germany and, against Stalin's
wishes, Churchill insisted that France should have a voice in
German affairs. They differed more strongly over Poland's
future because Britain had entered the war to secure her
freedom but Russia was now in possession of most of the country
and Stalin had no intention of allowing the anti-Communist
London Poles to form a government. Poland, he insisted, would
have " free " elections without outside supervision and her new
frontiers would be decided at a later date. Churchill's protests
were not supported by Roosevelt because Stalin had promised,
for a price, to attack Japan when the European war was over.

Potsdam, in August 1945, proved that Churchill's fears had
been well-founded. He himself, having ceased to be Prime
Minister, was replaced by Attlee and in Roosevelt's place was
President Truman. Stalin, sole survivor of the earlier meetings,

CHURCHILL, ROOSEVELT AND STALIN AT YALTA

was in an unassailable position and he had his own way in all matters that affected Russia. His armies had taken every capital in Central Europe and he saw to it that each had a government which took its orders from Moscow. Poland's fate was sealed, German minorities were sent, or driven, back to Germany from Hungary, Czechoslovakia and Poland, and, *Potsdam* alone of the Powers, Russia took reparations from Germany.

At Potsdam, Attlee and Bevin, the British Foreign Secretary, were fully aware that Russia's new style imperialism was a threat to the freedom of Europe; but they were unable to impress the Americans with a sense of danger. Misjudging both the British Prime Minister and the Soviet leader, the Americans believed that Britain was still trying to play the role of an old-fashioned imperialist power, whereas they and the Russians, the two " big boys ", could settle affairs amicably. In this minority position, Attlee and Bevin had to accept Russian demands on many points, though they tried hard to ensure that the people of Poland should be allowed to choose their own government. Eventually a joint government was formed of London Poles and Russian-dominated " Lublin Poles ". It was not long, however, before the latter, supplied with Soviet weapons, were able to liquidate all their opponents.

Thus the Second World War, which was fought to save Europe from Nazi tyranny, ended by delivering about half the continent into the hands of another tyrant. Hitler and the worst of his gang perished; Germany, divided into four occupied zones, lay at the mercy of her conquerors and Japan was deprived of all her short-lived gains. But nothing could be done for Poland, Czechoslovakia and the other countries * that had fallen into Russia's grip and were now, in Churchill's phrase,

* By 1948 the following countries were Communist states: Czechoslovakia, Hungary, Rumania, Bulgaria, Yugoslavia, Albania. (Estonia, Latvia and Lithuania had been absorbed into Russia.)

behind the "Iron Curtain" which had come down across Europe.

The loser of the war was not just Germany but Europe. Almost every country was damaged and impoverished; the empires of Britain, France, Belgium and Holland were about to disappear and the continent which for so long had been the greatest force in world history was dwindling in importance. New states in Asia and Africa would emerge from the collapsed empires but, from 1945 on, the world would be dominated by two non-European giants, Russia and the United States. As time went by, it would be seen that a third giant, China, was growing up faster than either.

America quickly shed Roosevelt's benevolence towards Russia and during the years that have passed since Potsdam, the two giants have glared at each other with varying hostility. At times they have well-nigh agreed to co-exist peaceably; at others, they have been close to war and have been restrained only by the knowledge that full-scale war would lead to annihilation of both sides. Always, they have competed fiercely for prestige and for the allegiance of smaller nations, and in the outcome of this rivalry, complicated now by the rise of China, lies the future of the world.

In this situation, the major countries of Western Europe, except perhaps Britain, made an astonishing recovery. Germany climbed back rapidly to a position of affluence and dignity; Italy, at least in the north, made marked industrial progress and France, for a time apparently broken by defeat, found an aggressive self-confidence under de Gaulle's rule. With the formation of N.A.T.O. and the Common Market, a union of Western Europe promised to be a new force in world affairs.

The United Nations Organisation The aim to replace the old League of Nations by a new organisation was fulfilled at San Francisco in 1945 when the United Nations Charter was drawn up by fifty nations. In simple words, they agreed that they were

" determined to save succeeding generations from the scourge of war . . . to reaffirm faith in fundamental human rights, in the dignity and the worth of the human person and in the equal rights of men and women of the nations large and small."

The permanent headquarters of the United Nations was set up in New York and all the member states (114 by 1964) are entitled to be represented in the *General Assembly* where each has one vote. Important decisions are taken by a two-thirds majority of members and there is a permanent staff, the *Secretariat*, headed by the Secretary-General. This post, one of the most important in the world, was first held by Trygve Lie, a Norwegian, and next, from 1953 to 1961, by Dag Hammar-skjöld, a Swede. The third Secretary-General was U Thant of Burma.

The *Security Council*, which is always on duty, has considerable power, for it is responsible for keeping the peace and may ask for armed forces from member nations. It consists of eleven members—five of them permanent and six of them elected by the General Assembly for two-year terms. The five permanent members are the United States, the U.S.S.R., Britain, France and " China ", though this came to mean only Formosa, the last refuge of Chiang Kai-Shek's Nationalist China, for the Chinese People's Republic, i.e. China proper, was refused membership. Each of the permanent members has the right to " veto " or prevent any action of the Security Council. This right was agreed upon because it was felt that it would be unwise to force the Great Powers to agree but, in practice, the use of the veto has been very much abused by the Soviet Union. However, the General Assembly decided that if the Council failed to agree to take action, it could itself recommend action.

Three other important parts of U.N.O. are the *International Court of Justice* which meets at the Hague in Holland to give legal rulings on questions of international law (e.g. fishing rights, boundaries, interpretations of treaties), the *Trusteeship Council* which does the work of the former Mandates Commission in looking after enemy colonies and the *Economic and Social Council* which carries out vital work through its Specialised Agencies.

THE
UNITED NATIONS
GENERAL
ASSEMBLY,
NEW YORK

Some of these agencies were in existence well before 1945, e.g. the *World Meteorological Organisation* and the *International Labour Organisation,* and new ones were set up to meet the needs of a troubled world. The *International Monetary Fund* (headquarters at Washington) helps trade by making short-term loans to countries requiring assistance, and the *International Bank* (" World Bank "), provides long-term loans for major projects such as atomic power stations or huge dams. Among the best known and most valuable agencies are the *World Health Organisation* (Geneva) to fight disease, the *United Nations Educational, Scientific and Cultural Organisation* (U.N.E.S.C.O.—headquarters in Paris) to promote education and the exchange of knowledge, the *United Nations International Children's Emergency Fund* (U.N.I.C.E.F.) to help children in devastated areas and where there is widespread poverty and the *Food and Agricultural Organisation* (F.A.O.—at Rome) to improve food production.

In many ways, the United Nations is an improvement on the League for most countries are members, including the United States and Russia, though the Chinese People's Republic (still not recognised by the U.S.A.) is a notable absentee. Decisions do not have to be unanimous, as in the past, and armed forces can be raised to enforce decisions.

Nevertheless, there are weaknesses. The use of the veto has become a weapon of rivalry and it is clearly impossible to compel nations to contribute troops to a U.N. army or even to pay their membership dues. No way has been found to make powerful nations work together unless they want to. In theory, the U.N. consists of equal, independent states but in practice it has been dominated by the two great rival powers, America and Russia, and this has led to blocs of the smaller nations supporting one side or the other, and to all kinds of manœuvres which have tended to discredit the noble aims of a world assembly.

The Peace Settlement   As with the Versailles Treaty, peace terms were not negotiated with the defeated enemy and the settlement was essentially a dictated one in which the only negotiations were between the victors.

A Council of Foreign Ministers of the five leading Powers drew up the peace treaties for Italy, Rumania, Bulgaria, Hungary and Finland.   Italy lost all her colonies and yielded territory to France, Yugoslavia and Greece; Trieste became a free United Nations territory.   Finland had to cede Petsamo and Karelia to Russia and there were territorial exchanges between Rumania, Hungary, Bulgaria and their neighbours, most being in Russia's favour.   There were some reparations which Italy, in particular, had to pay.

Agreement about Austria and Germany was very difficult to reach because Russia, helping herself freely to Austria's resources, would not consent to consider the countries separately. Not until 1955 was peace signed with Austria, which was to remain permanently neutral and to supply Russia with heavy reparations including one million tons of oil annually for ten years.

In theory, Japan was to be occupied by the victorious Powers but, in fact, American forces under General MacArthur took control.   Japan was completely disarmed and several of her war leaders, including Tojo, were executed.   By 1947 military occupation had become education for democracy and many reforms, astonishing to the Japanese, were introduced.   By this time the United States had decided to rebuild Japan as a buffer against Asiatic Communism.   A peace treaty was signed in 1951 (Russia refused to do so) followed by a treaty of alliance between the United States and Japan.   The recent enemy became a cherished ally.

In Germany there was chaos at first, with no government except that of the victorious army commanders.   Hordes of foreign workers, liberated from the forced labour-battalions, roamed the country taking frenzied revenge for their own ill-treatment.   Thousands of Germans were themselves homeless and near to starvation.

The American and British exerted themselves to bring relief to their enemy and U.N.R.R.A. (the United Nations Relief and Rehabilitation Administration) carried out what was called " the biggest piece of first aid in history ".

This merciful behaviour was all the more praiseworthy because the advancing Allies had uncovered evidence of the appalling nature of Nazi inhumanity.   At Buchenwald, near Weimar, and at Belsen in Hanover, Allied soldiers found pits filled with corpses and thousands of emaciated prisoners huddled together in the last stages of filth and disease. In one place 17,000 bodies had been cremated by the German guards just before the Allies arrived. Even worse was the concentration camp at Auschwitz in Poland whose commandant was sentenced to death for murdering 4 million people including, as he admitted, 1½ million Jews. Altogether some 5 million Jews— the exact number will never be known—perished in gas chambers and in other repulsive ways.

At Nuremberg in 1945 and 1946, twenty-two of the surviving Nazi leaders were put on trial for their crimes, and further trials continued to take place up until 1965 as more criminals and *Nuremberg* evidence came to light. Many of the accused were hanged or *trials* sentenced to terms of imprisonment and some, including von Papen and Krupp, the armaments-maker, were acquitted. Goering managed to commit suicide, as Hitler, Goebbels and Himmler had done before him.

These trials, unique in history, were criticised on the ground that the acts of victors would never impress the defeated. There was also the danger that the criminals might be elevated to heroes. However, responsible Germans have themselves meted out justice to those who disgraced their nation and the Western Allies, at least, refrained from taking mass reprisals against the German people.

Germany was divided into four zones occupied by British, French, American and Russian forces. Although Berlin was inside the Russian zone, the city was similarly divided into four sectors. Mindful of the mistakes made after the previous war, the Western Allies set about helping the Germans to solve the appalling problems of clearing up their devastated cities and of feeding and housing millions of " displaced persons " who poured into Western Germany from the east. The Russians, displaying no tenderness towards an enemy who had killed four million of their soldiers, were intent upon removing food and machinery to the ruined areas of the Soviet Union.

The Berlin From the beginning of the occupation, there were differences *Airlift* between the Western Allies and the Russians over the treatment of the Germans. Tension increased until, in June 1948, the Russians tried to drive the other Powers out of Berlin by blocking all the agreed routes to Western Germany. The United States and Britain answered this threat by using aircraft to supply their sectors of the capital with food and essential materials. The Berlin Airlift was maintained for nearly a year until the Russians

decided to call off the blockade. Twelve years later, the Communists built a wall across the city to prevent all communication between East and West Berlin.

In 1949 the Federal Republic of Germany, usually called Western Germany, came into being with its capital at Bonn and with Dr Adenauer, an old opponent of the Nazis, as the first Chancellor. Russia set up the German Democratic Republic for East Germany which was now of course a Communist state. A new German problem had been created. They might acquiesce for the time being but, in the long run, the Germans would never accept the permanent division of their country. On the other hand, having cut their dangerous neighbour in halves, the Russians would not willingly permit Germany to become united.

Meanwhile Western Germany went ahead by leaps and bounds. American aid and the people's prodigious capacity for hard work brought about an astounding recovery so that, within ten years, this occupied country, still without a peace treaty, had become the most prosperous state in Europe.*

* Two factors that contributed greatly to the " German miracle " of recovery were 1. the replacement of her ruined industry by new factories equipped with modern methods and machines and 2. the absence of defence expenditure. In 1938 Germany had spent a quarter of her total income on armaments but after the war she was allowed to spend virtually nothing.

19 The Cold War 1945–53

RIVALRY between America and Russia became so intense that, except for the actual firing of guns, a state of war existed between them. This was called the " Cold War " and it has been fought continuously since 1945 with the weapons of espionage, propaganda and finance.

At the end of the war, America was in a position of supremacy. Apart from her colossal productive powers, she was the only country capable of manufacturing atomic bombs, and Britain, whose scientists had been partly responsible for their construction, alone shared the secret. Rich in prestige, Britain was much reduced in strength for, considering her size, her war-effort had been tremendous and her people were very tired.

The rest of the Powers were in poor shape. France, still shocked by the enormity of her defeat, was weak and disunited and, as in most of the occupied countries, there was abiding bitterness between those who had suffered and resisted and those who had co-operated with the enemy. Italy, dejected and half-ruined, was veering towards Communism, Japan's defeat had engulfed China in a civil war from which the Communists had not yet emerged victorious. Only Russia stood up head and shoulders above the rest to challenge American might.

Russian losses had been vast but the country's industries had grown up so fast during the war that, with a huge population, disciplined and intensely patriotic, she was already far stronger than in 1939. In addition, Stalin had taken control of Eastern Europe and his hold did not depend entirely upon fear. In some countries Communists had played a leading part in fighting the Germans and, as the war ended, they were therefore able to assume power with local support and the prestige that their courage deserved. This was particularly true of Marshal Tito in Yugoslavia.

But, in 1945, few people in Britain and America entertained any suspicion of their " glorious Russian ally ". Churchill's *Fulton* warning speech at Fulton in America in 1946, when he urged the democracies to stand together, was dismissed as the utterance of an unconverted old war-monger. Almost at once, however, events in Greece changed the attitude of America.

214

The arrival of British troops at Athens in 1944 had helped to put down an attempt by the left-wing to seize power and, with a good deal of uneasiness in some quarters, a royalist government came into office in 1946. Civil war broke out again and the Security Council was told that Greek Communists were receiving arms from their Balkan neighbours. Behind them stood the figure of Stalin. Unable to afford the cost of operations in Greece, Britain asked the United States for help and President Truman persuaded Congress to make a massive grant for military and economic aid to Greece and Turkey.

The civil war in Greece came to an end in 1949 * and from then on, the " Truman Doctrine " expressed America's attitude towards Communism. President Truman declared, " It must be the policy of the United States to support free peoples who are resisting attempted subjugation by armed minorities or outside pressure ". In most cases, support took the form of dollars which were used to build factories and to encourage industry. The theory was that Communism was less likely to flourish when people were busy and prosperous than when they were suffering from hunger and injustice.

PRESIDENT
TRUMAN

A huge programme known as the Marshall Plan was introduced in 1948 and, in the next three years, some 12,500 million dollars were provided for various schemes of recovery.

Marshall Aid was offered to all European countries, but the Soviet Union and its satellites refused to accept and when the Czech Government appeared to hesitate, a *coup d'état* in Prague took Czechoslovakia firmly into the Communist camp. Democracy was snuffed out in that unhappy country but, remembering Munich, who could have asked the Czechs to resist?

The next step in the struggle was the Russian attempt to blockade Berlin, which, as already mentioned, was foiled by the Berlin Airlift. Then, in 1949, came the formation of N.A.T.O. (North Atlantic Treaty Organisation) which developed out of the Brussels Treaty of the previous year signed by Britain, France, Belgium, Luxembourg and the Netherlands for defence

N.A.T.O.

---

* A prime cause of the end of the civil war was the stopping of supplies from Yugoslavia to the Greek Communists. Marshal Tito, strong enough in his own country to be able to defy Stalin, refused to take orders from Moscow. Yugoslavia was expelled from the Communist Bloc in 1948.

against aggression. N.A.T.O. consisted of these five plus the U.S.A., Canada, Italy, Portugal, Iceland, Denmark and Norway. Greece, Turkey and Western Germany joined later. Similar steps taken in 1951 to provide security in the Pacific led to the creation of S.E.A.T.O. (South East Asia Treaty Organisation, 1954).*

Russia's reply on the economic front was the Cominform (Communist Information Bureau) which organised Communist activities in many countries. One of its principal aims was to undermine the Marshall Plan by fomenting strikes and in-dustrial unrest. To counter N.A.T.O., Russia created the Warsaw Treaty Organisation (1955), also known as the Warsaw Pact, to provide for the defence of the Communist countries. †

ERNEST BEVIN

During these critical years, Britain remained the close ally of the United States. This was not necessarily inevitable because, from 1945 until 1951, there was a Labour Government in Britain and Labour had for long tended to be suspicious of America and sympathetic towards Russia. At Potsdam and in the United Nations, Ernest Bevin, the British Foreign Secretary, tried hard to establish friendship with Russia but his efforts were received with hostility and abuse.

Bevin, who had received little education in his poverty-stricken boyhood but had risen by sheer ability to a position of great influence in trade union circles, had entered Churchill's government during the war as Minister of Labour. Now, as a shrewd, realistic Foreign Minister, he proved himself to be one of the most forceful personalities of the post-war world. Seeing no hope of an understanding with Moscow, he threw all his weight on to the side of the Atlantic Alliance and it was Bevin who supported Marshall Aid and the Brussels Pact which led to N.A.T.O. He accepted the need to set up a democratic government in Western Germany and to face the Russian challenge over Berlin. But while he did much to encourage co-operation among the countries of Western Europe, he did not entirely agree with those who wanted a union that would eventually lead to a United States of Europe.

It was in the Far East rather than in Europe that the Cold

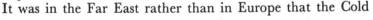

* S.E.A.T.O. consisted of the U.S., Britain, France, Australia, New Zealand, Pakistan, the Philippines and Thailand.

† In 1955 they were the U.S.S.R., Poland, East Germany, Albania, Bulgaria, Czechoslovakia, Rumania and Hungary.

War threatened to develop into a Third World War. The defeat of Japan had not brought peace to China, for civil war broke out between the Communist armies of Mao Tse-tung and the forces of Chiang Kai-shek's Nationalist Government. For years, Chiang Kai-shek had been recognised as his country's rightful leader by all the Allies, and Nationalist China became one of the permanent members of the Security Council. With generous help from the United States, it seemed possible that Chiang might bring order and peace to the country. However, the Communists had good reason to distrust the Nationalists.

After fourteen years of war, Chiang Kai-shek's government and army had become increasingly corrupt and inefficient. As their authority and appeal to the Chinese people declined, the position of the Communists grew stronger. From 1948 onwards, the Nationalists lost control of one great area after another until Chiang Kai-shek withdrew the remnant of his forces to the island of Formosa. On the mainland, Mao Tse-tung proclaimed the People's Republic of China.

The People's Republic of China

This was an event of enormous importance for it meant that the Chinese people, a quarter of the world's population, would now be given the discipline and control of Communism. Russia, at least for a time, had gained a colossal success and the Americans had suffered a major defeat. They refused to recognise the Chinese People's Republic and in 1966 were still doing so, whereas the Soviet Union (and most of the world, including Britain and France) recognised Mao as China's leader. This led to further friction in the United Nations.

The struggle now shifted to Korea, a Japanese-held peninsula of North China, which the Russians had entered as soon as they declared war on Japan in August 1945. By agreement, Korea was temporarily occupied by Soviet forces north of the 38th parallel of latitude, and by American troops south of that line. As a result, North Korea was given a Communist government while South Korea, under the supervision of United Nations officials, elected a right-wing government headed by Syngman Rhee.

Korean War

Numerous border incidents occurred and, in June 1950, North Korean forces invaded South Korea and captured Seoul the capital. The Security Council named North Korea as the aggressor and asked member states to send armed assistance to South Korea. This decision could not have been taken if the Russians had used the veto but they were absent from the Council

in protest against Communist China's exclusion from the United Nations. For the first time, therefore, a United Nations Army took the field.

British and Commonwealth units served in Korea but most of the troops and equipment were American. Led by General MacArthur, they quickly drove the North Koreans back to the Manchurian border. Mao Tse-tung sent a Chinese army to the rescue and MacArthur was forced to retreat to a line roughly along the 38th parallel. The American general, concerned only with the military situation, wished to bomb China in order to cut off the enemy's source of supplies and reinforcements, but Truman, who courageously dismissed MacArthur from his command, refused to agree. There was no telling how disastrously the war might have spread for it was reasonably certain that Russia now possessed atomic bombs.

The Korean War reached stalemate and it was not until 1953, when Stalin died and Eisenhower was President of the U.S.A., that an armistice was signed. The frontier was left more or less where it had been at the start but, at enormous cost (the country was devastated and some three million Koreans were killed), Communism had been halted and the United States was more deeply committed than ever to the unending struggle.

20 Labour Government 1945–50

AT the General Election of July 1945, the first for almost ten years, Britain elected a Labour Government by a majority of 145 over all other parties. To an astonished world, this seemed to be an act of base ingratitude to Mr Churchill who, having led the nation from the disasters of 1940 to victory in Europe, was in conference at Potsdam almost until the day of the election. " Don't let HIM down " pleaded the Conservative posters but, although the crowds and the soldiers acclaimed him with shouts of " Good old Winnie! ", they voted for Mr Attlee.

The reasons were not difficult to find. The Conservatives had little to offer apart from Churchill's leadership and only in dire extremity had they taken him back into the fold. Their pre-war record was not likely to appeal to those with long memories nor to the millions of men and women under thirty who were voting for the first time. Baldwin, Chamberlain, Munich and Norway were embarrassing names in 1945 and so were Jarrow, the Dole and the Means Test.

Even so, electors usually think not of the past but of the future and Labour's manifesto " Let Us Face the Future " was well named. It promised full employment, housing, public-owner-ship of coal, transport, gas and electricity, iron and steel. Above all, it promised the Beveridge Plan. Herbert Morrison, the sharp bouncy Londoner who so ably ran the Labour Party's election campaign, made the most of his opportunity. Scorn was poured upon the " Men of Munich ", the " guilty men " who had failed the nation in peace and war and who now asked for yet another term of office.

For all its evils, war gives rise to idealism. In trenches, jungles and prisoner-of-war camps, men think of a better world for themselves and their children. At the height of the war, in 1942, the Coalition Government had asked a civil servant, Sir William Beveridge, to make a survey of social insurance.

GEORGE VI WITH LABOUR MINISTERS, AUGUST 1945: MORRISON, ATTLEE,
GEORGE VI, GREENWOOD, BEVIN, ALEXANDER

*The
Beveridge Plan*

The Beveridge Plan was a best-seller from the day it appeared and its author became a public hero overnight. To the Government's astonishment, it found that it had brought out a statement of Human Rights. The " five Great Evils " of Want, Disease, Ignorance, Squalor and Idleness would be overcome by means of a system of social insurance that would provide full employment, family allowances and a comprehensive health service. Every citizen would enjoy these blessings as his right.

It was for the Beveridge Plan that the people voted, and because the Labour Party seemed the more likely to fulfil its promises. Clement Attlee became Prime Minister in 1945.

The Parliamentary Labour Party that filled the Government benches in the House of Commons was a different party from the one which MacDonald had led. Some of the veterans were still there, Ernest Bevin, once a van-driver and now Foreign Secretary, Herbert Morrison, a policeman's son, Lord President of the Council, George Tomlinson, a former mill-hand, Minister of Works, and numerous trade unionists and miners, including Aneurin Bevan, the Minister of Health. But there were also about 150 Labour M.P.'s from middle-class backgrounds—lawyers, economists, journalists and doctors, and their numbers included the new Prime Minister himself (Haileybury and Oxford), the Chancellor of the Exchequer, Hugh Dalton (Eton and Cambridge), the President of the Board of Trade, Sir Stafford Cripps * (Winchester and Oxford), and a few clever, well-educated youngsters like Hugh Gaitskell and Harold Wilson.

* Richard Stafford Cripps, 1889–1952, b. London, educated Winchester and Oxford. Became a very successful barrister; 1931, Solicitor-General, but refused to serve in National Government. Between wars a left-wing extremist. Expelled from Labour Party in 1939; 1940, Ambassador in Moscow; 1942, Lord Privy Seal; leader of Cripps Mission to India; Minister of Aircraft; 1945, President of Board of Trade; 1947, Minister of Economic Affairs and Chancellor of Exchequer. Resigned from ill-health 1950.

Attlee, much tougher than his mild demeanour suggested, *Attlee's*
controlled his team with the authority of a first-class chairman *task*
and he entrusted Labour's programme to his three senior
ministers. Bevin looked after overseas policy, including the
Commonwealth, Cripps was responsible for economic affairs
and Morrison took on the domestic and parliamentary work.
Each was faced with most formidable problems.

After six years of war, Britain was tired, shabby and bankrupt.
Her overseas investments had largely gone, almost half her
merchant shipping had been sunk, export trade had dropped to
one-third of its pre-war volume and her debts were enormous.

Food was strictly rationed and so was almost everything else—
clothes, fabrics, furniture, domestic fuel and petrol; many other
things, from bananas and pepper to motor-cars and children's
toys, were practically unobtainable. No houses had been built
for six years and five million had been destroyed or damaged.
Factories had to be brought back to peace-time production at a
time when raw materials were scarce and world trade was still
dislocated. Yet millions of men and women were about to leave
the Forces and war-factories wanting jobs and homes.

Abroad, the picture was equally gloomy. Hopes of lasting
friendship with Russia began to fade when at the Potsdam and
London conferences, Molotov, the Soviet Foreign Minister,
proved to be totally unco-operative. Many European countries,
struggling to clear up the mess of war and Nazi occupation, had
also to wrestle with the problems of refugees, traitors, Communist
sympathisers and returning exiles. In the Empire and in
Palestine, for which Britain was responsible, there were tides of
nationalism which could not be ignored.

In tackling these problems, the Labour Government showed
a good deal of courage and resolution. They did better than
Lloyd George's government in 1919 because, not being a
collection of " hard-faced men who looked as if they had done
well out of the war ",* most of them had come to the House
determined to make Britain a better country. Moreover, they
had the advantage of knowing what went wrong the last time.
Their policy ran along two lines; first, they had to deal with the
existing situation and get the country back to peace-time working, and second, they intended to keep their election promises
by introducing measures that would bring Socialism to Britain.

* Baldwin's description of his Conservative colleagues in 1919.

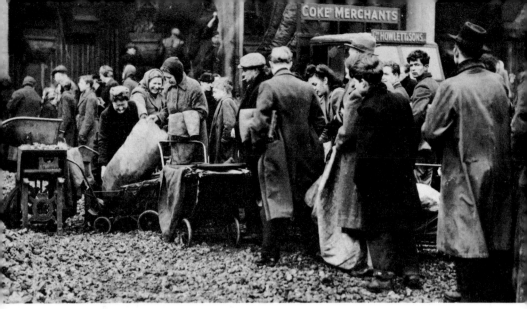

COAL SHORTAGE, 1947. PEOPLE QUEUE FOR A WEEK'S SUPPLY OF 56 LBS

At home, the first task was to get the men out of uniform and back to work. Demobilisation was managed very much better this time and every serviceman was given leave, an outfit of clothes, the right to have his old job back (if it still existed) or the chance to train for a new one. A new Ministry of Economic Affairs was set up and planning staffs helped to turn industry back to peace-time production. The lessons of the twenties had not been forgotten so that there was no mass unemployment after a brief boom.

New industries, such as man-made fibres and plastics, began to develop rapidly and there was marked expansion of some of the older industries, such as iron and steel, cars, aircraft, chemicals and electrical manufactures. At this period, shortage of coal was a serious problem and, in the bitter winter of 1947, stocks became exhausted and some power-stations and factories had to close down.

In putting the country back on its feet, it was vital to avoid inflation, that mounting spiral of wages and prices that would make orderly progress impossible. The Government therefore used its powers to plan and control industry, and to restrict private and public spending when it felt this was necessary.

Stafford Cripps This work fell mainly upon the shoulders of Sir Stafford Cripps, who succeeded Dalton as Chancellor of the Exchequer in 1947. No one could have been better suited for the task. An intellectual whose extreme Left-wing views were based upon his religious beliefs, Cripps lived as plainly as any monk and he seemed almost to relish the " Austerity " which he had to impose upon the rest of the nation. Not even Cripps could entirely prevent inflation but he managed to slow it down by high taxation and by persuading the trade unions to agree to a voluntary " wage-freeze ".

Britain's greatest problem was the balance of payments— that is, her exports were not sufficient to pay for the food and raw materials which she needed from foreign countries. In addition, there was a " dollar gap " caused by buying more from the United States than could be sold to that country. Lease-Lend stopped in 1945 and Britain was faced with a situation in which Cripps, at the Board of Trade and later at the Exchequer, had to persuade his countrymen to concentrate upon exporting their best goods and put up with " Austerity " at home.

A dollar loan worth £1,000 million was obtained from America in 1945 but this was spent so rapidly that a financial crisis occurred two years later. Fortunately Marshall Aid came to Britain's rescue, but another dollar crisis in 1949 led to devaluation of the pound. As in 1931, this made British goods cheaper for foreigners to buy and, by the end of the Labour Government's first term of office (1950), there was an improvement in the country's economic position. This of course was not due entirely to financial juggling, but to the recovery of industry and trade throughout the world.

While coping with immediate problems, the Government did not delay putting through the Acts of Parliament that were needed for its programme of nationalisation and social reform.

Nationalisation, that is, the compulsory transfer of industries and services from private owners to the State, was not a new idea. The Sankey Report of 1919 had recommended State-ownership of the coal-mines; the G.P.O. had long been an example of an efficient public service and the Conservatives themselves had created the B.B.C. and the Central Electricity Board. The Labour Party believed that fuel, transport and power, which everyone needed, should not make profits for private persons but should be owned by the public. As far as the mines and railways were concerned, there was not likely to be much opposition to this view. Private enterprise was not in a position to carry out the wholesale modernisation that these two services required.

Nationalisation

A start was made by nationalising the Bank of England and

the coal-mines. Compensation of £165 million was awarded to the mine-owners and on 1st January 1947 the National Coal Board took over the entire industry, except coke-ovens and by-product plants. A separate Act of Parliament created the British European Airways Corporation, thus putting civil aviation into public ownership. *

Next, the Transport Act (1947) merged the four railway companies into British Railways. A specially created British Transport Commission took over the various transport concerns, including long-distance road haulage companies, which became known as British Road Services.

From April 1948 electricity supply was completely nationalised and this was followed a year later by the purchase of all municipal and private gas-works. In each case, a Central Authority was set up with Area Boards to cater for the various regions of the country. Before long, Gas and Electricity Boards were competing against each other as vigorously as if they had been private companies.

So far, despite some opposition, these measures were approved by most of the public but nationalisation of iron and steel was another matter. These industries were modern, profitable and efficient so that the proposal to take them over was attacked with great vigour. Nevertheless, the Government persisted and the Iron and Steel Act was passed; but Labour's defeat in 1951 enabled the Conservatives to reverse nationalisation and hand the industry back to its shareholders. Even so, Government control could still be exercised through the Iron and Steel Board.

Nationalisation remained an issue but no longer a burning one. In 1966 the Labour Party was still promising to nationalise iron and steel and there were some who wanted to extend public ownership still further. Most of the public had lost interest in the question. The extreme hopes and fears of the supporters and opponents of nationalisation had never been realised. Conditions of work improved, notably in the mines where the Coal Board headed by Alfred Robens really did transform the industry, and there were earnest attempts to improve the railways. Here, partly because of proposals to reduce unprofitable sections, there was less confidence between workers and management. Conditions in State industries did

* B.O.A.C. (British Overseas Airways Corporation) had been set up in 1939.

not excite the envy and admiration of those in private employment; managers tended to be the same persons and the workers had hardly any more control, let alone sense of ownership, than formerly. In short, there was no revolutionary upheaval of British industry. The change-overs were put through with a minimum of fuss (thanks largely to Herbert Morrison) and nothing dramatic occurred. One very important thing had happened, however; business remained in private hands but the Government's control of the basic industries meant that it now held the whip hand over the country's economy.

The second part of Labour's domestic programme was concerned with social reform. This Government did not create the Welfare State but it put the Beveridge Plan into operation by building upon the work already carried out by Chamberlain in the thirties and by Lloyd George and Churchill earlier in the century.

FASHION 1949: THIS STYLE WAS CALLED THE "NEW LOOK"

The Welfare State

By the National Insurance Act of 1946, almost every citizen in the land was protected against illness, accident and unemployment. Old Age Pensions (for men at sixty-five and women at sixty) were raised to 42s for a married couple and 26s for a single person and there were also maternity allowances * and widows' pensions. The cost was to be met by contributions from every employed person, from employers and from the State.

Alongside the insurance scheme the National Health Service was set up in 1948 in order to provide medical, optical and dental treatment for everyone. As Minister of Health, Aneurin Bevan had to face strong opposition from doctors and dentists, but his persuasive gifts—and toughness—were enough to induce the majority to swallow their misgivings.

Reorganisation and extension of the country's inadequate hospital service was begun and local authorities were given the important task of providing accommodation for the aged and infirm. Owing to the cost, progress was slow and years passed

* Family Allowances had been introduced by the Coalition Government in 1945.

before new hospitals, clinics and Health Centres began to be built. Demand for medical treatment proved to be very high and the Health Service came under considerable strain, so that the doctors' misgivings appeared to be well justified. However, if there were abuses and disappointments, the nation as a whole benefited to a degree that would have seemed miraculous to an earlier generation.

For education no new law was needed because, in the 1944 Education Act (the " Butler Act "), the Coalition Government had already provided a plan that was to serve for at least the next twenty years. Hitherto, the State had been mainly concerned with " elementary " education but, under the new Act, the existing system was to be expanded to bring about " secondary education for all ".

Education

Three stages of education were laid down: primary, secondary and further; the minimum leaving age was raised to fifteen and fees at State schools were abolished. At the age of eleven, children were to be selected for the type of secondary school for which they were thought best suited. In most places this was either a grammar school or a secondary modern school (housed at first in the old senior elementary school building). For those leaving at fifteen, there was to be compulsory part-time attendance until the age of eighteen at County Colleges, though this part of the Act failed to come into being.

The Government * was therefore faced with the need to make sweeping improvements to the entire system of public education at a time when there were many other urgent calls for building materials and money. To its credit, it tackled the problem energetically, with an emergency scheme to train additional teachers and a building programme which presently produced some of the most imaginatively designed schools in the world. At long last Britain began to have a worthwhile system of State education. The new Act was not perfect and it remained constantly under discussion, for the British public had discovered a passionate interest in education. The most encouraging feature was that the spirit of the 1944 Act was progressive and good. It raised the function of the State from the lowly one of doling out instruction to the masses to providing a real education for all the nation's children.

In affairs outside Britain, Attlee and Bevin were faced with *Foreign* the problems of Britain's relations with the two giant Powers, *affairs* with her European neighbours and with the Commonwealth. As we have seen, Russia's inflexible attitude drove Bevin to abandon his hopes of establishing good relations with the Soviet Union and to work ever more closely with the United States. By helping to draw the peoples of Western Europe closer together and to form the Brussels Pact, he paved the way for N.A.T.O. and for collective security against the threat of further Soviet advances.

Bevin was, however, less favourably impressed with the idea of complete European unity. He believed that Britain had special Commonwealth obligations and it was only with reluctance that he agreed to join the Council of Europe,† a Committee of Foreign Ministers, formed in 1948.

As the Ruhr, Europe's greatest industrial area, began to revive, fears arose that the steel barons and armament kings who had formerly financed Hitler might again support nationalist forces in Germany. Robert Schuman, France's Foreign Minister, therefore put forward the Schuman Plan to pool the coal and steel resources of France and Germany. After a series of discussions, Belgium, the Netherlands, Luxembourg and Italy

* In Ellen Wilkinson and George Tomlinson, Labour had two outstanding Ministers of Education.
† The members were France, Britain, Denmark, Belgium, Italy, Luxembourg, Ireland, the Netherlands, Norway, Sweden, Turkey, Austria, West Germany, Greece and Iceland.

European Coal and Steel Community

joined them in an association called the European Coal and Steel Community. They agreed to place their coal and steel with West Germany's under the control of a nine-man High Authority but Britain, suspicious of foreign ways and pre-occupied with nationalising her own mines, did not join. She signed an Association Agreement which kept a link with the others but the opportunity to be in at the start of a great enterprise was refused. The European Coal and Steel Community developed into the Common Market, still without Britain.

Meanwhile Palestine was proving to be a most painful problem for Britain. This former province of the Turkish empire had become a British Mandate after the First World War and Britain had clear obligations to the Arab population. But the Balfour Declaration,* promising to give the Jews a national home, made the task of governing the country exceptionally difficult. For years there had been clashes between the Arabs and the incoming Jews who, aided by American funds, established themselves as a vigorous, rapidly increasing community. Terrorist activity was widespread and both sides laid the blame on Britain.

Israel

After 1945 tens of thousands of European Jews who had survived the Nazi persecution managed to evade the British attempts to impose an immigration quota and, with the Arab countries (which had set up the Arab League to resist the Jews) becoming increasingly angry, the chances of avoiding war were very small. Bevin, who almost fell out with the Americans over their desire for unlimited entry of the Jews, decided to hand the problem over to the United Nations and, in 1947, the U.N. voted for partition of Palestine into a Jewish state (Israel) and an Arab state (Jordan). Fighting had broken out before the British troops departed in 1948.

Ben Gurion proclaimed the Republic of Israel and in the war that followed, the Jews triumphed over the badly organised forces of the Arab States.† In 1949, when Israel had secured more territory than had been awarded to her by the U.N., a truce was declared. But the story had a sequel in 1956 at Suez.

* The Balfour Declaration was made in 1917 when Britain was hoping that the Americans would enter the war on their side. Sympathy for the Jews was strong in America where Jewish interests were very influential. Ben Gurion, father of the Republic of Israel, said that the Declaration owed much to Anglo-Saxon love of the Bible.

† Egypt, Iraq, Jordan, Lebanon, Syria.

BEN GURION

If Clement Attlee had no other claim to fame, his name would always be associated with Britain's decision to leave India. No doubt existed that the Indians were determined to rule themselves but imperial Powers rarely hand over their empires without a struggle and it was fortunate that when the time came there was in office a Labour Prime Minister who, unlike his great predecessor Winston Churchill, did not regard the end of British rule in India as " a frightful prospect ".

For well over a century India had been by far the most valuable part of the Empire. It absorbed a great many of Britain's exports and, in return, a handful of officials and soldiers brought order and justice to a vast country where despotism had previously reigned. The British always tried to rule well and they intended to grant self-government when the Indians were ready for it but, as happened in other parts of the Empire, there was no agreement about readiness. The Hindu National Congress had been agitating since 1885 and the All-India Muslim League was formed to put forward the views of the millions of Muslims who lived in ill-concealed hostility towards the Hindus. But although measures were introduced from time to time to include Indians in the Viceroy's Council and as advisers to the provincial Governors, most Britons living in India made no secret of their belief that Indians were not fit to govern themselves.

This was wounding to Indian pride, especially as many of the leaders were clever, educated men, well aware that their country possessed a culture much older than Britain's. After the First World War, when over a million Indians served in the British Forces, the first real steps towards independence (i.e. Dominion status) were granted by the India Act of 1919. This established an Indian Assembly and Indian control of certain aspects of government such as agriculture and education; but the Viceroy could override the Assembly and issue emergency laws.

Congress, led now by a saintly politician named Gandhi, *

* M. K. Gandhi, 1869–1948, known as Mahatma or " Holy One ", studied at London University and became a barrister. He went to South Africa where there was a large Indian population, formed a Red Cross unit during the Boer War, and became the leader of the Indian community. In the First World War he returned to India where he was revered for his saintly life and for the spiritual guidance he gave to his millions of followers.

rejected the proposals and organised a campaign of civil disobedience. Despite Gandhi's appeal for non-violence, riots occurred in which some Europeans were killed, and at Amritsar in the Punjab (1919) a large crowd of Indians was fired upon by order of the local commander and 379 Indians were killed. The Indian Nationalists never forgave the British for this massacre and the chances of co-operation became less as Indian leaders, including Gandhi and Nehru, his chief assistant, were sent to prison.

In 1935 a new India Act gave self-government to the provinces under appointed governors. At this level, Congress co-operated but there was less agreement over the powers given to the princes ruling the native states and already there were violent clashes between Hindus and Muslims. During the Second World War, Sir Stafford Cripps, an old friend of Nehru, went to India to promise complete self-government after the war in return for Indian help but Gandhi and Mohammed Ali Jinnah, the Muslim leader, refused the offer.

As it happened, only a few Indians assisted the Japanese and the Indian Army fought extremely well in Burma and Africa so that in 1946 the newly-elected Labour Government was ready to fulfil Cripps's promise. But it was easier to talk about self-government than to grant or accept it. The semi-independent princes were one difficulty but far greater was the implacable hatred between Hindus and Muslims. The latter were in the minority but there were nevertheless seventy million of them, and Jinnah, having abandoned his earlier attempts to co-operate with Congress, had for some time been putting forward the idea of a separate Muslim state to be named Pakistan. In this, he had the support of all leading Muslims, including Liaqat Ali Khan, a man of fine character and more moderate views.

When negotiations dragged on and mounting tension led to riots, Mr Attlee suddenly threw out a challenge in order to bring both parties to their senses. He set a time-limit. He announced, in February 1947, that the British would leave India by June 1948, and this date was presently brought forward to August 1947. It was therefore essential for the rival leaders to find a speedy solution to their differences. With his usual flair for picking the right man, Attlee chose Lord Mountbatten, lately Supreme Allied Commander in south-east Asia, to be the last Viceroy of India. His task was to

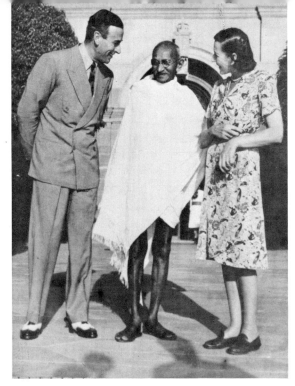

MAHATMA
GANDHI WITH
LORD AND LADY
MOUNTBATTEN,
NEW DELHI,
1947

arrange the settlement and it could only be partition. On 15th August 1947, the separate states of India and Pakistan came into existence as free and equal members of the Commonwealth. Mountbatten * had so impressed the Indian leaders that he was invited to become India's first Governor-General. Jinnah became Governor-General of Pakistan, and both countries found men of first-rate ability to be their first Prime Ministers—Nehru and Liaqat Ali Khan.

Partition

Even so, partition was a tragic, if unavoidable, decision. Appalling massacres took place of Hindus and Muslims who found themselves on the wrong side of a dividing line. Millions of refugees set out to find safer homes among their own people and many perished on the way. Still worse for the future outlook, Pakistan itself consisted of two widely separated parts and there was Kashmir,† precious for many reasons to both sides, with a mainly Muslim population and a Hindu ruler who chose union with India.

* Louis, 1st Earl Mountbatten of Burma (b. 1901), was younger son of Admiral Prince Louis of Battenburg, who changed his German name during the First World War. Lord Mountbatten's mother was a granddaughter of Queen Victoria and he himself was uncle to the future Duke of Edinburgh.

† War between India and Pakistan over Kashmir broke out in 1965.

One of the innumerable casualties was Gandhi himself who had done his utmost to bring the bloodshed to an end. In 1948, in New Delhi, he was murdered by a fanatical young Hindu, as he was walking among the people who loved him. Not long afterwards, Pakistan's leader Ali Jinnah also died, Ali Khan was assassinated in 1951 and, following a series of political wrangles, Ayub Khan, an Army officer, emerged as the country's " strong " President.

Pandit (" Wise Man ") J. Nehru, who succeeded Gandhi as India's leader, became one of the world's foremost statesmen, endeavouring to exert a moderating influence, to soothe international tension and to keep India " uncommitted " to either America or Russia. But when he died in 1964 Nehru * had suffered many disappointments. India, despite much industrialisation and many schemes for progress, was poorer and more overpopulated than ever; China was issuing threats on her border, the Kashmir situation was worse and a spirit of aggressive nationalism was on the increase.

NEHRU

The Second World War swept away the empires of victors and vanquished alike. In Africa and Asia, one country after another acquired its independence, as the flags of Britain, France, Holland and Belgium were hauled down. Italy and Japan also lost their briefly-held empires and only Portugal clung to her overseas possessions. Unfortunately, whereas the war brought independence to many countries, it also brought a loss of freedom to European nations behind the Iron Curtain, though this did not prevent Russian spokesmen from continuing to use such words as " colonialism " and " imperialism " as terms of abuse.

Nationalism   Nationalism became an explosive force among peoples who, before the war, had never thought of self-government and nationhood. This was particularly true of Africa and of some less-advanced territories of Asia which, unlike India, had no long-established movements towards independence.

In most cases, the situation was the same; young men, educated in Britain or France, usually as lawyers, returned to their own countries to form nationalist parties, to go to prison for organising defiance of the colonial power, and to emerge as popular leaders of an independent country. The white man's supremacy was over. The Japanese had destroyed it and there

* He was succeeded by L. B. Shastri, who died in 1966 and was succeeded by Mrs Gandhi, daughter of Pandit Nehru.

was no going back. Ceylon became a Dominion a few months before India and Pakistan; and Burma, freed from the Japanese, left the Commonwealth (the word " Empire " had been tactfully dropped) and took complete independence under a Socialist Government. In 1948 Eire, renamed the Republic of Ireland, also severed the last ties with Britain and the Commonwealth.

At this stage, Attlee's benign attitude was of great value in emphasising British sincerity. " We want no unwilling partners in the British Commonwealth," he remarked when Burma decided to leave, and he insisted that Irish citizens should enjoy the same rights in Britain as formerly. Thus, a fund of goodwill was built up which had the remarkable effect of inducing former colonies to remain in the Commonwealth after receiving independence. When the Commonwealth Prime Ministers' Conference met in 1949, a way was found of preserving the union without injuring the feelings of those who had newly acquired their freedom. Even the countries which decided to become Republics found that they could accept " *the King as the symbol of the free association of its independent member nations and as such the Head of the Commonwealth* ".

For the moment, the Labour Government did not attempt to hurry matters in other parts of the Commonwealth. Movements towards independence were gaining momentum particularly in West Africa, where Dr Nkrumah had come to the fore, and in Malaya, where progress was delayed by the activities of Communist guerrilla forces. As we shall see, these movements came to a head in the fifties and sixties.

One of Ernest Bevin's last achievements before his death was to bring the Commonwealth Foreign Ministers together in Ceylon in order to produce the Colombo Plan (1950). Economic development in south-east Asia would be financed by the World Bank, the United States and the leading Commonwealth countries and, whilst this could be seen as a plan to arrest the spread of Communism, it also sprang from a genuine desire to help the underdeveloped countries of the world.

Colombo Plan

During the next twenty years Britain handed over most of her colonial possessions with dignity and goodwill. This was not always apparent in Malta, Aden, Cyprus and Kenya but, although there were disturbances, usually due to disagreement about the timing of independence and safeguards for minorities, the British never intended to fight a full-scale war rather than give up their Empire.

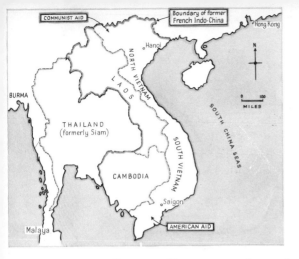

COMMUNIST AID

Boundary of former French Indo-China

Hong Kong

NORTH VIETNAM

Hanoi

N

LAOS

BURMA

THAILAND
(formerly Siam)

SOUTH CHINA SEAS

0   100
MILES

SOUTH VIETNAM

CAMBODIA

Saigon

Malaya

AMERICAN AID

21 Three Empires Lost

VIETNAM   IN 1945 France was determined to recover her overseas territories, apart from Syria and Lebanon which had declared their
independence during the war. However, when the French went
back to Indo-China after the Japanese surrender, their authority
was resisted by nationalists who had already proclaimed the
country a republic called Vietnam. A gruelling jungle war was
fought in which the nationalists received large-scale help from
Communist China and, in 1954, after a disastrous defeat at
Dien Bien Phu, the French were forced to give up the struggle.
Indo-China became the separate states of Laos, Cambodia and
Vietnam, the latter being divided into North Vietnam, under
Communist rule, and South Vietnam, a republic supported by
the United States. This was the Korean situation over again
and in 1962 war broke out in Laos and Vietnam between the
Communists and their right-wing opponents.

The loss of Indo-China made France all the more determined
to retain her empire in North Africa where Algeria, with a
million French inhabitants, was regarded as part of France itself.

The Algerian   Attempts were made to placate Tunisia and Morocco but, after
War   much unrest, both provinces became independent in 1956. The
struggle for Algeria reached atrocious depths of bitterness because
the Algerian rebels, known as F.L.N., besides fighting the
French armies, conducted a campaign of terrorism against the
African Algerians who wished to remain citizens of France.
Half a million French soldiers could not subdue the country and
only when General de Gaulle came to power in France was the
war brought to an end.

De Gaulle, contemptuous of the instability of French politics,
had waited for three years at his home for the call to assume
power. It came in 1958 from a group of generals who thought
that he would win the war in Algeria. But, when de Gaulle

234

realised the hopelessness of the struggle, he repudiated the generals and made peace. In 1962 Algeria became independent with Ben Bella, a former prisoner and rebel leader, as President.

In the Far East, Holland never recovered the East Indies. There had been an independence movement before the war, led by a young nationalist named Soekarno and in 1945, when the Japanese departed, he proclaimed the Indonesian Republic. Like the French, the Dutch fought for nearly five years to regain these rich territories but in 1949 they had to accept Indonesia's independence. President Soekarno, a flamboyant dictator, created a large army, flirted with the Communists and in 1957 expelled all persons of Dutch birth and descent from Indonesia. His corrupt and inefficient régime did not prevent him from trying to play a dominant role in south-east Asia and to bring Malaysia and Singapore into his sphere of influence.

SOEKARNO

In Africa, Belgium possessed an area one hundred times as large as Belgium itself. The Belgian Congo, a vast equatorial region with rich deposits of uranium and copper in the Katanga province, was ruled with firmness but not perhaps with much foresight by the Belgians. When demands for self-government were raised and rioting broke out in Leopoldville in 1960, they hurriedly granted independence and departed. Chaos resulted. The Congolese had had little or no education and training for self-government, and within a week bloodthirsty disorders broke out on a wide scale. Belgian troops, flown in to restore order, were attacked as colonial aggressors and the U.N. was called in.

A strong U.N. force had to deal with undisciplined government troops, armed rebels and white mercenaries as well as with the forces of Katanga which, under Mr Tshombe, broke away to try to become a separate state. During the fighting, Prime Minister Lumumba was murdered and Dag Hammarskjöld, Secretary-General of the United Nations, was killed in an air accident. Gradually some kind of order was imposed and Mr Tshombe returned from exile to become Prime Minister under Mr Kasavubu, the President. Behind them stood the powerful figure of General Mobutu, chief of the army; and by 1965 both politicians had been dismissed. Congo's descent into barbarism had shocked those who believed in self-rule by Africans, and had hardened the attitude of those who opposed it.

TSHOMBE

22 The Early Fifties

THE British General Election of 1950 showed that Labour's popularity had declined. It won the election but only just. The number of Labour M.P.'s fell from 393 to 315, giving a majority of only 9 over the combined Conservative and Liberal total.

Several factors produced this result: people were bored with " austerity " and with Labour's apparent fondness for all kinds of controls; the war had been over for five years and they felt that life should be less grim and restricted. While it was unfair to blame the country's economic difficulties upon the Labour Party, it was easy to point to the costliness of the Welfare State and to such expensive failures as the Tanganyika groundnut scheme. Taxation was very high, but the biggest cause of discontent was the housing shortage. Although Britain actually built more houses in this period than any other country in Europe, the much-talked of target of 200,000 new houses a year was not reached and even this figure compared poorly with pre-war building.*

However, Labour lost only 3 per cent of votes and Attlee returned to office as Prime Minister. A few months later, in July 1950, the Korean war began; British troops were included in the U.N. forces, rearmament became necessary and a financial crisis made one of its regular appearances.

In October, Hugh Gaitskell, who succeeded Cripps as Chancellor, decided to cut the cost of the National Health Service by imposing a charge for spectacles and false teeth. Aneurin Bevan and Harold Wilson resigned in protest and it became apparent that the Government was not only tired after its exertions (Attlee, Cripps and Bevin fell ill and Bevin died), but that it was losing the drive and unity that had enabled it to do so much since 1945.

It was far from easy to govern with so small a majority and,

* Between 1919 and 1939, nearly 4 million houses were built in England and Wales—1,112,000 by local authorities and 2,885,000 by private enterprise. 266,000 were built in 1933, 329,000 in 1934 and 346,000 in 1936.

THE FESTIVAL OF BRITAIN.　ON THE RIGHT IS THE DOME OF DISCOVERY

in September 1951, Attlee went to the country again and this time he lost to the Conservatives, who came in with 321 M.P.'s to 295. But at least Labour went out on a brighter note, for 1951 saw the Festival of Britain, a well-designed and successful exhibition of British products, staged mainly by Morrison, who did his best to furbish up the shabbiness of London (where bomb-damage was still mostly uncleared). The Festival Hall and Battersea Fun Fair were left as permanent reminders of his enterprise. *Labour defeated*

The Labour Party had governed Britain for six years and proved that it could do so with scrupulous regard for the traditions of Parliament and, despite what its opponents said, without creating bitter divisions inside the country. In fact, Britain became more united as a community than ever before— Disraeli's " two nations " were fusing into one—and Labour had provided two or three of the major political figures of the century, Attlee himself, Ernest Bevin and, perhaps, Cripps. Its failure to retain office was due not so much to the fact that it tried to do too much too quickly or that it turned its back on the opportunity to take the leadership of Europe, but that it could not sustain the crusading spirit of 1945 and did little to foster in younger people the idealism that had brought men like Tomlinson and Chuter Ede to Westminster.

At the age of almost seventy-seven, Churchill was again Prime Minister, with Eden, R. A. Butler, Harold Macmillan and Lord Salisbury as the leading figures in his government which had come, said Churchill, " to set the people free " from the intolerable shackles that Labour had imposed. However, it was easier to talk about controls than to remove them in the *Churchill's government* face of economic difficulty and it was quite impossible to reverse most of the measures of nationalisation.

Iron and steel and road transport were restored to private ownership and there was a gradual easing of controls. Restrictions on building private houses were taken off and council housing was pushed ahead in order to reach Macmillan's promised target of 300,000 houses a year. Private landlords were permitted to raise rents, and council rents also tended to go up since the new Government did not favour Labour's policy of keeping rents low by means of subsidies. Food and farming subsidies were reduced so that, with dearer food and higher rents, there were strikes and demands for increased wages.

However, as in the late twenties, improvement of world trade helped Britain's recovery. The balance of payments difficulty became less when the Korean war ended in 1953 and, with increasing production, standards rose steadily. By 1954 food rationing had been abolished, there was a drop in world prices of raw materials, Mr Butler took sixpence off income-tax and Britain at last began to take on an air of prosperity. One pointer to this was the passing of the Television Act of 1954 (due perhaps more to a skilful pressure group than to a widespread demand) which set up an Independent Television Authority and allowed firms to advertise their goods in return for large fees. The B.B.C. monopoly was broken and another long stride towards inflation had been taken.

King George VI, a most courageous and conscientious monarch, died in 1952 and was succeeded by his daughter, Elizabeth II, whose Coronation took place in the following year. Churchill himself became seriously ill and in 1955 he retired at the age of eighty. He was succeeded by Sir Anthony Eden, who had made his reputation in foreign affairs and had long been regarded as the " crown prince " of politics, the certain successor to his great leader.

Eden
Prime Minister

Eden decided to hold a General Election at once and, in May 1955, the Conservatives increased their majority by sixty. They were helped by dissensions within the Labour Party in which the old guard of Attlee and Morrison, supported by moderates like Gaitskell, were opposed by Aneurin Bevan and his followers,

GAITSKELL AND
MORRISON

the " Bevanites ", who included Harold Wilson.* Attlee's retirement intensified the feud between Bevan and Gaitskell, who gained the leadership by a large majority. They were partially reconciled later and Gaitskell had reunited the Party when he died suddenly in 1962 at the age of fifty-six. Bevan had died two years earlier and the leadership fell to Wilson, an economist who had been by far the youngest member of Attlee's Cabinet.

In domestic affairs, Eden's outstanding minister was Macmillan † who, having succeeded with the housing programme (over one million houses had been built since 1951), became Chancellor of the Exchequer. The upper and middle classes still had scope for grumbling at the high taxation but, with full employment and, in many industries, high wages, the country had never appeared more prosperous, so that Macmillan was able to promote savings, to cut Government expenditure and to try to stabilise wages and prices.

Colonial and foreign affairs caused Eden far more anxiety than the situation at home. Cyprus, a British colony regarded, though wrongly, as a valuable military and naval base in the Mediterranean, had long been seething with discontent. Most of the islanders, Greek-Cypriots, wanted " enosis " or union with Greece, while the Turkish minority, one-fifth of the population, dreaded domination by the Greeks. By 1955 Eoka, a terrorist organisation led by Colonel Grivas, began extensive attacks upon the British troops and the Turkish communities. The leader of the Greek-Cypriots, Archbishop Makarios, was suspected of complicity in this savage campaign

Cyprus

* Harold Wilson, b. 1916, educated Oxford University; lecturer in economics; M.P. 1945; Parliamentary Secretary to Ministry of Works 1945–47; President of Board of Trade 1947–51; Leader of the Labour Party 1962, Prime Minister 1964–

† Harold Macmillan, b. 1894, educated Eton and Oxford; M.P. 1924; Parliamentary Secretary to Ministry of Supply 1940; Colonial Under-Secretary 1942; Minister Resident at Allied H.Q. North Africa 1942; re-entered Parliament 1951; Minister of Housing 1954; Minister of Defence 1955; Foreign Secretary 1955; Chancellor of Exchequer 1955–57; Prime Minister 1957–63.

ARCHBISHOP
MAKARIOS
(CENTRE)
ARRIVING AT
HIS PLACE OF
EXILE IN THE
SEYCHELLES
ISLANDS

but deporting him to the Seychelles only increased the violence of his followers. As had happened so often in the past, no solution was possible until the imprisoned leader was brought back. After four murderous years, agreements in Zurich and London (1960) resulted in Cyprus becoming an independent republic with a Greek-Cypriot President and a Turkish-Cypriot Vice-President. Britain retained two military bases and Cyprus entered the Commonwealth, but it was soon evident that peace between the two hostile communities was only temporary.

Mau-Mau

Kenya provided another instance of the difficulties which faced Britain when trying to be just to all sections of the population in a colony that was demanding self-government. Here, the country had been developed economically by some 60,000 Europeans, mostly farmers, and 160,000 Asians and Arabs who were traders and shopkeepers. The African population, numbering 8 million, demanded a greater share of land and prosperity, with the Kikuyu, the strongest tribe, taking the lead.

From 1952 until 1956, Mau-Mau, a terrorist society, waged war against Europeans and peaceable Africans so that British troops had to go into action—giving the impression that an old-style colonial Power was crushing a local movement for independence, but this was not so. Although Mau-Mau was suppressed and Jomo Kenyatta, the Kikuyu leader, placed under arrest, Britain's intentions remained unaffected by violence. " The interests of the African natives must be paramount," declared Iain Macleod, the Colonial Secretary, and, in 1962, Kenyatta was released and a London Conference reached agreement upon self-government. When the Kenya African National Union

MAU-MAU SUSPECTS AWAIT QUESTIONING, APRIL 1953

NIKITA KRUSHCHEV, MAY 1960

Party gained a majority in the elections, Jomo Kenyatta became Prime Minister of Kenya.

During these disturbances in Cyprus and Kenya, world tension was temporarily eased by the death of Stalin in 1953 and by the emergence of Krushchev as leader of the Soviet Union. Bald, stout and, when he chose, as vulgarly jovial as a peasant, Krushchev seemed to be a much more human personality than his menacing predecessor. He may have lacked Stalin's absolute power but, strong enough to curb the dreaded political police, he revealed to the astounded masses some of his dead master's tyrannies. With Stalin's name disgraced, it became possible to speak of " peaceful co-existence " between Russia and the West, talk that was undoubtedly helped by the fact that both sides now possessed the hydrogen bomb, equivalent to 850 Hiroshima bombs.

Krushchev

Krushchev's apparent mildness towards the capitalist world was virulently attacked by the Chinese Communist Party which, having achieved miracles inside China itself, was beginning to devote itself to the old doctrines of spreading Communism throughout the world. This split between the two great Communist Powers was a startling development in world affairs at a time when Western Europe was drawing still closer together in the vital matters of trade and defence.* However, the hopes of those who believed in democracy and peaceful negotiation received a severe setback in the Middle East.

* E.D.C. (European Defence Community) was set up in 1952 by France, Italy, West Germany, Belgium, Luxembourg and the Netherlands. The Paris Agreement of 1954 formed the Western European Union in which Britain agreed to keep forces on the continent and West Germany joined N.A.T.O. The European Coal and Steel Community (E.C.S.C.) began to work in 1952.

COLONEL NASSER AND GENERAL NEGUIB (WITH HANDKERCHIEF) AUGUST 1953

23 The Suez Affair

SINCE the war British influence in Egypt had been on the wane. Her Protectorate over Egypt had been abandoned in 1919, but for various reasons—fear of Italy, defence of the Canal Zone, interests in the Sudan and then the Second World War—British troops and advisers had remained in the country. But the Egyptian Army officers were determined to get rid of Western control. They also intended to put an end to the corrupt rule of King Farouk and the abysmal poverty of the Egyptian peasants. Above all, they longed to unite the Arab world by destroying Israel and avenging their humiliating defeat in 1948.

Nasser

In 1952 General Neguib led a revolution that deposed King Farouk and challenged the British position. Two years later, Neguib was ousted by his former supporter, Colonel Nasser, a much more able and forceful man who opened negotiations with Britain for a peaceful evacuation of the Canal Zone by 1956. In agreeing to this, Eden, then Foreign Secretary, was making a bid for Egypt's friendship and, in any case, despite criticism from fellow Conservatives, he knew that there was nothing for it but to withdraw gracefully. Britain was in retreat in the Middle East (the Palestine Mandate had been given up, Persia's seizure of the Anglo-Persian Oil Company had been accepted and by now control of Egypt had gone) and Eden was well aware that America, the senior ally, had no sympathy with or understanding of Britain's position.

Baghdad Pact

The chances of friendship with Nasser were destroyed in 1955, when Eden, now Prime Minister, formed the Baghdad Pact of Iraq, Turkey, Persia, Pakistan and Britain in order to protect the Middle East against a possible attack by Russia. There were intense rivalries among the Arab nations and Nasser was enraged by Britain's support for Iraq at the very time when he himself was assuming leadership of the Arab world. Therefore he accepted Russia's offer of military and economic aid to Egypt.

242

Meanwhile Ben Gurion began to talk of a " preventive war " by Israel before Egypt became too strong, and the French, convinced that Nasser was helping the Algerian rebels, sent secret shipments of arms to Palestine.

In an attempt to woo Nasser away from Russia, Britain suggested an Anglo-American loan for the building of the Aswan Dam, a colossal project that would do much to feed Egypt's rapidly increasing population. Nasser appeared likely to accept the offer but, at this point, the small Arab state of Jordan came into the picture. King Hussein was induced, supposedly by pressure from Nasser, to dismiss General Glubb, *Jordan* his British military adviser, and this incident (1956) convinced Eden that Nasser must be regarded as the arch-enemy of British interests.

However, Nasser had decided to accept the Anglo-American loan for the Aswan Dam but he also announced Egypt's recognition of Communist China. Nothing could have been more likely to antagonise American opinion. In a Presidential election year (Eisenhower was elected for a second term), no one was going to lend American money to a pro-Communist country and Mr Dulles, the American Secretary of State, withdrew the proffered loan. Britain seconded his decision.

A few days later, 26th July 1956, Nasser declared that Egypt would nationalise the Suez Canal Company (whose concession had twelve years to run) and pay for the dam out of its profits. *The Canal* Shareholders would be compensated and the Canal would be open to all nations.

There seems little doubt that Nasser was entitled to take this action but France and Britain made strong protests and even Gaitskell, the Labour leader, said that Nasser had behaved in a high-handed, Hitler-like manner. In Eden's view, the Canal would be closed to British shipping through a combination of malice and inefficiency and therefore there was no alternative but to use force to secure it.

The French agreed with Eden and, although President Eisenhower and Dulles were obviously disturbed, there seemed to be no thought of asking for United States' support or even of frank consultation with a great ally. This breach in Anglo-American friendship was partly caused by the dislike which Dulles and Eden entertained for each other. Eden, the suave diplomat, felt that Dulles was tricky and overbearing; he had failed to support the Arab League and made no attempt to understand Britain's difficulties in the Middle East. But although Britain and France were resolved to take strong action, they were hard put to rake up the necessary forces, because the French were heavily involved in Algeria and Britain could not bring even two air-borne divisions to readiness. In any case, with Cyprus lacking a good harbour, there was no suitable base nearer than Malta.

There was therefore a delay during which a conference of maritime nations discussed plans for international control of the Canal and Mr Menzies, the Australian Prime Minister, headed a committee that went to Egypt to see Nasser. Not surprisingly, Nasser rejected the plan, pointing out that although the Canal was still operating as usual, he was being threatened with force. At this, Britain and France withdrew the Company's pilots in the pathetic belief that no other pilots could be found to carry out a comparatively easy job and Dulles put forward his plan for a Suez Canal Users' Association, though no one was clear what its function would be. In September, Eden asked the Security Council for international control of the Canal but the matter was vetoed by Russia.

The meeting in Paris

On 16th October, Eden and Selwyn Lloyd (the Foreign Secretary) met M. Pineau and M. Mollet, the French ministers, in Paris. What they decided is not known, nor is it certain that Ben Gurion was present. What is certain is that, on 29th October, despite warnings from the U.S. to Israel not to launch an attack on any Arab state, an Israeli army invaded the Sinai peninsula, threw back the Egyptian Army and captured masses of Russian equipment.

At once the U.S.A. called for an emergency meeting of the Security Council, but Eden announced that Britain and France had sent an ultimatum to Egypt and Israel ordering them to withdraw their forces to positions ten miles on either side of the Canal (i.e. Israeli troops would be about a hundred miles *inside* the Egyptian frontier!). If Egypt did not accept within twelve hours, Anglo-French forces would occupy the Canal Zone. This attempt at "Hitler-like" action was farcically mismanaged. Instead of the swift descent of invading forces, there were only a few bombs dropped upon Egyptian soil and some threatening broadcasts from Cyprus radio!

Nasser ordered blockships to be sunk in the Canal, the United Nations demanded withdrawal of Egyptian and Israeli troops to their respective frontiers and Britain used the veto for the first

BLOCKSHIPS SUNK IN THE SUEZ CANAL, NOVEMBER 1956

time to prevent condemnation of Israel's aggression. Meanwhile, moving slower than in Nelson's time, the invasion force approached Egypt from Malta and when all fighting between Egyptian and Israeli forces had ceased, Anglo-French paratroops landed at Port Said and next day a sea-borne force stormed the beaches and prepared to move down the Canal.

Anglo-French attack

By this time the British public, recovering from stupefaction at the news that Eden of all people had ordered the attack, was more bitterly divided than at any time since the days of the Irish question. While some rejoiced at the thought of Britain asserting herself, as many others were angrily ashamed that their country, a founder member of the United Nations, should have committed an act of naked aggression. Eden, surprised by the intensity of public criticism and by being booed in the House, began to waver. Everything was going wrong. The Anglo-French forces had not caused Egypt to collapse, Nasser had not been overthrown and the Syrian oil pipe-line had been blown up. Russia threatened to intervene against the aggressors; India, Canada and the United States were scathingly hostile and foreign investors were withdrawing their money from London at an alarming rate.

As suddenly and as surprisingly as they had issued their ultimatum, France and Britain ordered their troops to cease operations. On 6th November they agreed to withdraw from Egypt in favour of an international police force and, apart from the arguments which would continue for years, the Suez affair was over. It remains one of the most astonishing episodes in British history.

Eden, the League of Nations man, the negotiator at countless peace conferences, had played the major role in a secret plot to make war on Egypt. Hardly anyone was consulted. The Opposition, the Foreign Office, the Commonwealth Prime Ministers, the United States and most of the Cabinet were kept in the dark about the Prime Minister's intentions. The only feasible explanation could be that Eden was a very sick man, for his health broke down almost at once and he resigned from office early in 1957. For the rest, Nasser, although defeated by Israel, won enormous prestige and he still held the Suez Canal. The French Army, feeling let down once again by the British, resumed the Algerian war with added bitterness, and some of their Suez parachutists were to play a leading part in overthrowing the politicians in Paris two years later. The United Nations gained somewhat in authority because two Powers had obeyed the order to cease fire. On the other hand, preoccupation with Suez had enabled Russia to triumph over Hungary.

Revolt in Hungary

In October 1956, Budapest had risen in arms to drive out the Russian occupation troops and, for a short time, it looked as if Hungary might win independence. But on 4th November, Soviet tanks returned to crush the uprising with vengeful brutality. The conduct of Britain and France now appeared to be much less atrocious than that of the Russians and, to some extent, attention was diverted from their behaviour.

For the British people, Suez was a bitter pill to swallow. It brought home to them the truth that Great Britain was now a Power of the second rank and that, in a pitifully mismanaged attempt to intimidate a lesser country, she had revealed her military and economic weakness to the entire world. It was a sad position for the country which had ended the war with such prestige that moral leadership could have been hers for the taking; and it was frightening to reflect that in a democracy the Prime Minister possessed the power to plunge the country into war without the genuine consent of people and Parliament.

RUSSIAN
SOLDIERS RETURN
TO BUDAPEST

24 After Suez

STRANGELY enough, Suez did not break the Conservative Party
or even compel it to resign from office. Harold Macmillan, who
succeeded Eden in January 1957, did not appear to be at all
overwhelmed or dejected by the low state of the country's
fortunes. On the contrary, as shrewd and " unflappable " as
Baldwin, he displayed an air of cheerful confidence at every
turn. In his sprightly, curiously old-fashioned way, he suggested
that he was just the man to put awkward things right.

As Prime Minister for a longer continuous period than anyone
since Asquith, Macmillan was able to concentrate upon five ob-
jectives: to heal the wounds of his own Party, to restore the
damaged partnership with the United States, to encourage
economic progress at home, to improve relations with Russia
and to bring about a series of settlements in Africa.

The " Suez rebels " in the Conservative Party soon faded
into the background and, when the General Election occurred in
1959, the public had so far forgotten the humiliations of Suez as
to re-elect a Tory Government with an increased majority of
more than a hundred. Macmillan's authority was firm and he
was able to give the Foreign Office to a peer, Lord Home, in
1960 and to dismiss seven Cabinet Ministers in 1962 without
provoking a rebellion. But when, after holding the Premiership
for nearly seven years, Macmillan resigned in October 1963, he
did not hand to his successor a popular and united party. The
important matter of grooming a young and vigorous minister
for leadership had been neglected; Reginald Maudling and
Edward Heath had " arrived " too recently, R. A. Butler, the
discreet, liberal-minded Deputy Prime Minister, was passed
over and the Party found itself led by Lord Home who renounced
his title and became Sir Alec Douglas-Home in order to take
the helm in the House of Commons. Within a year of Macmillan's departure, Home had been defeated and Labour was
back in office.

The efforts to mend relations with the United States and
to come to a better understanding with Russia were reasonably
successful thanks partly to Macmillan's personal meetings with
President Eisenhower, with Krushchev and with President

Macmillan
Prime
Minister

MACMILLAN

247

HOLY LOCH, SCOTLAND, 1961. THE MAN IN THE CANOE IS ONE OF THOSE WHO DEMONSTRATED AGAINST THE ARRIVAL OF THE ' POLARIS ' SUBMARINE

John F. Kennedy, who succeeded Eisenhower in 1960. Meetings between heads of government usually take place when one or more than one have something to gain and at this time there were good reasons for cordiality. Eisenhower continued Truman's policy of checking Communism by military and economic aid and this accorded with Britain's interests. Agreement was reached about production of certain weapons and U.S. nuclear-powered Polaris missile submarines were to operate from a British base at Holy Loch in Scotland.

Russia, well aware of Communist China's increasing influence in Asia and Africa, agreed to a cease-fire in Laos but Macmillan's hopes for a " Summit " conference in 1960 were wrecked by the shooting down of a United States U.2 reconnaissance aircraft over Russian territory. This incident led to a return of bad feeling which was to reach its zenith in the Cuba crisis of 1962.

The election of President Kennedy brought a welcome warmth to Anglo-American relations, for his youth and enthusiasm for good causes immediately endeared him to the British public. Here, they felt, was the man whose vision and ideals could transform the world by bridging the gulf between East and West and by helping the underprivileged peoples of many countries, including his own.

At home, Kennedy was fully engaged in securing Civil Rights for America's eighteen million negro citizens and pressing social reforms upon a Congress that was deeply

248

suspicious of British-type Welfare State legislation. But an even greater challenge was to face him in Cuba, an island of the West Indies lying only 130 miles from the American coast.

A Cuban revolution in 1958 had overthrown a corrupt dictatorship and had brought to the top a dynamic lawyer named Fidel Castro. Finding no support for his Left-wing aims in America, Castro turned to Russia for help, and by *Cuba* 1962 the island was supplied not merely with Russian tractors and technicians but with Russian aeroplanes and nuclear missile bases. Kennedy reacted strongly by ordering a blockade of shipping to Cuba and appealing direct to Krushchev while asking the Security Council to intervene.

As Russian ships approached the Caribbean and both sides prepared for war, Kennedy and Krushchev exchanged letters. At the eleventh hour, Krushchev gave way and agreed to dismantle the missile sites. The world sighed with relief as the tension gradually subsided, for it was clear that when it came to the crunch, the two greatest Powers did not want atomic war. Perhaps they would confine their rivalry to the exploration of Space.*

During these perilous weeks, the British Prime Minister could do little but he played a leading part in the sequel to the Cuba crisis—the signing of the Nuclear Test Ban Treaty in Moscow in July 1963. Three months later, Macmillan resigned from office, and within another month President Kennedy

* In 1957 the Russians put the first earth satellite into orbit; in 1959 they hit the moon with a rocket; in 1960 both countries brought animals safely back from journeys in space and on 12th April 1961 the Soviet airman, Yuri Gagarin, orbited the earth in a spaceship. Twenty-three days later the American Commander Alan Sheppard also travelled into space.

was dead.   He was assassinated at Dallas, Texas, on 23rd November 1963.

At home Macmillan's period of office saw Britain reach a very high level of prosperity.   All the wartime shortages had disappeared and although the national economy might be shaky and the balance of payments problem unsolved, most of *Prosperity in* the people, in Macmillan's own words, had " never had it so *Britain* good ".   Generally speaking, they were better fed, better clothed, better housed than at any time in their history.   They owned more goods, spent more money on drink, gambling and entertainment, and even those who were old and needy were far better cared for than in the days when Britain was looked upon as the wealthiest country on earth.

This improvement in the people's standard of living was not, of course, entirely due to Macmillan's leadership.   The effects of full-employment and mass-production became particularly apparent at this time.   Between 1951 and 1963 prices rose by 45 per cent but wages rose by 72 per cent and actual earnings by 95 per cent.   Since Macmillan's remark about " never having had it so good " was sometimes derided and denied, it is worth examining the position a little more closely.

The average earnings of men in industry rose from £8 6s a week in 1951 to £16 3s 1d in 1963 when Macmillan resigned, but this would only be a large gain if the £ remained steady. In fact, it declined in value during that time to 14s 6½d which brought the real value of £16 3s 1d down to £11 17s, an increase of 42.7 per cent.   This was still a very substantial figure because the rise in prices was also offset by the lower value of the £. The earnings figures apply to men over 21 in industry, so one ought also to consider workers not included in that category, e.g. miners and agricultural workers.   For them the position was:

	1951			1963			1963 Corrected*			Increase %
	£	s	d	£	s	d	£	s	d	
Miners	10	11	11	18	5	0	13	7	9	26.4
Agricultural Workers	5	19	5½	11	9	11	8	8	8	41.1

(* To allow for falling value of £)

But it was claimed that pensioners fell behind in the race. Here again, the figures are instructive:

	1951			1963			1963 Corrected			Increase
	£	s	d	£	s	d	£	s	d	%
Insured person or widow	1	10	0	3	7	6	2	9	6	65
Uninsured wife	1	0	0	2	1	6	1	10	5	52
	(or 16s)									

Taxation became less heavy, purchase-tax was reduced (on cars and television sets it fell from 66 per cent to 25 per cent) and personal savings doubled between 1959 and 1963. People's spending on comfort and enjoyment increased to a remarkable degree. At constant prices, the figures were:

Beer	$+14\%$
Food	$+21\%$
Furniture, carpets, etc.	$+25\%$
Clothing, footwear	$+39\%$
Wines, spirits, etc.	$+61\%$
Radios, electrical and other durable goods	$+120\%$
Cars, motor-cycles	$+530\%$

In 1959, at the Labour Party Conference, Hugh Gaitskell made this observation:

" The recent improvements in living standards have been of a special kind. There has been a particularly notable increase in comforts and pleasures and convenience in the home. Television has transformed the leisure hours of the vast majority of our fellow citizens. Washing machines, refrigerators, modern cookers have made women's lives easier.

" Holidays show another profound change. It is still true that many people do not go away from home but obviously more do. It is inconceivable that twenty years ago *Reynolds News* could have organised three weeks' tours for its readers in the United States at £200 per person and in the Soviet Union at £100 per person."

Thus the possessions and way of life that had belonged to the middle classes in pre-war years were shared increasingly by the weekly wage-earner but, strangely enough, the well-to-do society seemed to feel neither contented nor secure.

The trade figures for November 1957 were the best for seven years, yet the same year produced the highest number ever recorded (2,859) of stoppages due to industrial disputes. More goods to buy and more hire-purchase to pay seemed to bring more demands for higher wages. Many were successful, so that Macmillan's Chancellors of the Exchequer (four of them in five years) were constantly warding off inflation by cutting Government expenditure and raising the Bank Rate. The "credit squeeze", as it was called, was used every now and again to check home consumption (it worked chiefly by making hire-purchase more expensive); the Chancellor would appeal for a "pay pause", an "export drive" would be launched and then, when the crisis was over, the Bank Rate would come down and the financial merry-go-round would start again.

This lack of stability produced several results. People bought cars, refrigerators, clothes, furniture and gadgets of every kind in vast quantities, but many of the things which the Welfare State needed—hospitals, health centres, more new schools and universities—could not be afforded. The most impoverished country in Europe could hardly have built fewer motor-ways or have done less for public transport and the docks. Efforts to grapple with the country's problems by long-term planning, such as a National Economic Development Plan, an "incomes policy" and Dr Beeching's plan for British Railways, were received with suspicion by the trade unions.

The unions   The unions were criticised for their apparent unwillingness to co-operate in schemes for controlling wages (and therefore prices) and for their inability to impose discipline upon their own members. Unofficial strikes were commonplace, particularly in the docks and in the transport and motor industries, and there were many signs of lost confidence between leaders and the rank-and-file. It had to be remembered, however, that the unions came into existence to obtain the best conditions and wages for their members that could be wrung from the employers, and the prosperity which wage-earners now enjoyed was a very recent phenomenon. Most of the union leaders could recall the days of the Dole and the Means Test. In a competitive society, where yesterday's luxuries had become today's necessities, they saw it as their duty to push their own members' claims and to let the economy take care of itself.

In 1962 an old bogey reappeared. Unemployment increased in those parts which had once been known as Depressed Areas, the north-east, south Wales, parts of Scotland and Northern Ireland. The number of unemployed reached 500,000 and rose in January 1963 to over 800,000, nothing like the old figures but nearer to the million mark than for more than twenty years.

Steps were taken to encourage new industries in the worst-hit areas and to prevent a further flow of population to the southern half of Britain. But old fears had come to the surface and the uneasy feeling that prosperity itself was in danger led to fresh demands for shorter working weeks and " redundancy " guarantees.

However, in spite of many difficulties, Macmillan had done remarkably well up until the end of 1962. One crisis after another had been surmounted and negotiations were going on which might lead to a new and more vigorous spirit in British industry.

The European Coal and Steel Community, which, as we have seen, was set up in 1952, developed into the European Economic Community (E.E.C.) or " Common Market ", when France, West Germany, Italy, Belgium, the Netherlands and Luxembourg (" The Six ") signed the Treaty of Rome in 1957. They agreed that, as with coal, iron and steel, they would gradually abolish tariffs on all commodities in order to trade freely with each other. These arrangements were intended to lead eventually to political unification. Only a United Europe, it was felt, would be able to trade and negotiate on equal terms with the two Great Powers.

The Common Market

Britain, however, remained doubtful. Political union with European countries would conflict with British sovereignty and Commonwealth ties, but the trading implications were so important that she proposed a looser association. At Stockholm, in 1960, Britain, Austria, Denmark, Portugal, Sweden, Norway and Switzerland (" The Seven ") joined together to form the European Free Trade Association (E.F.T.A.) but the existence of two rival groups could not be regarded as a happy development in Europe's progress towards unity.

E.F.T.A.

By 1961 Macmillan's Government decided to apply for membership of the thriving E.E.C., provided adequate safeguards were made for the Commonwealth, E.F.T.A. and British agriculture. R. A. Butler opened negotiations on Britain's

EDWARD HEATH (LEFT) AT THE COMMON MARKET NEGOTIATIONS, 1963

behalf and was succeeded by Edward Heath who throughout
1962 displayed great skill and patience in the protracted
discussions. He appeared to be nearing success when, in
January 1963, de Gaulle curtly demanded an end to the
negotiations. The other five members of the Common Market
were in favour of Britain's entry but, by the Treaty of Rome,
decisions had to be unanimous and France was able to keep
Britain out.

This was a calamitous blow to Macmillan. Instead of being
able to relinquish his leadership in a moment of triumph, with
Britain about to take up the exciting challenge of a new phase
in her history, he was left empty-handed. Not many of the
public had understood what the negotiations were about but
they were indignant at the outcome; was there never to be an
end to the humiliations that Britain had to suffer? Unfairly,
they saw the Prime Minister no longer as " Wondermac " but
as a tired old failure. He and his colleagues found themselves
increasingly under attack from various directions and especially
from younger people, including a group of satirical writers and
television producers who were zestfully engaged in poking fun
at " the Establishment ", i.e. all those in authority. Behind the
irreverent gibes there was genuine disillusionment with an
ageing Government that seemed to have been in office for too
long.

In October, Macmillan resigned and Sir Alec Douglas-Home
became Prime Minister for one year until, in the autumn of
1964, Labour gained an overall majority of four in the General
Election and Harold Wilson took office as the third Labour
Prime Minister.

COMMONWEALTH PRIME MINISTERS' CONFERENCE 1965. HAROLD
WILSON, DR HASTINGS BANDA OF MALAWI, DR MILTON OBOTE OF UGANDA

25 The New Commonwealth

WHEN the Second World War ended, the British Empire and Commonwealth was made up of Britain, the four senior Dominions (Australia, New Zealand, Canada and the Union of South Africa) which were fully independent nations, the empire of India, which was partly self-governing, and a number of colonies and protectorates. Britain's policy was described by the Colonial Secretary in 1943 in these words:

" We are pledged to guide colonial people along the road to self-government within the framework of the British Empire, we are pledged to build up their social and economic institutions, and we are pledged to develop their natural resources."

There was, particularly in America and Russia, a great deal of scepticism about the real intentions of Britain. Roosevelt had thought that an aggressive revival of British Imperialism after the war was a greater danger to peace than Russian Communism. Fine words and noble aims were part of the self-righteousness which Britons always assumed when speaking of their Empire. But the habit of ruling would be too hard to give up and the colonial peoples would have to wade through blood to reach their freedom.

In less than twenty years Britain proved her critics wrong. She gave up her power over some 600 million people and helped nineteen countries to reach nationhood, most of them peacefully and with expressions of goodwill on both sides. Where there were delays and disorder, as in Kenya and Cyprus, these were usually due to racial difficulties and the need to safeguard minorities. Generally speaking, there was little argument about a people's readiness for self-government or their level of education. Britain herself had evolved a system of parliamentary government when the bulk of the population was illiterate, and men like Attlee, Macmillan, Iain Macleod and R. A. Butler realised that nationalism was a force that could not be denied. To those longing to rule themselves, self-government was better than the good government of a Colonial Power. As far as possible, they must be helped and guided, but where there were responsible leaders, a party system and a firm intention to respect the wishes and rights of all the population, the arrival of self-government was assured.

There were, of course, cases of special difficulty. In Malta and in some of the islands of the West Indies, for example, it was doubtful whether the economic position was strong enough; and in Malaya the presence of Communist terrorists delayed independence for several years.

The most surprising thing was that when this empire was dissolved, the new Asian and African nations did not throw aside all connections with the imperial power which they had so often opposed in the past. Naturally, there were solid advantages to be considered—the need for friends and protection, economic help and British capital—but there were less tangible reasons too for remaining in a group of nations that believed in freedom and decent behaviour to one another. The Commonwealth had no fixed constitution or rules, it imposed no domination but was flexible enough to include members with widely differing views. Its existence depended upon tolerance and goodwill, and it remained to be seen whether the links of friendship were strong enough to stand the strain of the kind of situation which, by the sixties, was developing in Southern Rhodesia.

As we have seen, India, Pakistan and Ceylon attained independence during Attlee's premiership. All three decided to enter the Commonwealth. Burma did not choose to do so and the Republic of Ireland resigned membership, though the Ireland Act of 1949 provided that it should not be treated as a foreign country.

Then followed the period of Churchill and Eden when there was less encouragement for colonial self-rule but this pause was succeeded by Macmillan's readiness to recognise the claims of emerging countries. As he said himself, there was " a wind of change " blowing through Africa and it could not be denied or stifled. In seven years, between 1957 and 1964, independence was granted to fifteen countries.

They were:

1957—Ghana
    The Federation of Malaya (renamed Malaysia in 1963 and then including North Borneo, Sarawak and Singapore)
1959—Singapore
1960—Nigeria

1961—Cyprus
      Sierra Leone
      Tanganyika (later Tanzania)
1962—Jamaica
      Trinidad and Tobago
      Uganda
1963—Zanzibar (later Tanzania)
      Kenya
1964—Malawi (formerly Nyasaland)
      Malta
      Zambia (formerly Northern Rhodesia)

During this period of expanding freedom, there occurred the withdrawal from the Commonwealth of one of its senior members, the Union of South Africa. This was the one country in Africa with a large population of Europeans, 3½ millions *South Africa* mostly of British and Dutch stock, whose forbears had settled there from the seventeenth century when the country was sparsely inhabited. In developing South Africa's great mineral and agricultural riches, they employed large numbers of Africans most of whom came from territories to the north. Besides 12 million Africans, there were about 2 million persons of mixed race. The existence of this large non-white population, well-paid by comparison with workers in the rest of Africa, caused anxiety to the Europeans. They feared that they would lose control of the country which was their home and which they and their ancestors had brought to a high stage of prosperity.

From 1948, therefore, the South African Government of Dr Malan (who succeeded the liberal-minded General Smuts as Prime Minister) adopted the policy of *apartheid* or " separateness ". The Africans were separately housed and educated; they had their own townships and areas of development but

APARTHEID.
THE LOCAL
AFRICAN
POPULATION WAS
DUE TO BE
MOVED TO A
NEW TOWNSHIP
AND ITS CAFÉ
TO BE
DEMOLISHED

ENG. BK. V—17

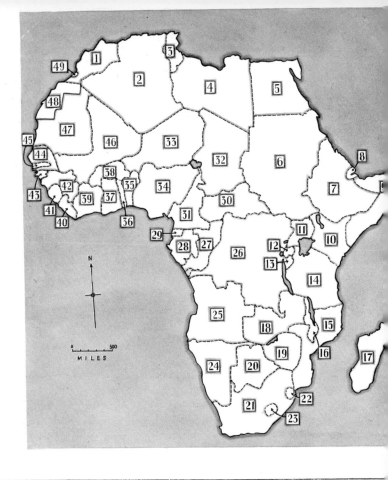

AFRICA
1966

1 MOROCCO. Partitioned; French, Spanish and Tangier sectors; independent 1956

2 ALGERIA. Ex-French department; independent 1964

3 TUNISIA. Ex-French protectorate; independent 1956

4 LIBYA. Ex-Italian colony; independent 1951

5 U.A.R. (EGYPT). Occupied by Turks, French and British; British occupation ended in 1936

6 SUDAN. Ex-British and French colony; independent 1956

7 ETHIOPIA. independent since 11th century B.C.

8 FRENCH SOMALILAND. French colony autonomous since 1957

9 SOMALIA. Ex-British and Italian colony; independent 1960

10 KENYA. Ex-British colony; independent 1963

11 UGANDA. Ex-British colony; independent 1962

12 RWANDA. U.N. Trust Territory; independent 1962

13 BURUNDI. Ex-Belgian colony; independent 1962

14 TANZANIA. Ex-British, French and German colony; independent 1961; renamed Tanzania 1964 after union with Zanzibar

15 MOZAMBIQUE. Portuguese colony

16 MALAWI. Ex-British protectorate; independent 1964

17 MADAGASCAR. Ex-French colony; independent 1960

18 ZAMBIA. British colony; independent 1964.

19 SOUTHERN RHODESIA. Self-governing colony under British Crown.

20 BECHUANALAND. Ex-British protectorate now High Commission Territory

21 SOUTH AFRICA. Ex-British and Dutch colonies became Union 1910 and Republic 1961

22 SWAZILAND. British High Commission Territory

23 BASUTOLAND. Ex-British protectorate now High Commission Territory

24 SOUTH WEST AFRICA Ex-German colony now South African administration under U.N.

25 ANGOLA. Portuguese colony

26 CONGO LEOPOLDVILLE. Ex-Belgian colony; independent 1960

27 CONGO BRAZZAVILLE. Ex-French colony; independent 1960

28 GABON. Annexed by France in 1888; independent 1960

29 SPANISH GUINEA. Formed by two Spanish provinces

30 CENTRAL AFRICAN REPUBLIC. Annexed by France in 1888; independent 1960

31 CAMEROON. Ex-German colony mandated to Britain and France in 1922; independent 1960

32 CHAD. Ex-German and French colony; independent 1960

33 NIGER. Separate territory within French West Africa; independent 1960

34 NIGERIA. Ex-British colony; independent 1960

35 DAHOMEY. Ex-French colony; independent 1960

36 TOGO. Ex-British and French colony; independent 1960

37 GHANA. Ex-British colony; independent 1957

38 UPPER VOLTA. Ex-French colony; independent 1960

39 IVORY COAST. Annexed by France in 1893; independent 1960

40 LIBERIA. Independent Negro Republic proclaimed 1847

41 SIERRA LEONE British colony; independent 1961

42 GUINEA. Ex-French and Portuguese colony; independent 1958

43 PORTUGUESE GUINEA. Portuguese province

44 SENEGAL. French colony; independent 1960

45 GAMBIA. Independent 1965

46 MALI. Ex-French colony; independent 1960

47 MAURITANIA. French colony; independent 1960

48 SPANISH SAHARA. Spanish province 1958

49 IFNI. Spanish province

they were not allowed the same civil rights as white persons. This policy was continued more rigorously by Dr Verwoerd.

The new leaders of Africa and their supporters in the United Nations were hotly opposed to apartheid, especially after the tragedy of Sharpeville in 1960 when police fired upon a crowd of African demonstrators. Feeling that a substantial part of the Commonwealth was hostile to its policies, South Africa ended its own membership upon becoming a Republic in 1961.

It now remains to outline the transformation from Empire to Commonwealth. West Africa posed fewer problems than most territories because, owing to the climate, there was no large body of white settlers, and the Crown Colony of the Gold Coast (population about seven million) had been steadily moving towards self-rule. The country had a very long connection with European ideas, there was an educated upper class and the economic position was reasonably good. Elections were first held in 1951 and the Convention People's Party, with the slogan " Self Government Now! ", was victorious. Its leader, Dr Kwame Nkrumah, became Prime Minister. On 6th March 1957 the *Ghana* Gold Coast, now called Ghana, became an independent country within the Commonwealth and in 1960 it followed the example of India and Pakistan by declaring itself a Republic.

Ghana got away to a good start but subsequent developments aroused some disquiet. President Nkrumah gradually assumed dictatorial powers that would have been unthinkable at the time when his country's democratic future was under discussion. Opposition was suppressed, and in 1963 the Chief Justice was dismissed from office when three former ministers were acquitted of charges brought against them. Nkrumah was empowered to quash decisions of the courts, he assumed supreme command of all the armed forces, and in 1964 he made Ghana into a one-party state in which only his own Party was allowed to operate.

It could well be that the British parliamentary system was not wholly suitable for newly-emerged countries where democracy was in its infancy, but it was disturbing to find in this British-sponsored country the familiar devices of totalitarian states—political trials, preventive detention and government-controlled justice.*

Nigeria, the most populous country in Africa, with more than fifty million people, had also known European traders, missionaries and administrators for a very long time. Since 1914 *Nigeria*

* In Feb. 1966, an Army revolt removed Nkrumah from office.

the colony had acquired an increasing share in its own government, and during the post-war years progress was so steady that in October 1960, a federation of the four regions became an independent country and, three years later, a Republic within the Commonwealth. On Independence Day, Nigeria's Prime Minister, Sir Abubakar Tafawa Balewa, declared:

" I don't think there has ever been such an organisation in the history of mankind as the Commonwealth, where you have people of all races and religions, where peoples have become independent but voluntarily agree to associate with the imperial power . . .

" We are grateful to the British officers whom we have known first as masters, then as leaders and finally as partners, but always as friends . . . To all, on behalf of my countrymen, I say ' thank you ' . . ."

Sierra Leone Next, in West Africa, the much smaller colony of Sierra Leone (with Sir Albert M. Margai as Prime Minister) became an independent member of the Commonwealth in 1961 and the United Nations 100th member-state. Then, in 1965, the tiny colony of Gambia, with a population of only 315,000, felt able to assume independence under the leadership of D. K. Jawara.

The first East African country to achieve independence was Tanganyika, the former German colony which was administered by the British under a mandate of the League of Nations. Led by Dr Julius Nyerere, the people of Tanganyika ($9\frac{1}{4}$ million Africans, 92,000 Asiatics and 21,000 Europeans) seemed likely to work together harmoniously when self-government arrived *Tanzania* in 1961 and a republic was declared in December 1962. However, union with Zanzibar in 1964 under the name of Tanzania brought its own problems, because the Afro-Shiruzu Party, which overthrew the Sultan and established the People's Party of Zanzibar, drew support from China, East Germany and other Communist countries.

Just to the north and astride the equator, Uganda progressed steadily towards self-rule despite difficulties over the position of Buganda, an ancient kingdom which formed part of the territory. When full independence was reached in October 1962, Sir *Uganda* Edward Mutesa, the Kabaka of Buganda, was elected President and Dr Milton Obote became Prime Minister.

With only 10,000 Europeans to 7 million Africans, Uganda did not have to face the same problems as its neighbour Kenya, where, besides over 8 million Africans, there were about

KENYA'S INDEPENDENCE: JOMO KENYATTA BEING SWORN IN AS PRIME
MINISTER

160,000 Asiatics and Arabs, and 60,000 Europeans. The latter, being the principal owners of property and land, had deep misgivings about majority rule and, as we have seen, there was the period of Mau-Mau violence in the fifties which threatened the country's political development. However, with responsible African leaders refusing to approve Mau-Mau's terrorism, order was restored and progress could be resumed.

Independence was granted in December 1963 when Jomo Kenyatta took office as President. He tackled Kenya's problems with restraint and tolerance which had not hitherto been associated with his reputation. Land reforms were introduced and the white population, as long as they did not claim to be a privileged class, were encouraged to remain in the country as Kenyans. Political and tribal rivalries existed, and among the leading figures were the left-wing Vice-President, Mr Oginga Odinga, and the able Minister of Economic Planning, Mr Tom Mboya. A pointer to the future may have been the announcement that Kenya was to become a one-party state from November 1964 when the leader of the Opposition declared the dissolution of his own party, leaving K.A.N.U. (the Kenya African National Union) as one official party in the Republic. *Kenya*

The anxieties that existed in a multi-racial society were also present in Central Africa. In 1953 the Federation of Rhodesia and Nyasaland was formed to assist economic co-operation between the two Rhodesias and Nyasaland. Sir Roy Welensky was a forceful Prime Minister of the Federation but opposition arose in all three territories. In Northern Rhodesia and Nyasaland the African leaders felt that the politics of the white minority in Southern Rhodesia were coming to resemble those of her southern neighbour, the Union of South Africa. *Central Africa*

When it was clear that the Federation could not succeed, R. A. Butler, minister in charge of Central African affairs, called a conference at Victoria Falls to discuss those matters in which co-operation could still continue and to arrange for the future of the three territories. As a result, Nyasaland—renamed Malawi

Malawi —became an independent member of the Commonwealth in July 1964 with Dr Hastings Banda, a well-known politician who had lived and studied for several years in London, as the first Prime Minister.

After ten months of internal self-government following the end of the Federation, Northern Rhodesia achieved independence—

Zambia and the name Zambia—on 24th October 1964. The President of this new republic was Dr Kenneth Kaunda.

Meanwhile, the situation in Southern Rhodesia was causing great ,anxiety to all who cared about the Commonwealth. Out of a population of about 4 million, 217,000 white citizens, nearly all of British descent, possessed political control of the

Southern country which Cecil Rhodes had taken from the Matabele
Rhodesia tribe. Since 1923 Southern Rhodesia had been a self-governing colony but under Sir Godfrey Huggins' twenty-year premiership so little progress was made in giving a share in government to the Africans that by 1958 only about 1,000 had achieved the right to vote. With Mr Garfield Todd as premier (1953–58) a voting roll with lower educational qualifications was introduced but it was limited to one-sixth of the electorate.

Thus, although Southern Rhodesia had enjoyed a large measure of self-government for nearly forty years, it had not acquired full independence because successive British Governments, Tory and Labour, insisted that this could be granted only on terms acceptable to *all* Rhodesians. A new Constitution was negotiated in 1961 whereby Africans would have fifteen seats in an Assembly of sixty-five and the chance to acquire more seats as African education advanced. This was meant to be a step towards majority rule but, with education in the hands of white administrators, the pace of advance was questionable. Mr Ian Smith, leader of the Rhodesia Front Party, stated that he would not accept the idea of an African Government within his own lifetime.

By 1962 a novel situation had arisen in which most of the white population, led by Prime Minister Smith, were demanding independence based upon the 1961 Constitution whereas the African leaders (some in exile or confinement) were opposed to independence on those terms. The danger was that the Rhodesian Government, if it made a unilateral (one-sided) declaration of independence (U.D.I.), which it did in November 1965, would not merely embarrass Britain but might provoke hostile action by other African states. By destroying the goodwill which had been created since 1945, this could threaten the very existence of the Commonwealth.

IAN SMITH

The problems of granting self-rule were not confined to Africa. Cyprus, as we have seen, gained independence without settling the differences between the Greek and Turkish communities and in Malta there was much discontent.

The war-time heroism of Malta gave Britain a special regard for this small island, so that a measure of self-government in 1947 was accompanied by the offer of actual union which *Malta* could have permitted Malta to send M.P.'s to the House of Commons. This was not accepted by Dom Mintoff, the Prime Minister, and, following his resignation and the outbreak of disturbances in 1958, a state of emergency was declared. The island returned to direct rule by the Governor. A new constitution was introduced in 1961 giving semi-independence, and grants were provided to assist economic development. After a London conference and a referendum on the island, Malta became an independent state in 1964 under the Premiership of Dr Borg Olivier.

Malaya was formed into one country by the union of nine separate states, some of them ruled by Sultans with British advisers. There were many races in the narrow, rich peninsula, *Malaysia* about half the population being Malays and the rest mostly Chinese, with some Indians, Arabs, Sinhalese and English. After the Japanese occupation, gangs of Communist guerrillas continued to operate in the jungle, terrorising the civilian population and damaging the economy. By the time British troops had exterminated these pests, the various states and races had come to realise the advantages of combining together, and the Federation of Malaya was formed in which Malays, Chinese and Indians put aside their differences under the leadership of Tunku Abdul Rahman. In 1957 Malaya became an independent monarchy, with a monarch elected from among the royal families, but the Queen was accepted as Head of the Commonwealth.

After the neighbouring port of Singapore had gained internal self-government, Abdul Rahman put forward a plan for a wider federation which led to the creation of a new state called Malaysia. This consisted of Malaya, North Borneo (renamed Sabah), Sarawak and Singapore (which presently withdrew) but the emergence of a prosperous federation on his doorstep aroused the active hostility of President Soekarno of Indonesia.

West Indies
Federation seemed to be the most promising form of development for the scattered islands of the West Indies and in 1958 the British territories in that area formed the West Indian Federation. However, there were differences between those members who felt capable of ruling themselves and those who were not yet able to stand on their own feet. Britain did not impose a solution but left it to the West Indians themselves; in 1961 Jamaica decided to leave the Federation but to remain in the Commonwealth as an independent country, with a Governor General as the Sovereign's representative, and a Parliament headed by Sir Alexander Bustamente.

Near to the coast of South America, the islands of Trinidad and Tobago, with their asphalt and petroleum riches, also decided to accept independence, and in 1962 the West Indian Federation was dissolved. The best hope for the future of the islands still dependent upon Britain seemed to lie in the creation of an East Caribbean Federation.

In the dwindling remainder of the colonial empire there were still problems to be solved, notably in British Guiana, Aden and Rhodesia, but, by 1965, a great and, one hoped, an enduring association of free nations had been founded. In proving that an ideal could be made to come true, Britain had shown that it was possible to cease being a Great Power and yet to remain a great nation.

WEST INDIAN IMMIGRANTS AT VICTORIA STATION, LONDON. BY 1965, ABOUT 800,000 COMMONWEALTH IMMIGRANTS HAD SETTLED IN BRITAIN SINCE THE WAR

Prime Ministers and Principal Ministers since 1902

PRIME MINISTER	CHANCELLOR OF EXCHEQUER	FOREIGN SECRETARY
1902 A. J. Balfour	C. T. Ritchie	Lord of Lansdowne
1906 Sir H. Campbell-Bannerman	H. H. Asquith	Sir Edward Grey
1908 H. H. Asquith	D. Lloyd George R. McKenna	Sir Edward Grey
1916 D. Lloyd George	A. Bonar Law	Sir Edward Grey
1919 D. Lloyd George	A. Chamberlain Sir R. Horne	A. J. Balfour Lord Curzon
1922 A. Bonar Law	S. Baldwin	Lord Curzon
1923 S. Baldwin	S. Baldwin N. Chamberlain	Lord Curzon
1924 J. Ramsay MacDonald (Jan.)	P. Snowden	J. Ramsay MacDonald
1924 S. Baldwin (Nov.)	W. S. Churchill	A. Chamberlain
1929 J. Ramsay MacDonald	P. Snowden	A. Henderson
1931 J. Ramsay MacDonald	P. Snowden N. Chamberlain	Lord Reading Sir J. Simon
1935 S. Baldwin	N. Chamberlain	Sir S. Hoare A. Eden
1937 N. Chamberlain	Sir J. Simon	A. Eden Lord Halifax
1940 W. S. Churchill	Sir K. Wood Sir J. Anderson	Lord Halifax A. Eden
1945 C. R. Attlee	H. Dalton Sir S. Cripps	E. Bevin
1950 C. R. Attlee	Sir S. Cripps H. Gaitskell	E. Bevin H. Morrison
1951 W. S. Churchill	R. A. Butler	Sir A. Eden
1955 Sir A. Eden	R. A. Butler H. Macmillan	H. Macmillan S. Lloyd
1957 H. Macmillan	P. Thorneycroft D. Heathcoat-Amory S. Lloyd R. Maudling	S. Lloyd Lord Home
1963 Sir A. Douglas-Home	R. Maudling	R. A. Butler
1964 H. Wilson	J. Callaghan	P. Gordon Walker R. Stewart

Summary of dates

1906 Liberal victory	1925 Locarno Pact
1908 Old Age Pensions	1926 General Strike
1909 " People's " Budget	1927 Trades Disputes Act
Union of S. Africa	1928 Equal Franchise Act
1910 George V	Briand-Kellogg Pact
1911 Parliament Act	1929 Local Govt. Act
National Insurance Act	Second Labour Government
Agadir crisis	Discovery of penicillin
industrial strikes	Wall Street crash
1912 Balkan war	1930 Simon Report
Home Rule Bill	1931 Financial crisis
Revolution in China	National Government
1914 Curragh " Mutiny "	Statute of Westminster
First World War	Manchuria invaded
Marne: Tannenberg	1932 Ottawa Conference
1915 Gallipoli	1933 Hitler in power
1916 Verdun: Jutland:	1934 Unemployment Act
Somme	1935 India Act
Irish rebellion	Abyssinia invaded
Lloyd George P.M.	1936 Rhineland occupied
1917 Russian Revolution	Spanish Civil War
U.S.A. enters war	Edward VIII abdicated
Nivelle offensive	George VI
Passchendaele	BBC television
Caporetto	1937 N. Chamberlain P.M.
1918 Armistice	1938 Austria annexed
Fisher Education Act	Munich crisis
Votes for women	1939 Czechslovakia taken
1919 " Coupon " Election	Second World War
Versailles Settlement	Poland conquered
League of Nations	Russo-Finnish War
Sankey Report	1940 Norway occupied
1920 War in Ireland	Churchill P.M.
1921 Treaty of Ireland	Holland defeated
1922 Mussolini in power	Dunkirk
Lloyd George defeated	Fall of France
British Broadcasting Company	Battle of Britain
1923 French occupy Ruhr	1941 Wavell's campaign
1924 First Labour Government	Crete: Matapan
Dawes Plan	Hitler attacked Russia
Death of Lenin	Pearl Harbour

ACKNOWLEDGEMENTS

GRATEFUL acknowledgement is made to the following for their permission to reproduce photographs:
Associated Press, 213, 231; Dr Barnardo, 136; B.O.A.C., 131; Cambridge University Press, 135; Fox Photos, frontis, 86, 100, 113, 119, 144, 147, 157, 160, 167, 173, 177, 179, 181, 189, 206, 215, 222, 239, 245, 247, 254; *Glasgow Herald*, 248; Greater London Council, 19, 226; Imperial War Museum, 45, 49, 50, 53, 59, 60, 63, 170, 174, 183; Keystone Press, 185, 218, 235b, 240, 261; London Museum, 26; Mansell, 7, 8, 13, 15, 21, 31, 38, 39, 41, 142–3, 192, 194, 203; Popper, 75, 88, 121, 127b, 138, 141, 152, 197, 200, 216, 228, 235a, 237, 238, 241, 249, 253, 257, 264; Press Association, 57; Radio Times Hulton Picture Library, 6, 9, 10, 17, 23, 24–5, 28, 32, 36, 40, 43, 51, 64, 66, 68, 70, 71, 76, 77, 81, 82, 83, 89, 91, 93, 95, 97, 98, 103, 105, 107, 109, 115, 122, 124, 128, 133, 139, 140, 149, 155, 158, 195, 225, 232, 242, 246; E. H. Sargeant, 129; Sport and General, 127a; the *Sun* 220; Topix, 151, 164, 168–9; U.N.O., 209, 210; United Press International, 79, 80, 111, 146, 187, 201, 207, 219, 263.

The photographs on the cover are reproduced by permission of the The Press Association, Fox Photos, the Imperial War Museum, Camera Press and *The Sunday Times*. The maps are by Harold Johns.

Index